Contents

Contents (continued)

UNIT 3

Tens and Ones
Counting, Place Value, and Time

Contents (continued)

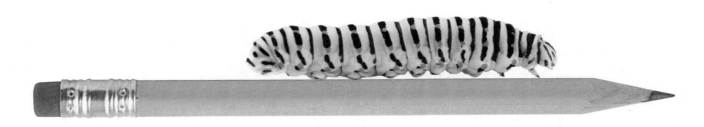

Contents (continued)

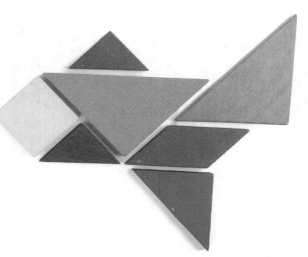

Prepare for Thinking About Tens

1 Think about what you know about tens and ones.
Fill in each box. Use words, numbers, and pictures.
Show as many ideas as you can.

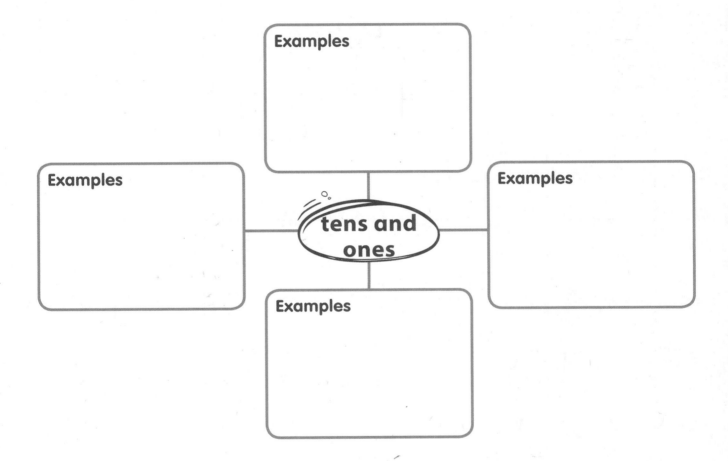

2 How many tens is the same as 40 ones?

3 **Fill the 10-frames. Write how many tens and ones.**

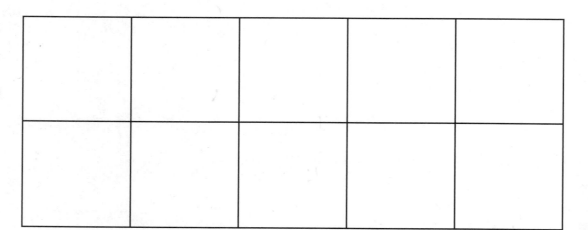

_____ tens   _____ ones

Counting to 120

Dear Family,

This week your child is learning about counting to 120.

Your child will learn to count to 120, starting at any number less than 120. He or she will recognize that these numbers are made up of tens and ones. He or she will also count groups of up to 120 objects.

Your child will explore counting using a 120 chart. A 120 chart shows the numbers 1–120 in rows of ten. Your child will learn that a 120 chart has rows and columns with numbers in certain patterns. He or she will become familiar with the numbers to 120, count on from a given number, and learn to use the chart to find numbers that are 1 more than any given number.

Using the 120 chart will help your child understand the relationships between numbers, as well as prepare to add and subtract two-digit numbers.

61	62	63	64	65	66	67	68	69	70
71	72	73	74	75	76	77	78	79	80
81	82	83	84	85	86	87	88	89	90
91	92	93	94	95	96	97	98	99	100
101	102	103	104	105	106	107	108	109	110
111	112	113	114	115	116	117	118	119	120

Invite your child to share what he or she knows about using a 120 chart by doing the following activity together.

Activity Counting to 120

Do this activity with your child to explore counting to 120.

Materials 120 chart

Have your child use the 120 chart to help as you give prompts such as:

- Say a number and have your child locate it on the chart.
- Point to a number and ask your child to say the number.
- Ask your child to point out patterns they see in rows and columns.
- Ask questions such as: *What is one more than 109?*
- Choose a starting number for your child to count on from, either for a short range or all the way up to 120.

Draw a number of objects. Have your child count the objects and then find the number on the 120 chart.

1	2	3	4	5	6	7	8	9	10
11	12	13	14	15	16	17	18	19	20
21	22	23	24	25	26	27	28	29	30
31	32	33	34	35	36	37	38	39	40
41	42	43	44	45	46	47	48	49	50
51	52	53	54	55	56	57	58	59	60
61	62	63	64	65	66	67	68	69	70
71	72	73	74	75	76	77	78	79	80
81	82	83	84	85	86	87	88	89	90
91	92	93	94	95	96	97	98	99	100
101	102	103	104	105	106	107	108	109	110
111	112	113	114	115	116	117	118	119	120

Explore Counting to 120

Learning Target
- Count to 120, starting at any number less than 120. In this range, read and write numerals and represent a number of objects with a written numeral.

SMP 1, 2, 3, 4, 5, 6, 7, 8

How can you count on a 120 chart?

Fill in the missing numbers.

Try It

Math Toolkit
- base-ten blocks

1	2	3	4	5	6	7	8	9	10
11	12	13	14	15	16	17	18	19	20
21	22	23	24	25	26	27	28	29	
31	32	33	34	35	36	37	38	39	40
41	42	43		45	46	47	48	49	50
51	52	53	54	55	56	57	58	59	60
61	62	63	64	65	66	67	68	69	70
71	72	73	74	75	76	77		79	80
81	82	83	84	85	86	87	88	89	90
	92	93	94	95	96	97	98	99	100
101	102	103	104	105	106	107	108	109	110
111	112	113	114	115	116	117	118	119	120

Connect It

Write the missing numbers.

31	32	33		35	36	37	38	39	40
41	42	43	44	45	46	47	48	49	
51	52	53	54	55		57	58	59	60

81	82	83	84	85	86		88	89	90
91		93	94	95	96	97	98	99	
101	102	103	104			107	108	109	110

Prepare for Counting to 120

1 Think about what you know about counting
starting from any number. Fill in each box.
Use words, numbers, and pictures.
Show as many ideas as you can.

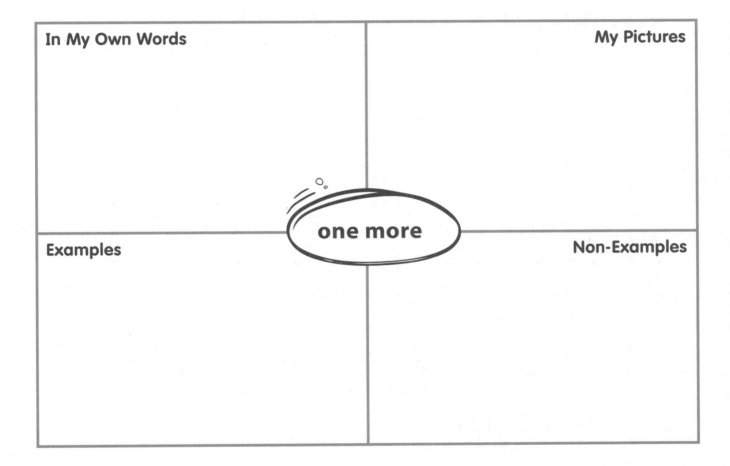

In My Own Words	My Pictures
Examples	Non-Examples

one more

2 There are 5 counters. Draw one more counter.
Now how many counters are there?

3 **Write the missing numbers.**

11	12	13	14	15	16	17	18	19	
21	22		24	25	26	27	28	29	30
31	32	33	34	35	36		38	39	40

91	92	93	94		96	97	98	99	100
101	102		104	105	106	107	108	109	
111	112	113	114	115			118	119	120

Develop Counting to 120

Celia counts by ones up to 106.
Then she continues counting.
Which three numbers does she say next?

Math Toolkit
- 120 charts
- counters

DISCUSS IT
I noticed . . .

> Celia counts by ones up to 106.
> Then she continues counting.
> Which three numbers does she say next?

Model It

Which three numbers come after 106?

Celia counts on 107, 108, 109.

Start at 106 on the 120 chart.

Count out loud.

Circle the next three numbers in the row.

91	92	93	94	95	96	97	98	99	100
101	102	103	104	105	**106**	107	108	109	110
111	112	113	114	115	116	117	118	119	120

Connect It

1 How is your way like **Model It**? How is it different?

2 How is counting numbers greater than 100 like counting up to 10?

Apply It

Fill in the blanks.

3 Count by ones: 104, _____, _____, 107, _____

4 1 more than 94 is _____.

5 1 more than 110 is _____.

61	62	63	64	65	66	67	68	69	70
71	72	73	74	75	76	77	78	79	80
81	82	83	84	85	86	87	88	89	90
91	92	93	94	95	96	97	98	99	100
101	102	103	104	105	106	107	108	109	110
111	112	113	114	115	116	117	118	119	120

Fill in the blanks.

6 Count by ones: 97, _98_, _99_, _100_, 101

7 Count by ones: 69, _70_, _71_, _72_, 73

8 Count by ones: 80, _81_, 82, _83_, _84_

9 1 more than _110_ is 111.

10 1 more than 119 is _120_.

Practice Counting to 120

Look at the Example. Then solve problems 1–4.

Example

Count by ones. Use the chart.

61	62	63	64	65	66	67	68	69	70
71	72	73	74	75	76	77	78	79	80
81	82	83	84	85	(86)	87	88	89	90

1 more than 80 is 81.   1 more than 87 is 88.

Count by ones: 78, 79, 80, 81, 82

1   Fill in the blanks. Use the chart.

1 more than 65 is __66__ .

1 more than 72 is __73__ .

2   Fill in the blanks. Use the chart.

Count by ones: 66, __67__ , 68, __69__ , __70__

Count by ones: __85__ , 86, __87__ , 88, __88__

81	82	83	84	85	86	87	88	89	90
91	92	93	94	95	96	97	98	99	100
101	102	103	104	105	106	107	108	109	110
111	112	113	114	115	116	117	118	119	120

3 Fill in the blanks. Use the chart.

1 more than 95 is _94_ .   1 more than 105 is _104_ .

1 more than 99 is _48_ .   1 more than 109 is _108_ .

1 more than 111 is _101_ .   1 more than 115 is _114_ .

4 Fill in the blanks. Use the chart.

Count by ones: 97, _98_ , 99, _100_ , _103_ , 102

Count by ones: _104_ , 103, 104, _105_ , _____

Count by ones: 115, _116_ , _____ , 118, _____

Develop Counting to 120

Pietro has these star stickers in his collection.

How many star stickers does he have?

Try It

Math Toolkit
• 120 charts

COUNT by 10s and
1s to go + 113
11 tens
3 ones

DISCUSS IT

How did you count
the stars?

Pietro has these star stickers in his collection. How many star stickers does he have?

★★★★★★ ★★★★★★ ★★★★★★ ★★★★★★
★★★★★★ ★★★★★★ ★★★★★★ ★★★★★★
★★★★★★ ★★★★★★ ★★★★★★ ★★★★★★
★★★★★★ ★★★★★★ ★★★★★★ ★★★★★★
★★★★★★ ★★★★★★ ★★★★★★ ★★★
★★★★★★ ★★★★★★ ★★★★★★

Model It

Count the stars.

★★★★★★ ★★★★★★ ★★★★★★ ★★★★★★
★★★★★★ ★★★★★★ ★★★★★★ ★★★★★★
   10   20   30   40

★★★★★★ ★★★★★★ ★★★★★★ ★★★★★★
★★★★★★ ★★★★★★ ★★★★★★ ★★★★★★
   50   60   70   80

★★★★★★ ★★★★★★ ★★★★★★ ★★★
★★★★★★ ★★★★★★ ★★★★★★
   90   100   110

Count the groups of 10 and then count on.

11 groups of 10 is __110__ .

Add __3__ more ones.

Pietro has __113__ star stickers.

Connect It

1 How is your way like **Model It**? How is it different?

I also by tens.

2 Buzz counts by ones from 110 like this:

111, 112, 114, 115. Is he right? How do you know?

No, Buzz skipped many.

Apply It

3 Find the number pictured here.

___7___ groups of 10 and ___5___ ones

Circle the total on the chart.

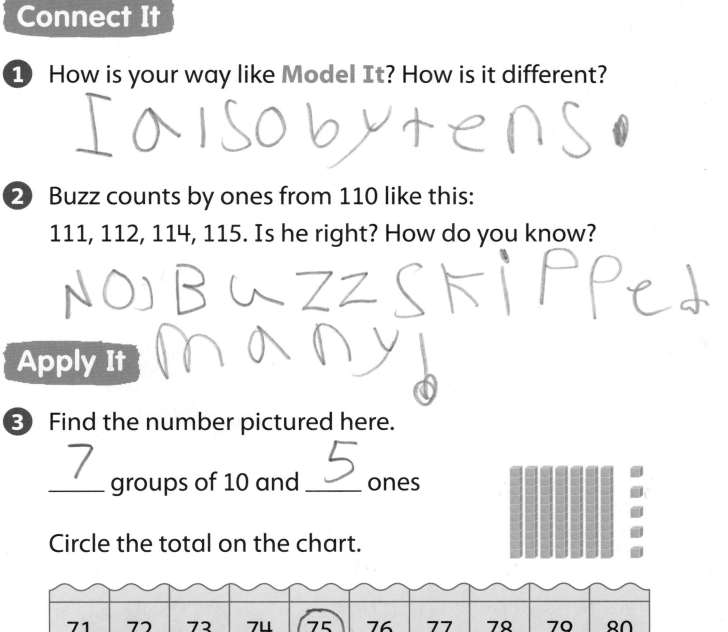

71	72	73	74	75	76	77	78	79	80
81	82	83	84	85	86	87	88	89	90
91	92	93	94	95	96	97	98	99	100

4 Gina counts these baseballs.
How many baseballs does she count?

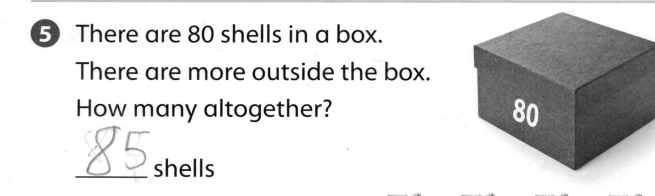

_106_ baseballs

5 There are 80 shells in a box.
There are more outside the box.
How many altogether?

_85_ shells

6 There are 110 pencils in a box.
There are more outside the box.
How many altogether?

_103_ pencils

Practice Counting to 120

Look at the Example. Then solve problems 1–4.

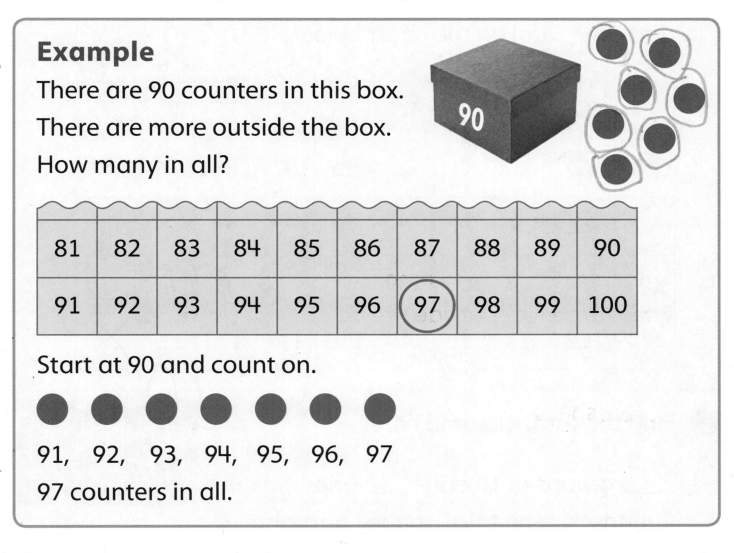

Example

There are 90 counters in this box.
There are more outside the box.
How many in all?

| 81 | 82 | 83 | 84 | 85 | 86 | 87 | 88 | 89 | 90 |
| 91 | 92 | 93 | 94 | 95 | 96 | 97 | 98 | 99 | 100 |

Start at 90 and count on.

● ● ● ● ● ● ●

91, 92, 93, 94, 95, 96, 97

97 counters in all.

1 60 flowers are in the box.
There are more outside the box.
How many altogether?

__64__ flowers

2 Find the total pictured here.

___8___ groups of 10 and ___2___ ones

Circle the total on the chart below.

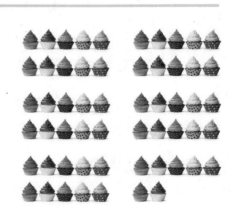

71	72	73	74	75	76	77	78	79	80
81	(82)	83	84	85	86	87	88	89	90
91	92	93	94	95	96	97	98	99	100
101	102	103	104	105	106	107	108	109	110
111	112	113	114	115	116	117	118	119	120

3 Find the total pictured here.

___12___ groups of 10 and ___0___ ones

Put an X on the total on the chart above.

4 Bo made these cupcakes.

How many cupcakes did he make?

___57___ cupcakes

©Curriculum Associates, LLC   Copying is not permitted.

Refine Counting to 120

Complete the Example. Then solve problems 1–3.

Example

Fill in the 2 blank spaces in the chart.

81	82	83	84	85	86	87	▲	89	90
91	92	■	94	95	96	97	98	99	100
101	102	103	104	105	106	107	108	109	●
111	112	113	**114**			117	118	119	120

Write the missing number for each shape in the chart.

■ is __93__.　　▲ is ____.　　● is ____.

Apply It

1 Fill in the 3 blank spaces in the chart.

61	62	63	64	65				69	70
71	72	73	74	75	76	77	78	79	80

1	2	3	4	5	6	7	8	9	10
11	12	13	14	15	16	17	18	19	20
21	22	23	24	25	26	27	28	29	30
31	■	33	34	35	36	37	38	39	40
41	42	43	44	45	46	47	48	49	●
51	52	53	54	55	56	57	58	59	60
61	62	63	64	65	★	67	68	69	70
71	72	73	74	75	76	77			
81	82	83	84	85	86	87	88	89	90
91	92	93	94	95	96	97	98	99	100
			104	105	106	107	⬠	109	110
111	112	113	114	115	116	117	118	119	120

2 Write the missing number for each shape in the chart.

⬠ is _____.   ■ is _____.

★ is _____.   ● is _____.

3 Fill in the blank spaces in the chart.

Practice Counting to 120

Look at the Example. Then solve problems 1–4.

Example

71	72	73	74	75	76	77	78	79	80
81	82	83	84	★	86	87	●	89	90
91	92	93	94	95	96	97	98	99	100
101	102	103	104	▲	106	107	108	109	110
111	112	113	114	115	116	117	118	119	120

Write the missing number for the ★ in the chart.

★ is 85.

Write the missing number for each shape in the chart.

1 ● is _____ .   ▲ is _____ .

1	2	3	4	5	6	7	8	9	10
11	12	13	14	15	16	17	18	19	20
21	22	23	24	25	26	27	28	29	30
31	32	33	♥	35	36	37	38	39	40
41	42	43	44	45	46	47	48	49	50
51	52	53	54	55	56	57	58	59	⬠
61	62	63	64	65	66	67	68	69	70
71				75	76	77	78	79	80
81	82	83	84	85	86	87	88	89	90
■	92	93	94	95	96	97	98	99	100
101	102	103	104	105	106	107	108	109	
		113	114	115	116	117	118	119	

2 Write the missing number for each shape in the chart.

■ is _____.   ⬠ is _____.   ♥ is _____.

3 Write the missing numbers in the chart.

4 Draw an X on the number that is 1 more than 99.

Refine Counting to 120

Apply It

Solve problems 1–11.

91	92	93	94	95	96	97	98	99	100
101	102	103	104	105	106	107	108	109	110
111	112	113	114	115	116	117	118	119	120

Fill in the blanks. Use the chart.

1 1 more than 100 is _____. **2** 1 more than 115 is _____.

3 1 more than 117 is _____. **4** 1 more than 119 is _____.

5 1 more than 99 is _____. **6** 1 more than 111 is _____.

Fill in the blanks. Use the chart.

7 104, _____, 106, _____, 108, _____

8 98, _____, _____, _____, 102

9 114, 115, _____, _____, _____

10 Gene has 60 cookies in a box.
There are some more on the tray.
How many cookies in all?

_____ cookies

---

11 Kadeem draws some faces.

How many faces?
Circle.

74 faces

84 faces

94 faces

Explore Tens and Ones

How many cubes do you have?

Try It

How many cubes?

My guess: __34__ cubes

Math Toolkit
- connecting cubes

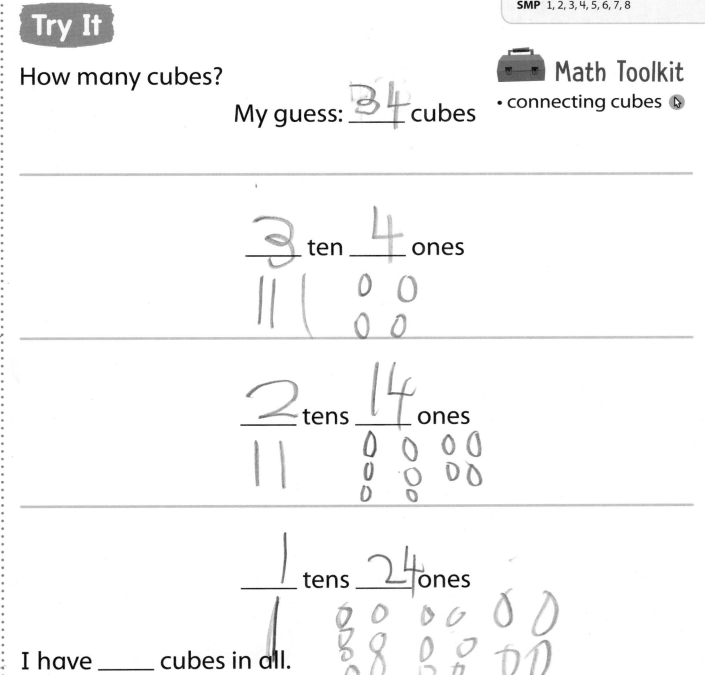

__3__ ten __4__ ones

__2__ tens __14__ ones

__1__ tens __24__ ones

I have _____ cubes in all.

Connect It

Ryan has 4 tens and 5 ones.

Kelly has 3 tens and 15 ones.

Draw to show how Ryan and Kelly have the same number of cubes.

Ryan has _____ cubes.

Kelly has _____ cubes.

Prepare for Exploring Tens and Ones

1 Think about what you know about digits.
Fill in each box. Use words, numbers, and
pictures. Show as many ideas as you can.

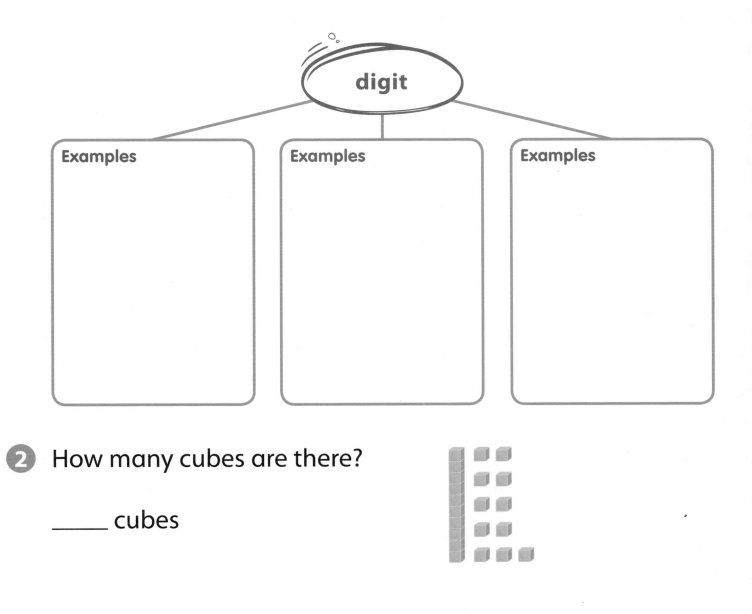

digit

Examples

Examples

Examples

2 How many cubes are there?

_____ cubes

Solve the problem.

Joy has 3 tens and 6 ones.
Alana has 2 tens and 16 ones.
Draw to show how Joy and Alana
have the same number of cubes.

Joy has _____ cubes.   Alana has _____ cubes.

Develop Understanding of Tens and Ones

How can you show ▯▯▯▯ as tens and ones?

One way is to use ▯▯▯
place value of ea▯ ▯igit.

36 is 3 tens 6 one▯

Another way:

36 is 36 ones.

3▯ ▯s 30 + 6

36

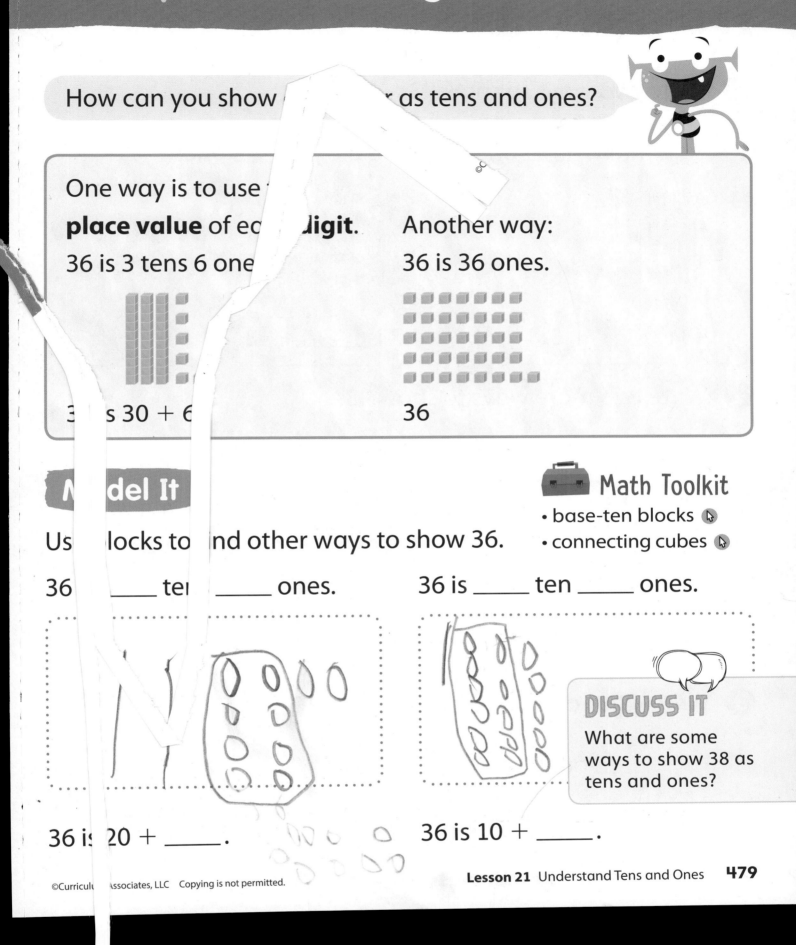

Model It

Us▯ ▯locks to ▯nd other ways to show 36.

Math Toolkit
• base-ten blocks ▯
• connecting cubes ▯

36 ▯___ te▯ ____ ones.

36 is ____ ten ____ ones.

DISCUSS IT

What are some ways to show 38 as tens and ones?

36 i▯ 20 + ____.

36 is 10 + ____.

Connect It

1 Write two ways to show 43.

43 is 4 tens __0__ ones.   43 is 3 tens __13__ ones.

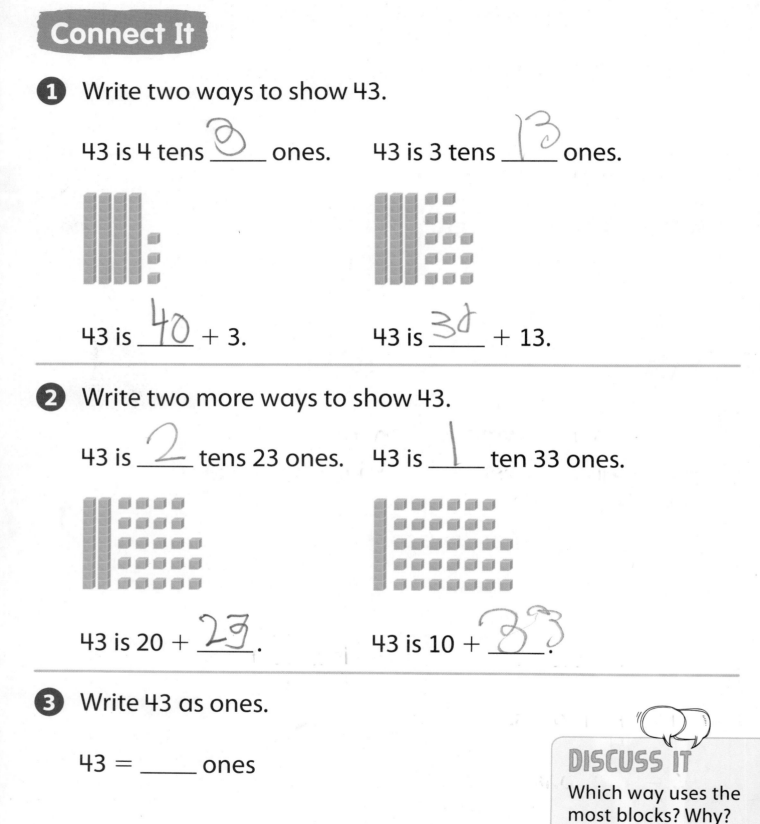

43 is __40__ + 3.   43 is __30__ + 13.

2 Write two more ways to show 43.

43 is __2__ tens 23 ones.   43 is __1__ ten 33 ones.

43 is 20 + __23__.   43 is 10 + __33__.

3 Write 43 as ones.

43 = ____ ones

DISCUSS IT
Which way uses the most blocks? Why?

Practice with Tens and Ones

Look at the Example. Then solve problems 1–5.

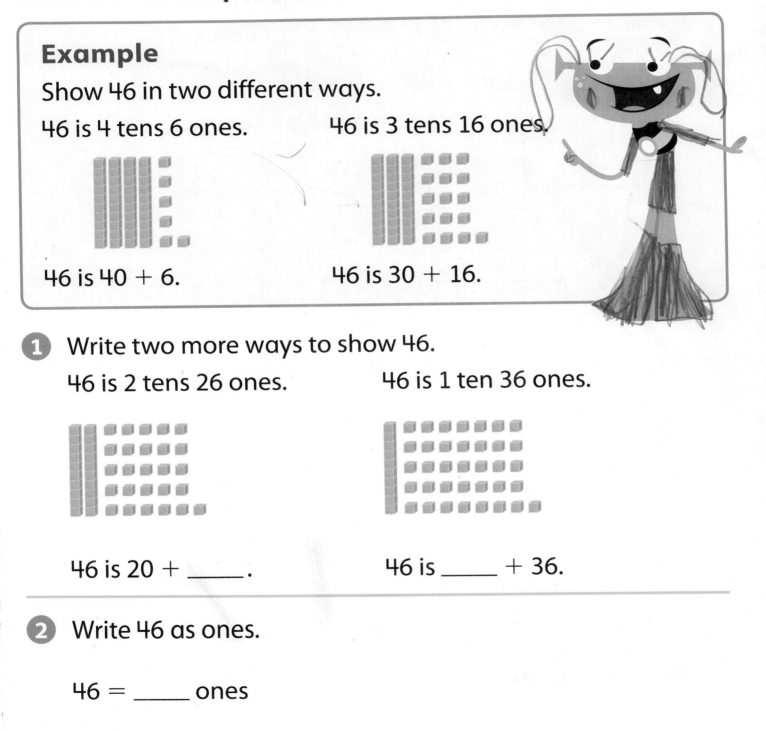

Example

Show 46 in two different ways.

46 is 4 tens 6 ones.

46 is 3 tens 16 ones.

46 is 40 + 6.

46 is 30 + 16.

1 Write two more ways to show 46.

46 is 2 tens 26 ones.

46 is 1 ten 36 ones.

46 is 20 + _____.

46 is _____ + 36.

2 Write 46 as ones.

46 = _____ ones

3 Write two ways to show 53.

53 is 5 tens _____ ones.   53 is 4 tens _____ ones.

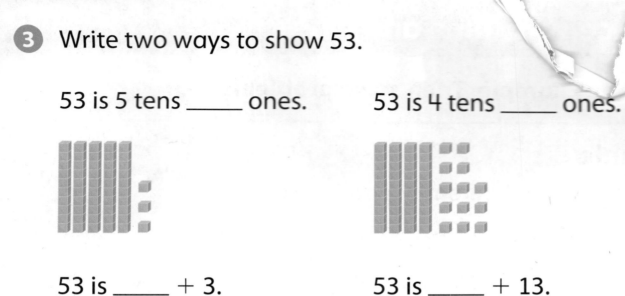

53 is _____ + 3.   53 is _____ + 13.

4 Write two more ways to show 53.

53 is _____ tens 23 ones.   53 is _____ tens 33 ones.

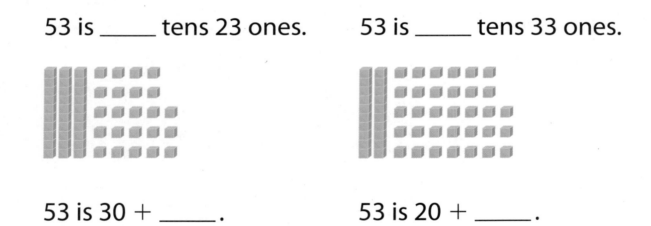

53 is 30 + _____ .   53 is 20 + _____ .

5 Show 53 in a way that is different from all
the ways above.

Develop Understanding of Tens and Ones

Model It

Use base-ten blocks. Choose any two-digit number. Show your number as tens and ones in different ways.

My number: _____

 **Math Toolkit**
• base-ten blocks

1 Circle the different ways to show 53.

 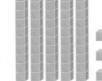 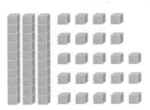

DISCUSS IT

The same number can be shown in different ways because . . .

Connect It

Fill in the blanks.

Base-Ten Blocks	Number	Tens and Ones
2	62	5 tens 12 ones 6 tens 2 ones
3	75	4 tens 35 ones 7 tens 5 ones
4	40	3 tens 0 ones 4 tens 0 ones
5	82	6 tens 22 ones 8 tens 2 ones

DISCUSS IT

When you see a two-digit number modeled with blocks . . .

Practice with Tens and Ones

Look at the Example. Then solve problems 1–6.

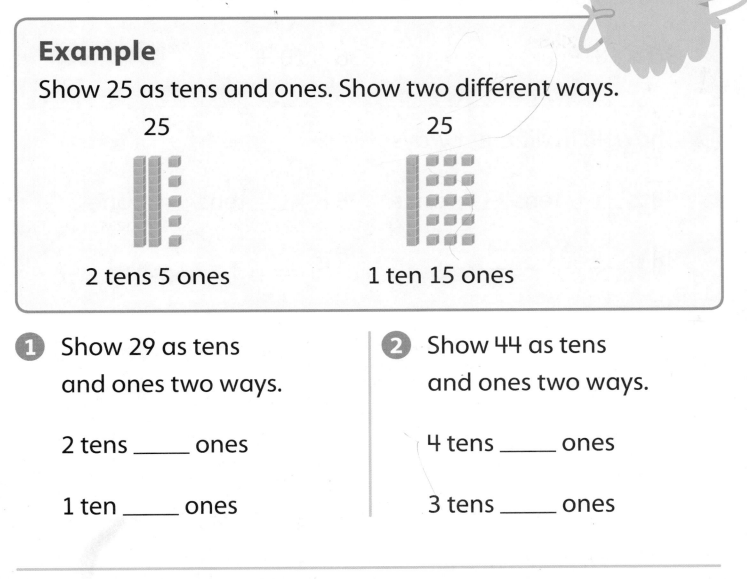

Example

Show 25 as tens and ones. Show two different ways.

25

25

2 tens 5 ones

1 ten 15 ones

1 Show 29 as tens and ones two ways.

2 tens _____ ones

1 ten _____ ones

2 Show 44 as tens and ones two ways.

4 tens _____ ones

3 tens _____ ones

3 Write 44 in a different way.

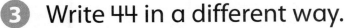

_____ tens _____ ones

4 Show 36 in different ways.

36 is 3 tens _____ ones.   36 is 2 tens _____ ones.

36 is 30 + _____.   36 is 20 + _____.

5 Show 48 in different ways.

48 is _____ tens _____ ones.   48 is _____ tens _____ ones.

48 is _____ + _____.   48 is _____ + _____.

6 Write all the different ways to show 52 as tens and ones.

_____ tens _____ ones

_____ tens _____ ones

_____ tens _____ ones

_____ tens _____ ones

_____ ten _____ ones

_____ tens _____ ones

Refine Ideas About Tens and Ones

Apply It

1 **Draw** Show why 34 ones is the same as
3 tens 4 ones.

---

2 **Identify** Circle all the ways that show 76.

7 tens 6 ones   6 tens 7 ones

60 + 7   70 + 6

5 tens 26 ones   6 tens 16 ones

---

3 **Explain** Boom says 5 tens 8 ones = 5 + 80.
Do you agree? Tell why or why not.

4 Think about how you can show numbers as tens and ones in different ways.

A: Circle some tens and ones. Write the two-digit number for the blocks you circled.

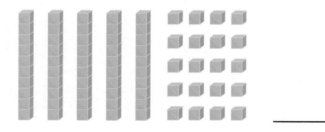 _____

Write the number you circled as tens and ones in two different ways.

_____ tens _____ ones   _____ tens _____ ones

B: Use the two digits from A. Write a different number. Show this number as tens and ones in two different ways.

Compare Numbers

Dear Family,

This week your child is learning to compare two-digit numbers.

To find which of two numbers is **greater than** the other (has more), or is **less than** the other (has fewer), you can compare the tens and compare the ones. Because tens have a greater value than ones, compare the tens first. If the tens are the same, then compare the ones.

Learning to compare two-digit numbers will help your child better understand the relationships between numbers and will be useful in real-life situations that involve comparing amounts or values.

You can use the **greater than symbol (>)** and **less than symbol (<)** to compare numbers.

• You can use place-value charts to compare numbers.

48 (?) 35

Tens	Ones		Tens	Ones
4	8		3	5

Compare tens. 4 tens is greater than 3 tens.
So, 48 > 35.

• You can also use quick drawings to compare numbers.

23 (?) 27

Each line represents ten. Each circle represents one.

2 tens 3 ones   **2 tens 7 ones**   The tens are the same, so compare the ones.

3 ones is less than 7 ones.
So, 23 < 27.

Invite your child to share what he or she knows about comparing two-digit numbers by doing the following activity together.

Activity Comparing Numbers

Do this activity with your child to explore comparing numbers.

Play a game with your child that involves comparing two-digit numbers.

- Cut out the cards shown below or use index cards to make your own set. Mix the number cards and place them facedown in a pile.

- Each player takes one of the symbol cards.

- Take turns picking two cards. Use the symbol card to make a statement that compares the two numbers, for example 33 < 42. You can position the symbol to show *less than* or *greater than*.

- Say what the statement shows, for example: *33 is less than 42.*

- When all cards are used, you can mix them up and play again.

21	24	29	33	34
35	38	42	45	46
47	51	53	59	60
62	67	68	>	>

Explore Comparing Numbers

Rosa carries 24 books. Ryan carries 37 books. Who carries more books? Who carries fewer?

Try It

Math Toolkit
- base-ten blocks

Rosa	Ryan

Write the names.

_____ carries more books than _____.

_____ carries fewer books than _____.

Connect It

There are 28 soccer balls.

There are 31 footballs.

Draw to compare the number of balls.

soccer balls	footballs
_____	_____

Fill in the blanks.

There are more _____ than _____.

There are fewer _____ than _____.

Prepare for Comparing Numbers

1 Think about what you know about comparing numbers. Fill in each box. Use words, numbers, and pictures. Show as many ideas as you can.

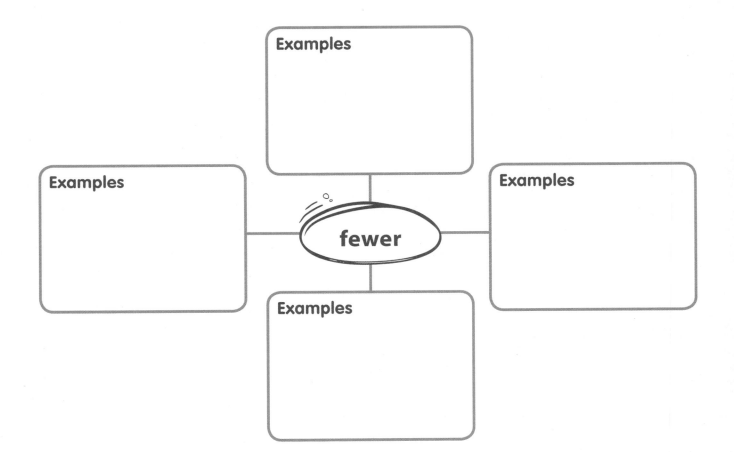

Examples

Examples

Examples

fewer

Examples

2 Circle the group with fewer books.

3 Solve the problem.

There are 34 apples. There are 27 bananas. Draw to compare the number of fruits.

apples | bananas

_____   _____

Fill in the blanks.

There are fewer _____ than _____.

There are more _____ than _____.

Develop Comparing Numbers

Nora picks 52 apples. Nick picks 25 apples.
Who picks more apples?

 **Try It**

 **Math Toolkit**
- base-ten blocks
- counters
- 10-frames
- tens place-value mats

DISCUSS IT
How can thinking about tens and ones help?

Nora picks 52 apples. Nick picks 25 apples. Who picks more apples?

Model It

Compare. 52 ⟮ ? ⟯ 25

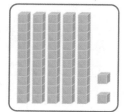 

Tens	Ones
5	2

Tens	Ones
2	5

Compare tens.

5 tens is **greater than 2** tens.

You can use the **greater than symbol (>):**

> **5** tens > **2** tens

> 52 ◯ 25

_____ picks more apples than _____ .

Connect It

1 How is your way like **Model It**? How is it different?

2 How did using base-ten blocks help you compare 52 and 25 to find the greater number?

Apply It

3 Dave has 13 crayons. Ari has 21 crayons.
Compare. 21 (?) 13

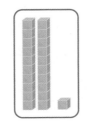

Tens	Ones
2	1

Tens	Ones
1	3

_____ tens is greater than _____ ten.

21 ◯ 13

Lesson 22 Compare Numbers   **497**

4 Roberto has 48 fish. Rena has 24 fish.
Who has more fish?
Compare. 48 ? 24

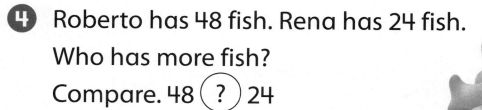

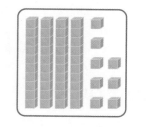

Tens	Ones
4	8

Tens	Ones
2	4

_____ tens is greater than _____ tens.

48 ◯ 24

_____ has more fish than _____.

5 Compare 45 and 63.
Which number is greater?

Tens	Ones
4	5

Tens	Ones
6	3

_____ tens is greater than _____ tens.

_____ ◯ _____

Practice Comparing Numbers

Look at the Example. Then solve problems 1–4.

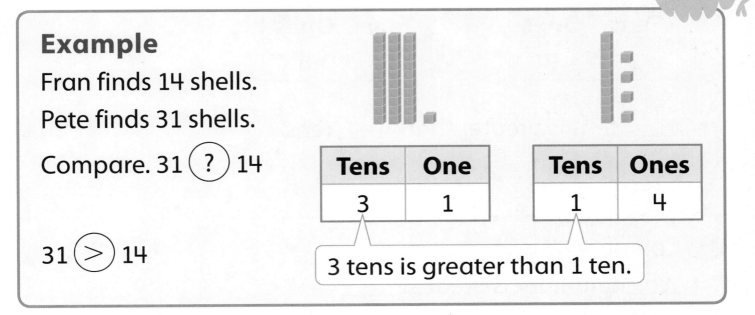

Example

Fran finds 14 shells.

Pete finds 31 shells.

Compare. 31 (?) 14

31 (>) 14

Tens	One
3	1

Tens	Ones
1	4

3 tens is greater than 1 ten.

1 Compare 65 and 42.

Which number is greater?

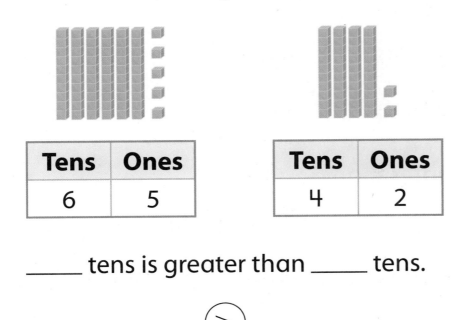

Tens	Ones
6	5

Tens	Ones
4	2

_____ tens is greater than _____ tens.

_____ (>) _____

Compare 29 and 88.

Which number is greater?

Tens	Ones
2	9

Tens	Ones
8	8

_____ tens is greater than _____ tens.

_____ ◯ _____

 Compare 37 and 47.

Which number is greater?

Tens	Ones
3	7

Tens	Ones
4	7

_____ tens is greater than _____ tens.

_____ ◯ _____

---

4 Find a number greater than 62.

Write it in the blank.

_____ > 62

Develop Comparing Numbers

Gabe collects 35 rocks.

Rose collects 39 rocks.

Who collects fewer rocks?

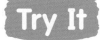 **Try It**

🧰 **Math Toolkit**
- base-ten blocks
- 120 charts
- tens place-value mats

DISCUSS IT

I found my answer by . . .

Gabe collects 35 rocks.
Rose collects 39 rocks.
Who collects fewer rocks?

Model It

Compare.

39 (?) 35

Compare the tens.
The tens are the same.

Compare the ones.

35 ◯ 39

Tens	Ones
3	**5**

Tens	Ones
3	**9**

5 ones is **less than 9** ones.
You can use the **less than symbol (<)**:

5 ones < **9** ones

5 ◯ 9

_____ collects fewer rocks than _____ .

Connect It

1 How is your way like Model It? How is it different?

2 Buzz collects 28 rocks. Boom collects 41 rocks.
Buzz says he has more rocks than Boom because 8 > 1.
Do you agree? Why or why not?

Apply It

3 Compare 62 and 67.
Which number is less?

Tens	Ones
6	2

Tens	Ones
6	7

_____ ones is less than _____ ones.

_____ < _____

---

4 Compare 98 and 94.
Which number is less?

Tens	Ones

Tens	Ones

_____ ones is less than _____ ones.

_____ < _____

5 Compare 52 and 57.
Which number is less?

Tens	Ones

Tens	Ones

_____ ones is less than _____ ones.

_____ < _____

---

6 Compare 89 and 83.
Which number is less?

Tens	Ones

Tens	Ones

_____ ones is less than _____ ones.

_____ < _____

---

7 Find two numbers with 5 tens.
One number is less than 54.
The other number is greater than 54.
Fill in the blanks.

_____ < 54   _____ > 54

Practice Comparing Numbers

Look at the Example. Then solve problems 1–5.

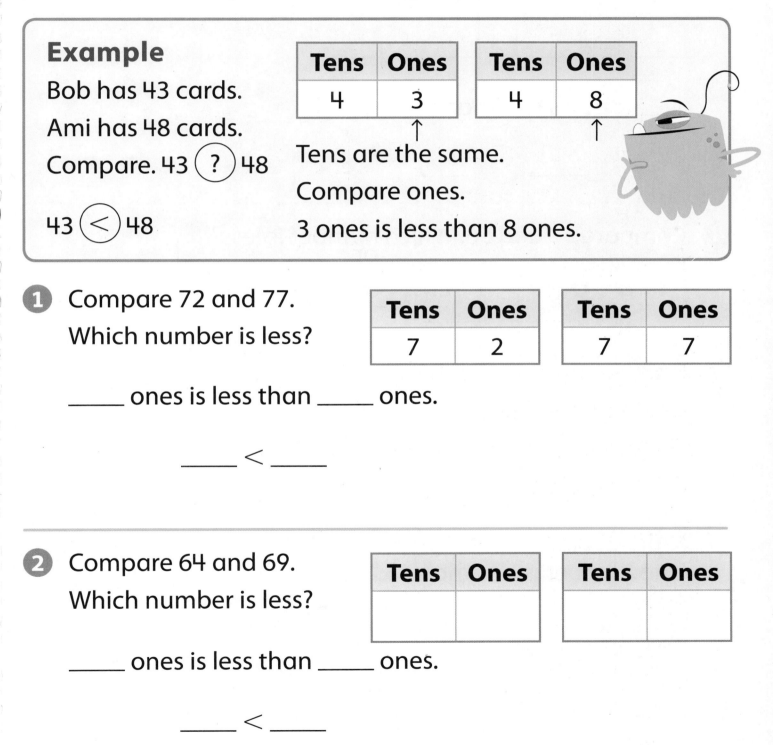

Example

Bob has 43 cards.

Ami has 48 cards.

Compare. 43 (?) 48

43 (<) 48

Tens	Ones
4	3

Tens	Ones
4	8

Tens are the same.

Compare ones.

3 ones is less than 8 ones.

1 Compare 72 and 77.
Which number is less?

Tens	Ones
7	2

Tens	Ones
7	7

_____ ones is less than _____ ones.

_____ < _____

2 Compare 64 and 69.
Which number is less?

Tens	Ones

Tens	Ones

_____ ones is less than _____ ones.

_____ < _____

3 Compare 95 and 93. Which number is less?

Tens	Ones

Tens	Ones

_____ ones is less than _____ ones.

_____ < _____

---

4 Compare 52 and 56. Which number is less?

Tens	Ones

Tens	Ones

_____ ones is less than _____ ones.

_____ < _____

---

5 Find two numbers with 6 tens.

One number is less than 65.

The other number is greater than 65.

Fill in the blanks.

_____ < 65   _____ > 65

Refine Comparing Numbers

Complete the Example. Then solve problems 1–5.

Example

Jen has 48 coins. Kim has 14 coins.

Who has more coins?

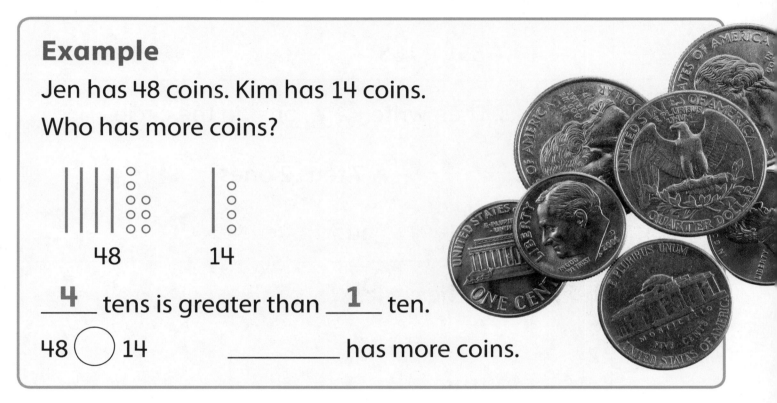

48   14

___**4**___ tens is greater than ___**1**___ ten.

48 ◯ 14   _____ has more coins.

Apply It

1 Anita packs 46 books.

James packs 27 books.

Who packs fewer books?

46   27

_____ tens is less than _____ tens.

_____ packs fewer books than _____.

27 ◯ 46

2 Fill in the blanks. Then write <, >, or = in the circle.

_____ tens _____ ones   _____ tens _____ ones

85 ◯ 85

---

3 Fill in the blanks. Then write <, >, or = in the circle.

7 tens 2 ones   7 tens 2 ones

_____ ◯ _____

---

4 Write <, >, or = in the circle.

23 ◯ 27

69 ◯ 64

---

5 Write <, >, or = in the circle.

74 ◯ 74

96 ◯ 99

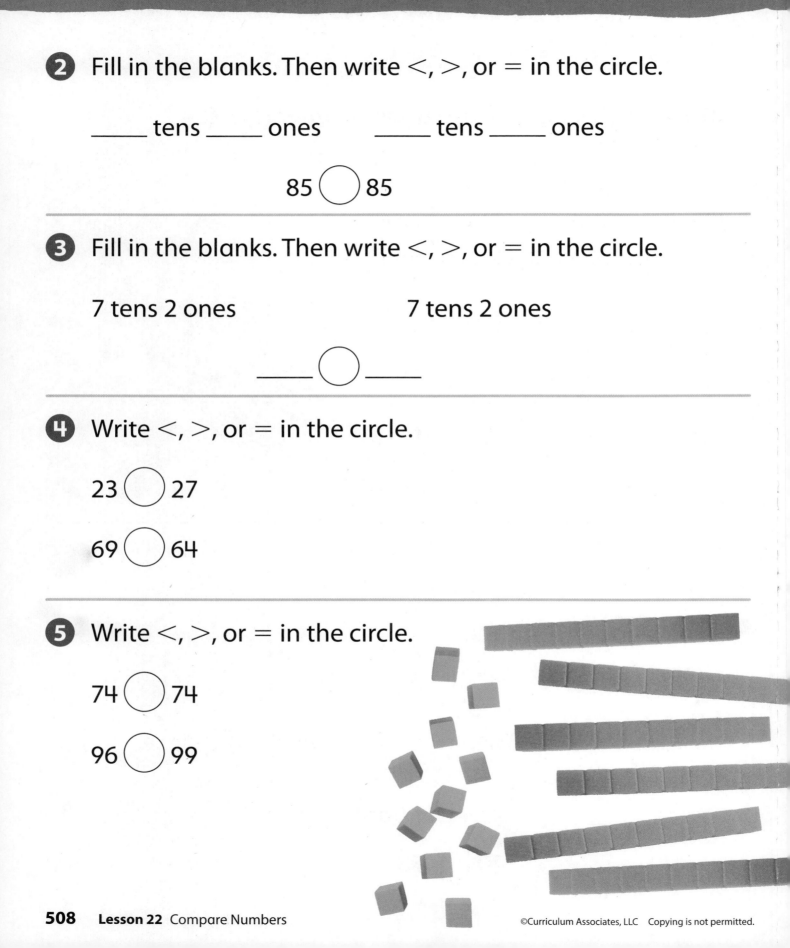

Practice Comparing Numbers

Look at the Example. Then solve problems 1–6.

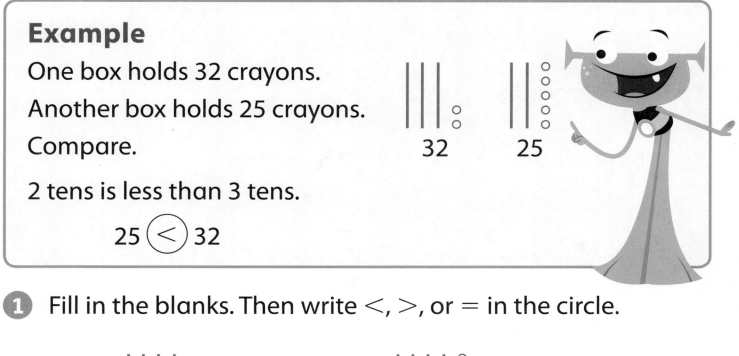

Example

One box holds 32 crayons.

Another box holds 25 crayons.

Compare.

2 tens is less than 3 tens.

25 $<$ 32

1 Fill in the blanks. Then write $<$, $>$, or $=$ in the circle.

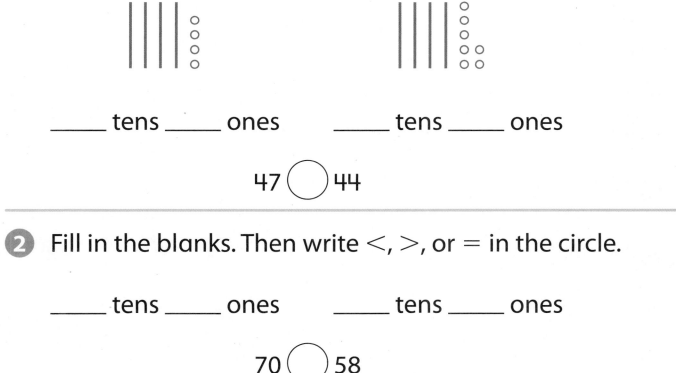

_____ tens _____ ones   _____ tens _____ ones

47 $\bigcirc$ 44

2 Fill in the blanks. Then write $<$, $>$, or $=$ in the circle.

_____ tens _____ ones   _____ tens _____ ones

70 $\bigcirc$ 58

3 Fill in the blanks. Then write <, >, or = in the circle.

3 tens 6 ones   3 tens 9 ones

_____ ◯ _____

4 Write <, >, or = in the circle.

91 ◯ 91

85 ◯ 82

5 Write <, >, or = in the circle.

54 ◯ 45

36 ◯ 63

6 Write <, >, or = in the circle.

26 ◯ 29

41 ◯ 40

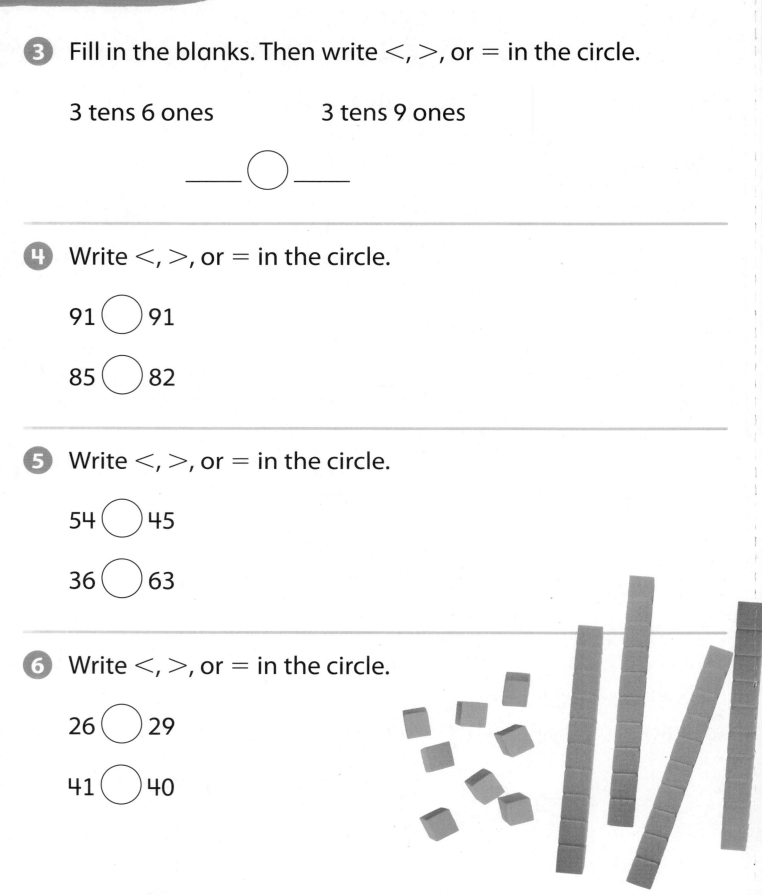

Refine Comparing Numbers

Apply It

Solve problems 1–6.

1 Fill in the blanks. Then write <, >, or = in the circle.

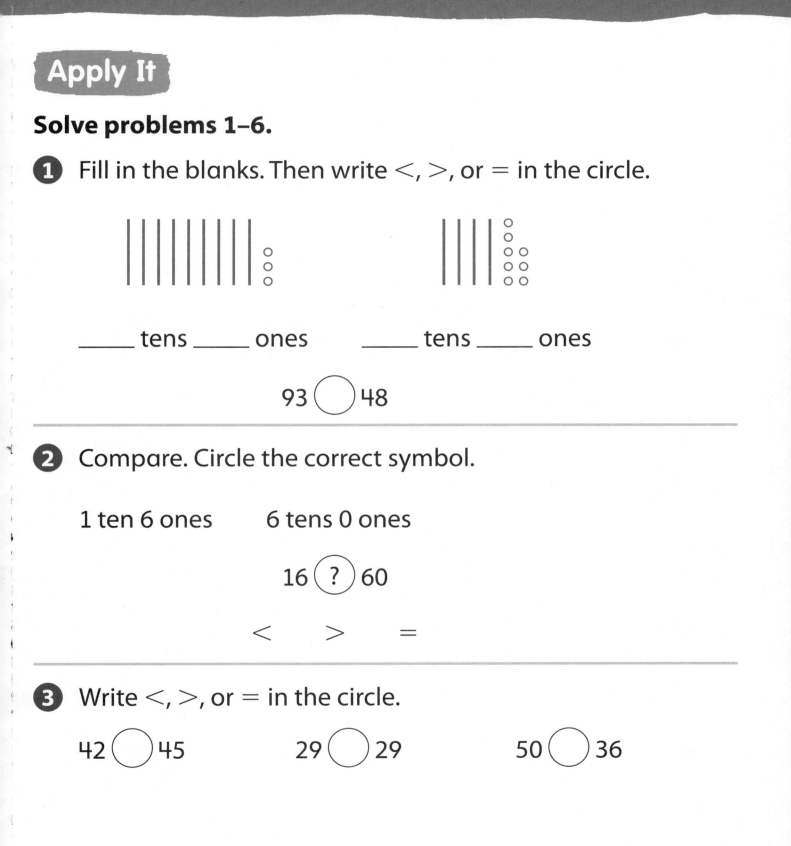

_____ tens _____ ones   _____ tens _____ ones

93 ◯ 48

---

2 Compare. Circle the correct symbol.

1 ten 6 ones   6 tens 0 ones

16 (?) 60

<   >   =

---

3 Write <, >, or = in the circle.

42 ◯ 45   29 ◯ 29   50 ◯ 36

4 Write <, >, or = in the circle.

74 ◯ 74

85 ◯ 87

63 ◯ 28

---

5 Write <, >, or = in the circle.

71 ◯ 65

34 ◯ 39

48 ◯ 48

---

6 Write <, >, or = in the circle.

54 ◯ 59

83 ◯ 83

60 ◯ 47

Tell Time

Dear Family,

This week your child is learning to tell time to the hour and half hour.

Your child is learning to tell time on analog clocks, like the one shown below.

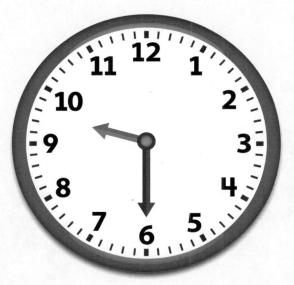

Your child will learn that the short hand shows the **hour (h)** and is called the **hour hand**. On the clock above, it is pointing between the 9 and 10, so the hour is 9.

He or she will also learn that the long hand shows the **minutes (min)** and is called the **minute hand**. On the clock above, the minute hand is halfway around the clock and is pointing to the 6, which represents one **half hour**. So, the time is 30 minutes after 9, **half past** 9, or 9:30.

Your child will also practice telling time on **digital clocks**.

The time is 5 **o'clock**.

Invite your child to share what he or she knows about telling time to the hour and half hour by doing the following activity together.

Activity Telling Time

Do this activity with your child to explore telling time.

Materials 2 crayons of different lengths

Help your child practice showing times to the hour and half hour on the clock below. Think of activities that your child does around the same time each day. Tell your child the time that an activity occurs and have him or her show the time by placing the crayons as the hands on the clock. The shorter crayon is the hour hand, and the longer crayon is the minute hand. Only suggest times that are on the hour or half hour.

For example:

- *We eat breakfast at 7:30.*

- *You get on the school bus at 8:00.*

- *Soccer practice starts at 4:30.*

Try It

4:00

🧰 **Math Toolkit**
- clock face model

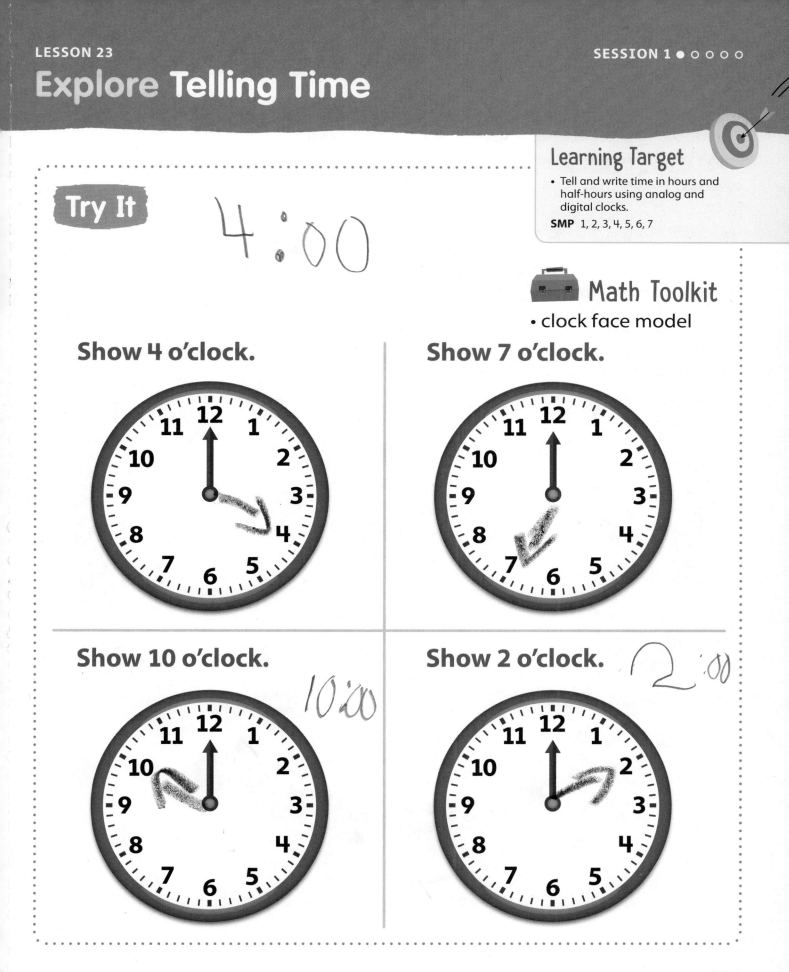

Show 4 o'clock.

Show 7 o'clock.

Show 10 o'clock.   10:00

Show 2 o'clock.   2:00

Connect It

_7_ o'clock

Prepare for Telling Time

1 Think about what you know about telling time.
Fill in each box. Use words, numbers, and pictures.
Show as many ideas as you can.

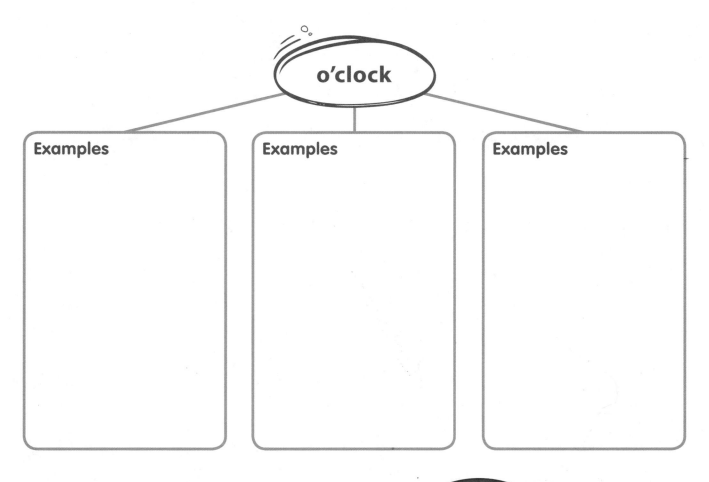

o'clock

Examples	Examples	Examples

2 Aiko tries to show 3 o'clock.
Is she right?

Circle: Yes   No

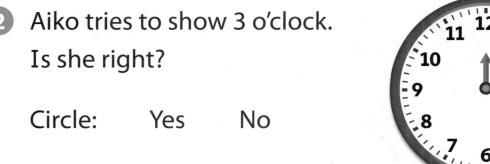

3 **Show 5 o'clock.**

Show 8 o'clock.

Show 11 o'clock.

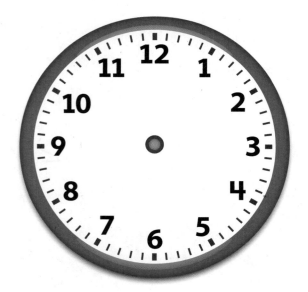

Show 6 o'clock.

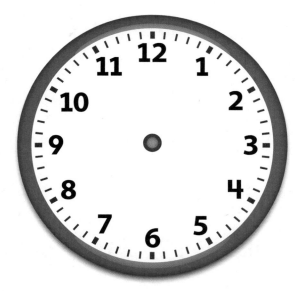

Develop Telling Time

It is 2 o'clock.

Next, it is just past 2 o'clock.

Then it is almost 3 o'clock.

Then it is 3 o'clock.

Where is the hour hand at each time?

hour hand

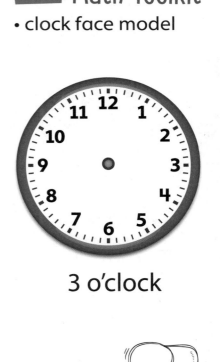

Try It

Draw the hour hand to show the time.

🧰 **Math Toolkit**
• clock face model

just past 2 o'clock

almost 3 o'clock

3 o'clock

DISCUSS IT

How did you know where to draw the hour hand?

It is 2 o'clock.

Next, it is just past 2 o'clock.

Then it is almost 3 o'clock.

Then it is 3 o'clock.

Where is the hour hand at each time?

Model It

The hour hand shows the time.

just past

_____ o'clock

almost

_____ o'clock

_____ o'clock

Connect It

1 How is your way like **Model It**? How is it different?

2 How did using the numbers on the clock face help you draw the hour hands?

Apply It

3 Draw the hour hand to show the time.

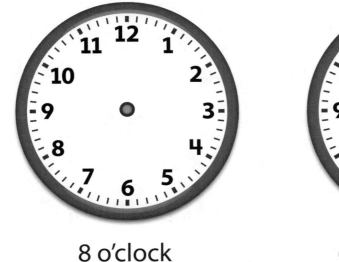

8 o'clock

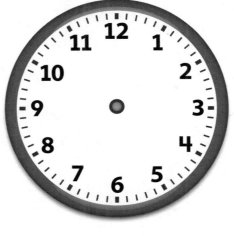

almost 9 o'clock

4 Which hour hand shows 11 o'clock?
Circle the clock.

5 Which hour hand shows almost 6 o'clock?
Circle the clock.

6 Draw the hour hand to show the times.

just past 7 o'clock   almost 8 o'clock   8 o'clock

Practice Telling Time

Look at the Example. Then solve problems 1–5.

Example

The hour hand on a clock shows the time.

hour hand

5 o'clock   just past 5 o'clock   almost 6 o'clock

1 Which hour hand shows 1 o'clock? Circle the clock.

2 Which hour hand shows 8 o'clock? Circle the clock.

3 Which hour hand shows almost 4 o'clock?
Circle the clock.

---

4 Draw a line from the time to the clock that shows that time.

| 11 o'clock | just past 11 o'clock | almost 12 o'clock |

---

5 Draw the hour hand to show the times.

just past 9 o'clock   almost 10 o'clock   10 o'clock

Develop Telling Time

What time do these clocks show?

How do you know?

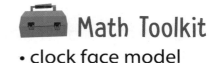 Math Toolkit

• clock face model

DISCUSS IT

What is the same about these two clocks? What is different?

What time do these clocks show?

How do you know?

Model It

Read the time.
The **digital clock** shows the same time with numbers.

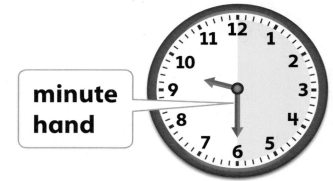

minute hand

It is 30 **minutes** after _____ .

It is _____ :30, or nine thirty.

It is **half past** _____ .

Connect It

1 How is your way like Model It? How is it different?

2 Buzz says 9:30 is halfway between the **hours** of 9:00 and 10:00. So, 30 minutes is the same as a **half hour**.

Do you agree? Why or why not?

Apply It

3 It is _____:30, or seven thirty.

It is 30 minutes after _____ .

It is half past _____ .

4 It is 30 minutes after _____ .

It is half past _____ .

It is _____:30.

5 Dan starts cooking at 4 o'clock. Dan finishes cooking at half past 4. Draw hands on the clocks to show the times.

Start

Finish

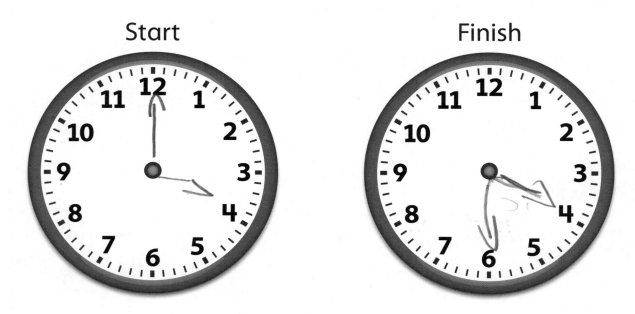

6 It is half past 12.

Show the time on both clocks.

Practice Telling Time

Look at the Example. Then solve problems 1–5.

Example

The minute hand is halfway around the clock.
The hour hand is halfway between 8 and 9.

It is half past 8.
It is 30 minutes after 8.
It is 8:30, or eight thirty.

minute hand

1 It is __11__ :30.

It is 30 minutes after __11:00__

It is half past __11:00__.

2 It is 30 minutes after _____ .

It is half past _____ .

It is _____ :30.

3 It is 1:30.

Show this time on both clocks.

4 It is half past 2.

Show this time on both clocks.

5 Imani starts eating at 6 o'clock.

Imani finishes eating at half past 6.

Draw hands on the clocks to show the times.

Imani starts eating.   Imani finishes eating.

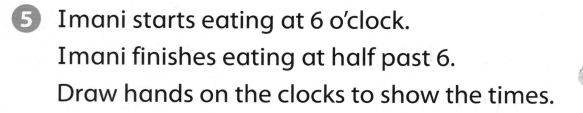

Refine Telling Time

Complete the Example. Then solve problems 1–5.

Example

These clocks show the same time.
What time is it?

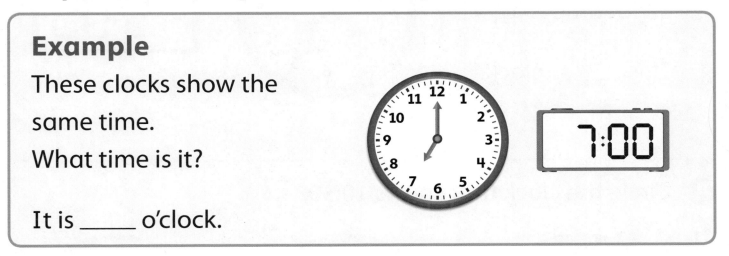

It is _____ o'clock.

Apply It

1 Circle the clock that shows 4:00.

2 It is half past 3. Show the time on these clocks.

3 These clocks show the same time. What time is it?

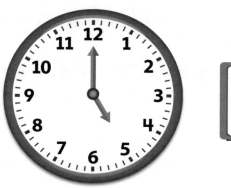 

It is _____ o'clock.

---

4 Circle the clock that shows 10:30.

---

5 It is half past 8.

It is _____ minutes after _____ o'clock.

Practice Telling Time

Look at the Example. Then solve problems 1–5.

Example

Both clocks show 4:30.

1 Circle the clock that shows 2:30.

2 Circle the clock that shows 10:00.

3 It is half past 7. Show the time on these clocks.

4 It is half past 1.

It is _____ minutes after _____ o'clock.

5 Draw lines to match the clocks that show the same times.

Refine Telling Time

Apply It

Solve problems 1–6.

1 Read the digital clock.

12:30

Draw the hands to
show the time.

---

2 Circle the clock that shows 11:00.

---

3 It is eight thirty. Show the time on these clocks.

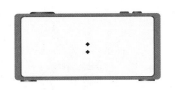

4 These clocks show the same time. What time is it?

It is _____ o'clock.

---

5 Circle the clock that shows 6:30.

---

6 It is half past 11.

It is _____ minutes after _____ o'clock.

Money

Dear Family,

This week your child is learning to identify coins and their values and find the total value of groups of coins.

quarter
25¢

dime
10¢

nickel
5¢

penny
1¢

When you count a group of coins, you can count coins with the greatest value first. Putting coins in order from the greatest to the least value is helpful. For example, to find the total value of 2 dimes and 3 pennies, count the dimes by tens first and then count on by ones to count the pennies. Counting the coins this way helps your child find the total value of the group of dimes and pennies.

Find the value of 2 dimes and 3 pennies.

Count by tens.   Count on by ones.

10¢   20¢   21¢   22¢   23¢

When a group of coins has a value of 100 **cents (¢)**, it is equal to one dollar. For example, a group of 100 pennies or 10 dimes is equal to one dollar.

Invite your child to share what he or she knows about coins and about counting groups of coins by doing the following activity together.

dollar ($)

Do this activity with your child to explore money.

Materials 2 quarters, 3 dimes, 3 nickels, 5 pennies

Help your child practice recognizing and counting coins. Have your child sort the coins by their values. Ask your child to name one of each coin and tell its value in cents. Your child should look at the pictures on both sides of each coin to help identify it.

Next, help your child practice counting the dimes and pennies to find their total value. Your child should put the coins in a row, count the dimes by tens first, and count on by ones to count the pennies. It may help your child to count aloud.

For example:

Start: 10¢, 20¢, 30¢   **Count on:** 31¢, 32¢, 33¢, 34¢, 35¢

- Make a different group with only dimes and pennies.

- Put the dimes and pennies in a row, with dimes first and then pennies.

- Count to find the total value of the dimes and pennies.

Look for other opportunities to practice recognizing coins and counting groups of dimes and pennies (up to 1 dollar) with your child.

Explore Money

Pretend you buy something at the store. How much does your item cost?

 Try It

Color the coins you used.

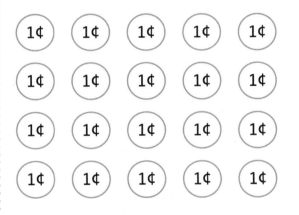

🧰 **Math Toolkit**
- play or real coins

_____ pennies

My item costs _____ ¢.

Connect It

Use a drawing and numbers to show 15 cents (¢) in two different ways.

Prepare for Counting Money

1   Think about what you know about the value of coins.
    Fill in each box. Use words, numbers, and pictures.
    Show as many ideas as you can.

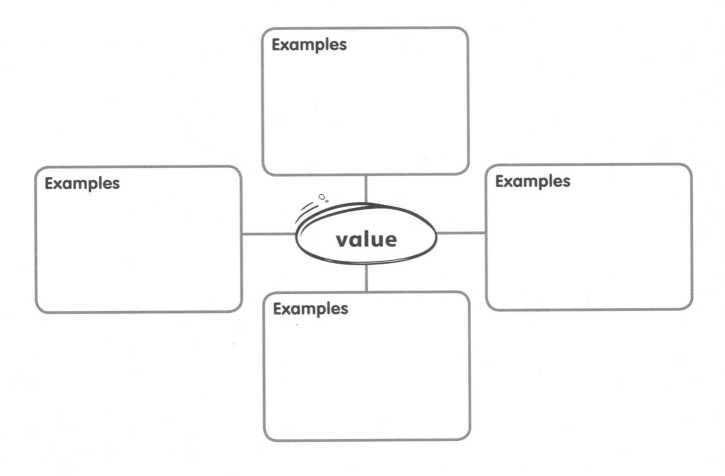

2   Berto buys a pencil that costs 13 cents.
    Color the coins he uses.

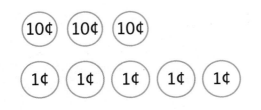

3 Solve the problem.

Use a drawing and numbers to show 13 cents in two different ways.

Develop Finding the Values of Coins

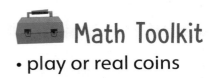

Put the coins in order from least value to greatest value. What is the value of each of these coins? Use the clues.

• **The largest coin is worth 25¢.**
• **Another coin is worth 5¢.**

 Try It

🧰 **Math Toolkit**
• play or real coins

DISCUSS IT
How did you know which coin to start with?

Put the coins in order from least value to greatest value. What is the value of each of these coins? Use the clues.

• The largest coin is worth 25¢.

• Another coin is worth 5¢.

Model It

Each coin has 2 sides. Name each coin.

Look at the value of each coin.

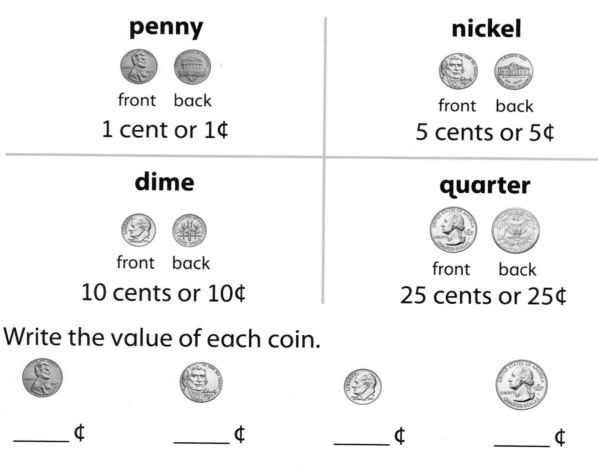

penny

front   back

1 cent or 1¢

nickel

front   back

5 cents or 5¢

dime

front   back

10 cents or 10¢

quarter

front   back

25 cents or 25¢

Write the value of each coin.

_____ ¢   _____ ¢   _____ ¢   _____ ¢

1 How is your way like **Model It**? How is it different?

2 How did you use the coins to know their values?

3 Write the value of each coin.

_____ ¢   _____ ¢   _____ ¢   _____ ¢

4 Circle each coin that has a value of 10¢.

5 Circle each coin that has a value of 25¢.

Practice Finding the Values of Coins

Look at the Example. Then solve problems 1–5.

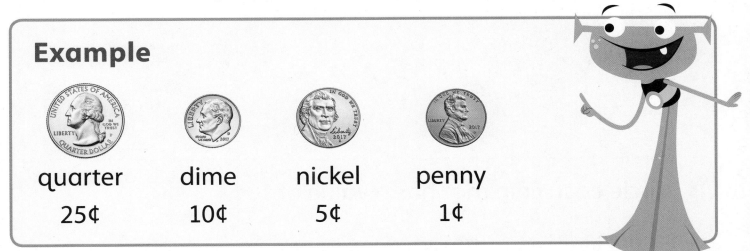

Example

| quarter | dime | nickel | penny |
| 25¢ | 10¢ | 5¢ | 1¢ |

1 Write the value of each coin.

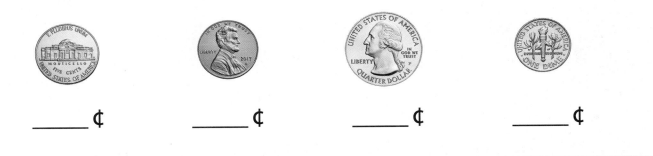

_____ ¢   _____ ¢   _____ ¢   _____ ¢

2 Write the value of each coin.

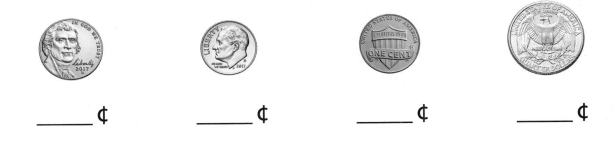

_____ ¢   _____ ¢   _____ ¢   _____ ¢

3 Circle each coin that has a value of 5¢.

4 Circle each coin that has a value of 10¢.

5 Draw a line to match the coin names and values.

quarter   1¢

dime   5¢

nickel   25¢

penny   10¢

Develop Counting Money

What is the total value of these coins?

Try It

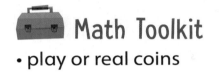 **Math Toolkit**
• play or real coins

DISCUSS IT
The coin I counted
first was . . .

What is the total value of these coins?

Model It

Count the coins. Put the coins in order.

Start with the coin with the greatest value.

Count by tens.   Count on by ones.

10¢   20¢   21¢   22¢   23¢

The value of these coins is _____ ¢.

Connect It

1 How is your way like **Model It**? How is it different?

2 How much money?

Buzz says 23¢.

Boom says 32¢.

Who is correct? How do you know?

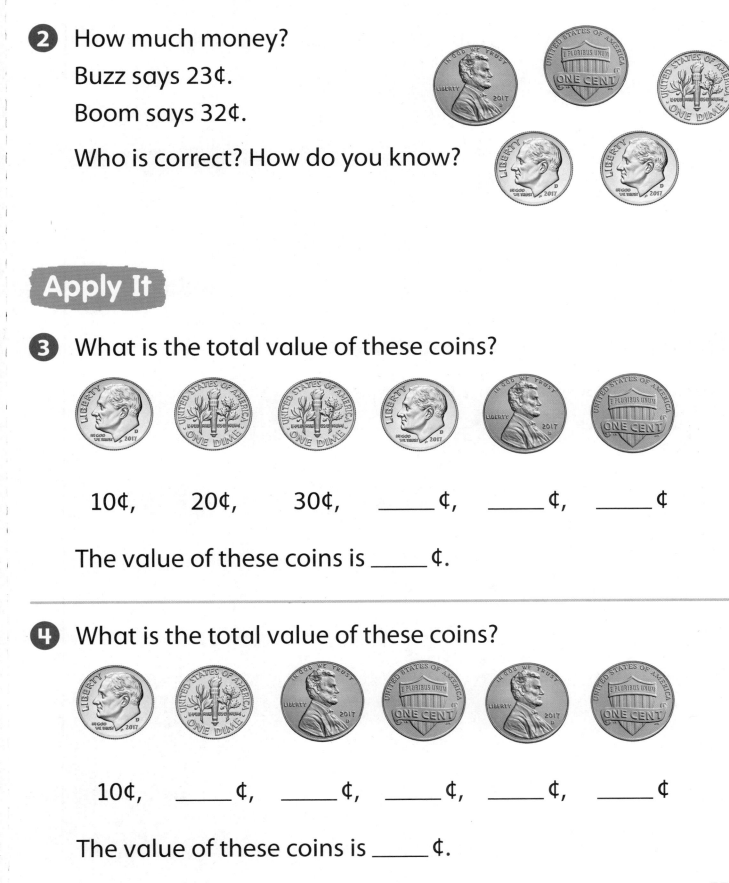

Apply It

3 What is the total value of these coins?

10¢,   20¢,   30¢,   _____ ¢,   _____ ¢,   _____ ¢

The value of these coins is _____ ¢.

4 What is the total value of these coins?

10¢,   _____ ¢,   _____ ¢,   _____ ¢,   _____ ¢,   _____ ¢

The value of these coins is _____ ¢.

    Lesson 24 Money **551**

5 What is the total value of these coins?

The value of these coins is _____ ¢, or 1 **dollar**.

---

6 What is the total value of these coins?

10¢, _____ ¢, _____ ¢, _____ ¢, _____ ¢, _____ ¢

The value of these coins is _____ ¢.

Practice Counting Money

Look at the Example. Then solve problems 1–4.

Example

What is the total value of these coins?

10¢, 20¢, 30¢, 40¢, 50¢, 51¢, 52¢

The value of these coins is 52¢.

1 What is the total value of these coins?

Count by tens.   Count on by ones.

10¢, _____ ¢, _____ ¢, _____ ¢, _____ ¢, _____ ¢, _____ ¢

The value of these coins is _____ ¢.

2 What is the total value of these coins?

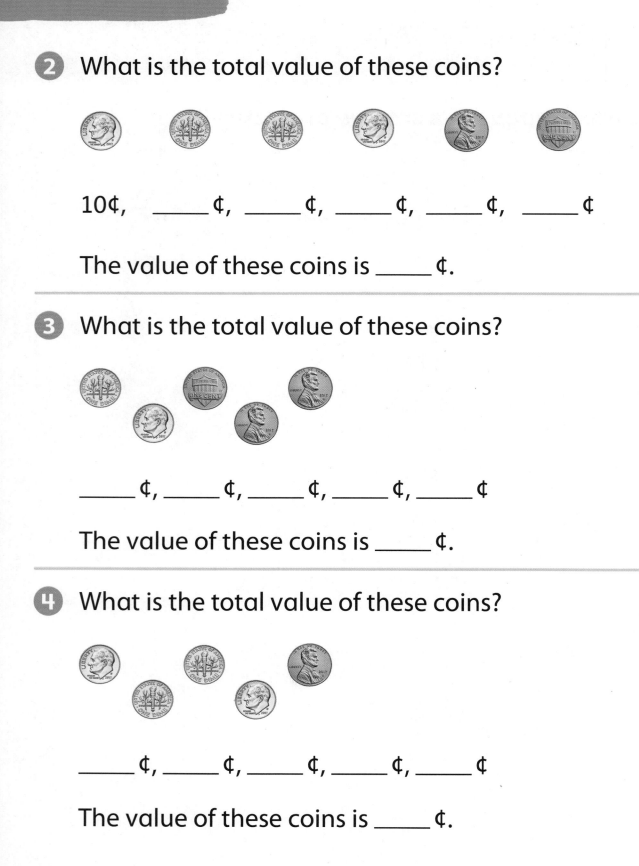

10¢,   _____ ¢, _____ ¢, _____ ¢, _____ ¢, _____ ¢

The value of these coins is _____ ¢.

3 What is the total value of these coins?

_____ ¢, _____ ¢, _____ ¢, _____ ¢, _____ ¢

The value of these coins is _____ ¢.

4 What is the total value of these coins?

_____ ¢, _____ ¢, _____ ¢, _____ ¢, _____ ¢

The value of these coins is _____ ¢.

Refine Counting Money

Complete the Example. Then solve problems 1–4.

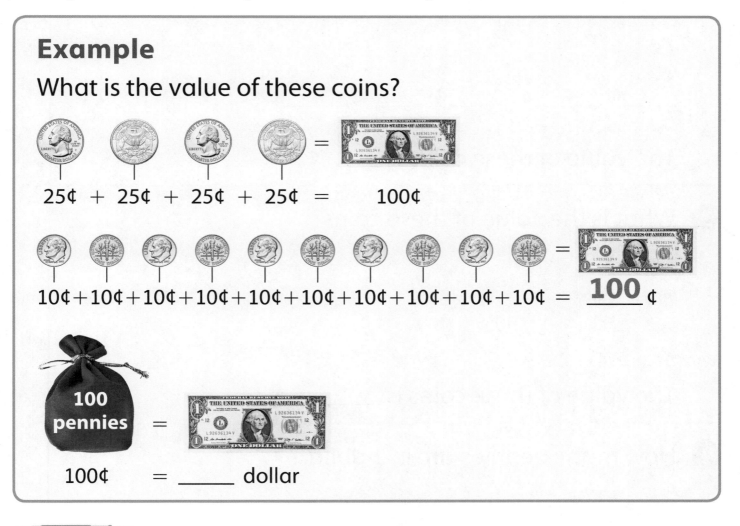

Example

What is the value of these coins?

25¢ + 25¢ + 25¢ + 25¢ = 100¢

10¢+10¢+10¢+10¢+10¢+10¢+10¢+10¢+10¢+10¢ = __100__ ¢

100 pennies =

100¢ = _____ dollar

Apply It

1 What is the value of these coins?

The value of these coins is _____ ¢.

2 What is the value of these coins?

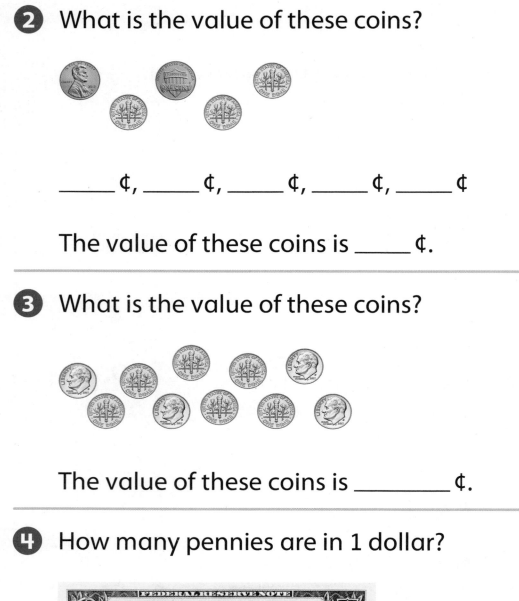

_____ ¢, _____ ¢, _____ ¢, _____ ¢, _____ ¢

The value of these coins is _____ ¢.

---

3 What is the value of these coins?

The value of these coins is _____ ¢.

---

4 How many pennies are in 1 dollar?

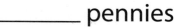 _____ pennies

Practice Counting Money

Look at the Example. Then solve problems 1–5.

Example What is the value of these coins?

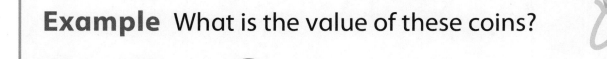

10¢, 20¢, 30¢, 40¢, 41¢, 42¢
The value of these coins is 42¢.

1 What is the value of these coins?

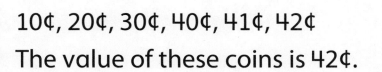

_____ ¢, _____ ¢, _____ ¢, _____ ¢, _____ ¢

The value of these coins is _____ ¢.

2 What is the value of these coins?

_____ ¢, _____ ¢, _____ ¢, _____ ¢, _____ ¢

The value of these coins is _____ ¢.

3 Circle each coin that has a value of 10¢.

---

4 What is the value of these coins?

The value of these coins is _____ dollar.

---

5 What is the value of these coins?

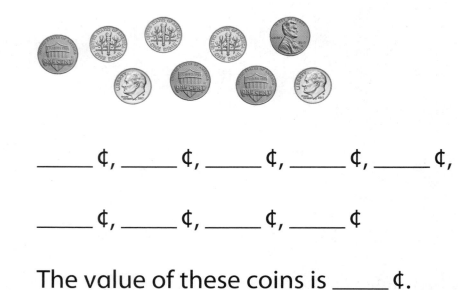

_____ ¢, _____ ¢, _____ ¢, _____ ¢, _____ ¢,

_____ ¢, _____ ¢, _____ ¢, _____ ¢

The value of these coins is _____ ¢.

Refine Counting Money

Solve problems 1–6.

 Apply It

1 What is the value of these coins?

10¢, 20¢, 30¢, 40¢, 50¢, 60¢, 61¢?

The value of these coins is _____ ¢.

2 What is the value of these coins?

10¢, _____ ¢, _____ ¢, _____ ¢, _____ ¢, _____ ¢, _____ ¢

The value of these coins is _____ ¢.

3 What is the value of these coins?

The value of these coins is _____ ¢.

4 What is the value of these coins?

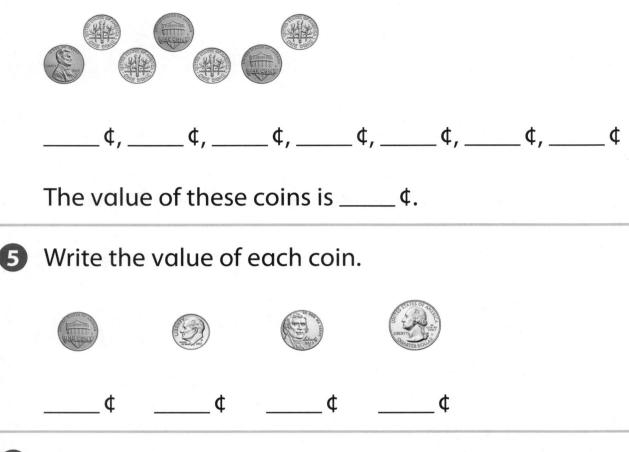

_____ ¢, _____ ¢, _____ ¢, _____ ¢, _____ ¢, _____ ¢, _____ ¢

The value of these coins is _____ ¢.

5 Write the value of each coin.

_____ ¢   _____ ¢   _____ ¢   _____ ¢

6 How many quarters are in 1 dollar?

_____ quarters

In this unit you learned to . . .

Skill	Lesson
Show numbers as tens.	19
Count on a 120 chart.	20
Show numbers as tens and ones.	21
Compare numbers.	22
Tell time to the hour and half hour.	23

Think about what you learned.

Use words, numbers, and drawings.

1 I am proud that I can . . .

2 I could use more practice with . . .

Solve the problems.

1 Compare. Circle <, >, or =.

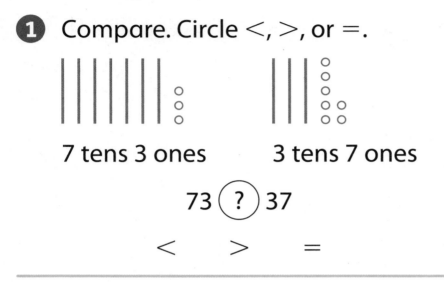

7 tens 3 ones   3 tens 7 ones

73 (?) 37

<   >   =

2 Sam gets to school at
eight o'clock.
Show the time on
these clocks.

3 Color to show 70.

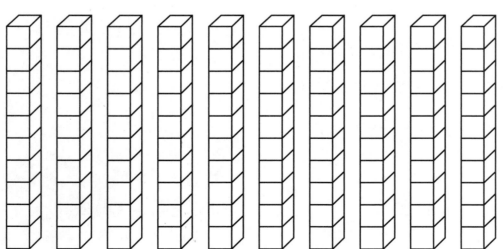

©Curriculum Associates, LLC   Copying is not permitted.

4 How many tens in all?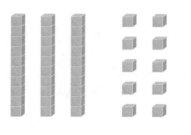

_____ tens

---

5 Fill in the blanks. Use the chart.

91	92	93	94	95	96	97	98	99	100
101	102	103	104	105	106	107	108	109	110
111	112	113	114	115	116	117	118	119	120

1 more than 92 is _____.

1 more than 99 is _____.

1 more than 110 is _____.

1 more than 118 is _____.

---

6 Use these tens and ones.
Write the two-digit number. _____
Write the number as tens and
ones two different ways.

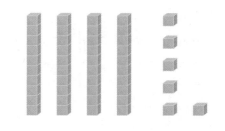

_____ tens _____ ones   _____ tens _____ ones

Put It Together

7 Abe, Ben, and TJ count trees.
Ben counts more trees than Abe.
Ben counts fewer trees than TJ.
Ben's number of trees has the
digit 8 in it.

Abe and TJ's trees are shown.
Show the trees Ben counts.

Abe's Trees	TJ's Trees
||| ∘∘∘∘	|||| ∘

Compare the number of trees each person counted.

Abe   **TJ**   **TJ**   **Ben**

___ ◯ ___   ___ ◯ ___

Vocabulary

Draw or write examples for each word. Then draw or write to show other math words in the unit.

cent (¢) the smallest unit of money. 100 cents is equal to 1 dollar.

My Example

digit a symbol used to write numbers. 0, 1, 2, 3, 4, 5, 6, 7, 8, and 9 are digits.

My Example

digital clock a clock that uses digits to show the time.

My Example

dime a coin with a value of 10 cents (10¢).

My Example

dollar ($) a unit of money. There are 100 cents in 1 dollar ($1).

My Example

greater than a group or number that has more.

My Example

greater than symbol (>) a symbol that means *is greater than*.

My Example

half hour a unit of time. There are 30 minutes in one half hour.

My Example

half past a time that is 30 minutes after an hour.

My Example

hour (h) a unit of time. There are 60 minutes in 1 hour.

My Example

hour hand the shorter hand on a clock. It shows hours.

My Example

less than the group or number with fewer, not as much, not as many.

My Example

less than symbol
(<) symbol that means *is less than*.

My Example

minute (min) a unit of time. There are 60 minutes in 1 hour.

My Example

minute hand the longer hand on a clock. It shows minutes.

My Example

nickel a coin with a value of 5 cents (5¢).

My Example

o'clock to tell time for an hour.

My Example

penny a coin with a value of 1 cent (1¢).

My Example

place value the value of a digit based on its position in a number. For example, the 2 in 24 is in the tens place and has a value of 2 tens or 20.

My Example

quarter a coin with a value of 25 cents (25¢).

My Example

My Word: _____

_____

_____

_____

My Example

My Word: _____

_____

_____

_____

My Example

My Word: _____

_____

_____

_____

My Example

My Word: _____

_____

_____

_____

My Example

☑ Self Check

Before starting this unit, check off the skills you know below. As you complete each lesson, see how many more skills you can check off!

I can . . .	Before	After
Add and subtract tens.	☐	☐
Add or subtract 10 from any number.	☐	☐
Add tens to any number.	☐	☐
Add one-digit and two-digit numbers.	☐	☐
Add 2 two-digit numbers.	☐	☐

Build Your Vocabulary

My Math Words

Read the sentences then write your answer.

What is the total number of stars Roberta has?

★ ★ ★ ★   _____

David has fewer stars than Roberta.

Draw the stars David could have.

Maria has more stars than Roberta.

Draw the stars Maria could have.

My Academic Words

Use the academic words to complete the sentences.

☐ always   ☐ plan   ☐ prepare

1 A teen number _____ has a one in the tens place.

2 Make a _____ to find out what kind of pet each student has.

3 I can _____ for the play by reading my lines.

Add and Subtract Tens

Dear Family,

This week your child is learning to add and subtract tens.

Your child will learn that adding or subtracting a number that is a multiple of ten (10, 20, 30, etc.) can be thought of as adding or subtracting a number of tens (1 ten, 2 tens, 3 tens, etc.) Similarly, your child will realize that $2 + 6 = 8$ can help him or her find $20 + 60 = 80$. Exploring strategies for adding and subtracting tens will help your child prepare to add and subtract all two-digit numbers.

Example: Find $40 + 20$.

Write the numbers as tens. Add the tens.

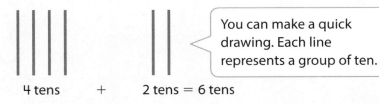

> You can make a quick drawing. Each line represents a group of ten.

4 tens   +   2 tens = 6 tens

$40 + 20 = 60$

Example: Find $70 - 30$.

Write the numbers as tens. Subtract the tens.

7 tens − **3 tens** = 4 tens
$70 - $**$30$**$ = 40$

Invite your child to share what he or she knows about adding and subtracting tens by doing the following activity together.

Activity Adding and Subtracting Tens

Do this activity with your child to add and subtract tens.

Materials pencil and paper

Help your child see how the addition he or she already knows can help with adding tens.

- Write an addition problem that has a total up to 10. For example, you could write $7 + 2 =$ _____ .

- Have your child find and write the answer using any strategy he or she prefers.

- Then rewrite the problem so that the first digit of each number remains the same and the second digit is zero. Using this example, you would write $70 + 20 =$ _____ .

- Have your child write the answer.

After your child solves several addition problems, adjust the activity for subtraction. Present subtraction problems in which the first number is less than 10 and greater than the second number, such as $9 - 2$, $5 - 4$, or $8 - 6$.

$$7 + 2 = 9$$
$$70 + 20 = 90$$

Explore Adding and Subtracting Tens

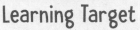

Jon uses 20 blocks.

He then uses 20 more.

How many blocks does Jon use in all?

Try It

Math Toolkit

• base-ten blocks
• hundred charts

Jon uses _____ blocks in all.

Connect It

Add in two different ways.

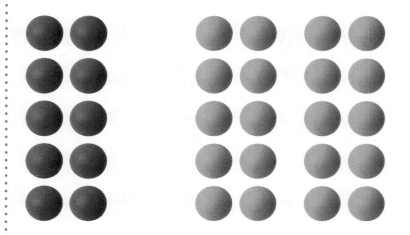

_____ balls and _____ more balls is _____ balls.

_____ ten and _____ more tens is _____ tens.

Prepare for Adding and Subtracting Tens

1 Think about what you know about groups of ten. Fill in each box. Use words, numbers, and pictures. Show as many ideas as you can.

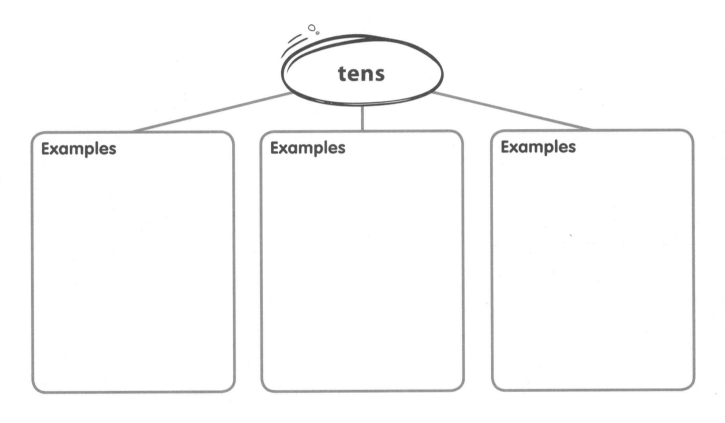

2 Fill in the blanks for the base-ten blocks shown.

_____ tens and _____ more tens is _____ tens.

3 Solve the problem.

Add in two different ways.

_____ balls and _____ more balls is _____ balls.

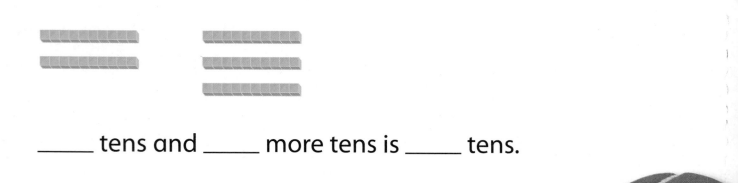

_____ tens and _____ more tens is _____ tens.

Develop Adding Tens

Tessa has 30 erasers in a jar.

She gets 20 more.

How many erasers does she have now?

 **Try It**

Math Toolkit
- base-ten blocks
- connecting cubes
- hundred charts

DISCUSS IT
How can thinking
about 3 + 2 help?

Tessa has 30 erasers in a jar.
She gets 20 more.
How many erasers does
she have now?

Model It

Find 30 + 20.
Write the numbers as tens.
Then add the tens.

3 tens + 2 tens = 5 tens

30 + 20 = _____

Tessa has _____ erasers now.

Connect It

1 How is your way like **Model It**? How is it different?

2 How is adding tens like adding ones?
How is it different?

Apply It

3 Mia has 40 shells.
She collects 30 more.
How many shells does Mia have now?

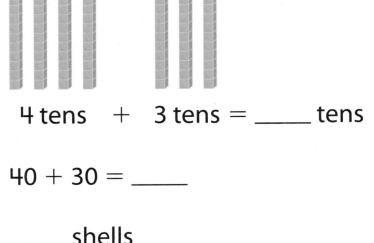

4 tens + 3 tens = _____ tens

40 + 30 = _____

_____ shells

4 Find 20 + 20.

2 tens + 2 tens = _____ tens

20 + 20 = _____

---

5 Find 20 + 60.

_____ tens + _____ tens = _____ tens

20 + 60 = _____

---

6 Find 50 + 30.

_____ tens + _____ tens = _____ tens

50 + 30 = _____

Practice Adding Tens

Look at the Example. Then solve problems 1–5.

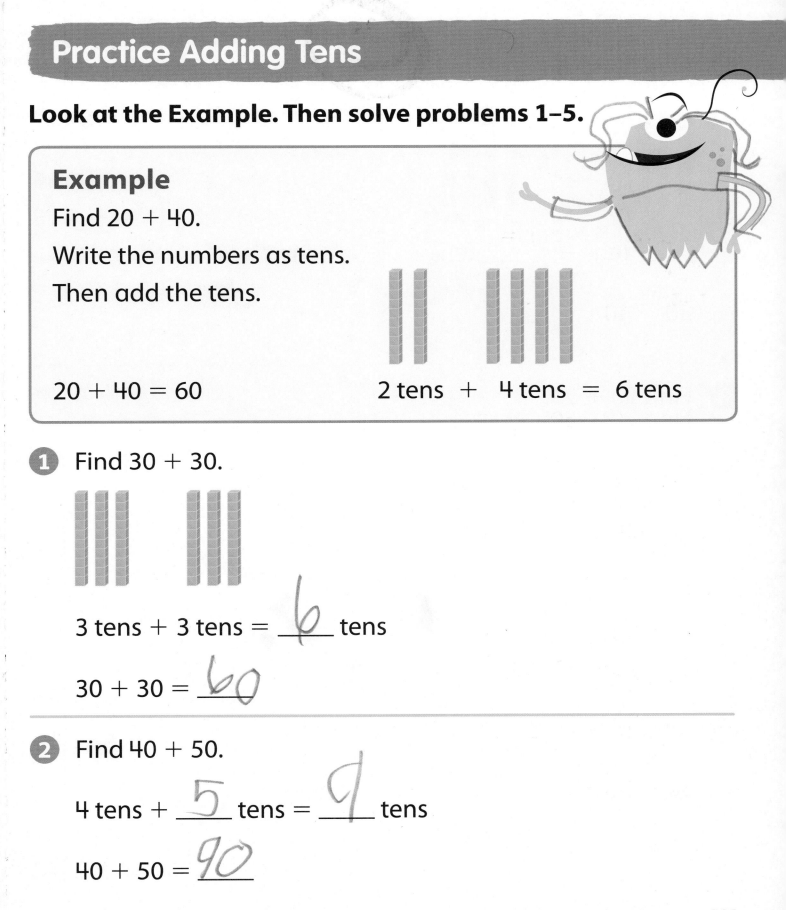

Example

Find 20 + 40.

Write the numbers as tens.

Then add the tens.

20 + 40 = 60

2 tens + 4 tens = 6 tens

---

1 Find 30 + 30.

3 tens + 3 tens = __6__ tens

30 + 30 = __60__

---

2 Find 40 + 50.

4 tens + __5__ tens = __9__ tens

40 + 50 = __90__

3 Find 30 + 40.

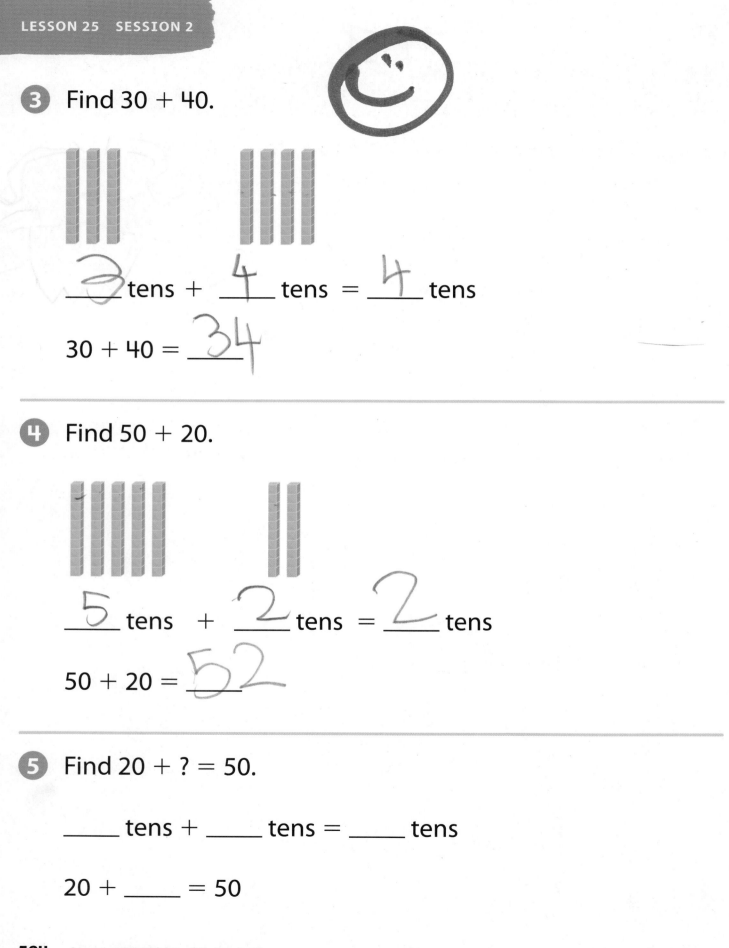

_3_ tens + _4_ tens = _4_ tens

30 + 40 = _34_

4 Find 50 + 20.

_5_ tens + _2_ tens = _2_ tens

50 + 20 = _52_

5 Find 20 + ? = 50.

____ tens + ____ tens = ____ tens

20 + ____ = 50

Develop Adding and Subtracting Tens

Julie picks 70 berries.
She gives 40 to Andy.
How many berries does
Julie have left?

Try It

🧰 Math Toolkit
- base-ten blocks 👆
- connecting cubes
- hundred charts

DISCUSS IT
I found my answer
by . . .

**Julie picks 70 berries.
She gives 40 to Andy.
How many berries does
Julie have left?**

Model It

Find 70 − 40.

Draw **7** tens.

Cross out **4** tens.

How many tens are left?

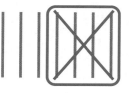

7 tens − 4 tens = _____ tens

70 − 40 = _____

Julie has _____ berries left.

Connect It

 How is your way like **Model It**? How is it different?

2 Boom says he does not have to use subtraction to solve $80 - 60$. He says he can think $60 + ? = 80$.

Is he right? How do you know?

Apply It

3 Jose counts 30 fish.
Kai counts 50 fish.
How many more fish does Kai count than Jose?

$30 + ? = 50$

3 tens +_____ tens = _____ tens

$50 - 30 =$ _____

_____ more fish

4 Find $60 - 20$.

_____ tens − _____ tens = _____ tens

$60 - 20 =$ _____

5 Find 80 − 40.

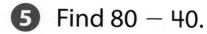

_____ tens − _____ tens = _____ tens

80 − 40 = _____

---

6 Find 50 − 50.

50 − 50 = _____

---

7 Find 90 − 70.

70 + ? = 90

7 tens + _____ tens = 9 tens

90 − 70 = _____

Practice Adding and Subtracting Tens

Look at the Example. Then solve problems 1–5.

Example

There are 50 children. 20 take the bus.

The rest walk.

How many children walk?

Find $50 - 20$.

$50 - 20 = 30$

30 children walk.

1 Find $40 - 30$.

4 tens $-$ 3 tens $=$ __1__ ten

$40 - 30 = $ __10__

2 Find $80 - 40$.

8 tens $-$ __4__ tens $=$ __4__ tens

$80 - 40 = $ __40__

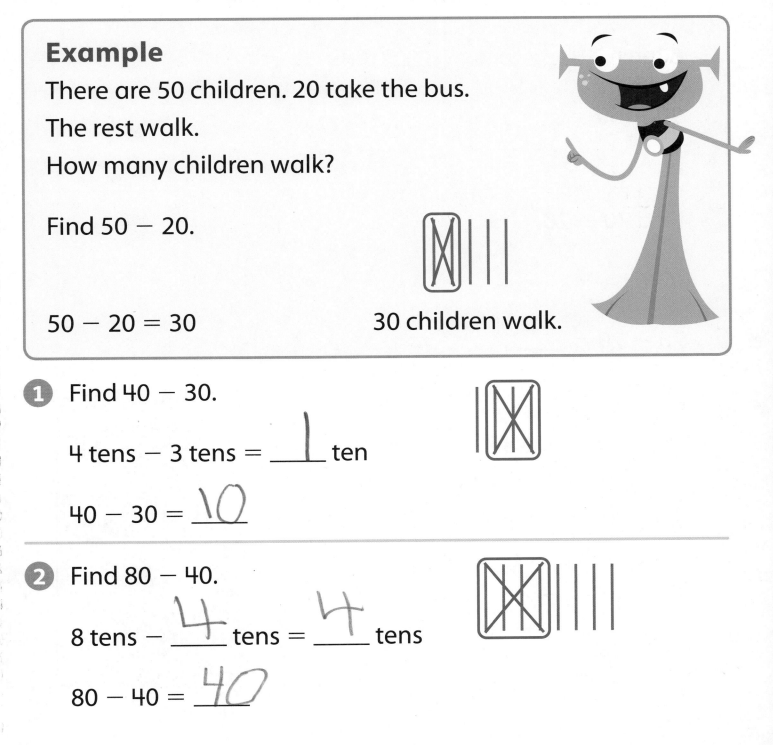

6 ✳ 9 = 3

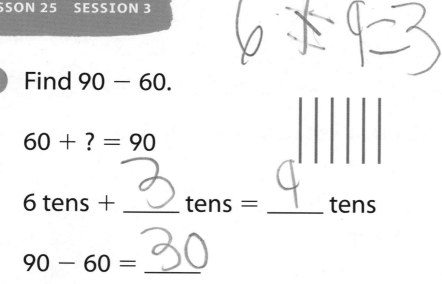

3 Find 90 − 60.

60 + ? = 90

6 tens + ___3___ tens = ___9___ tens

90 − 60 = ___30___

---

4 Find 70 − 20.

70 − 20 = 50

---

5 There are 80 seats.
   50 seats are taken.
   The rest are empty.
   How many seats are empty?

   80 − 50 = 30

   ___30___ seats are empty.

Refine Adding and Subtracting Tens

Complete the Example. Then solve problems 1–5.

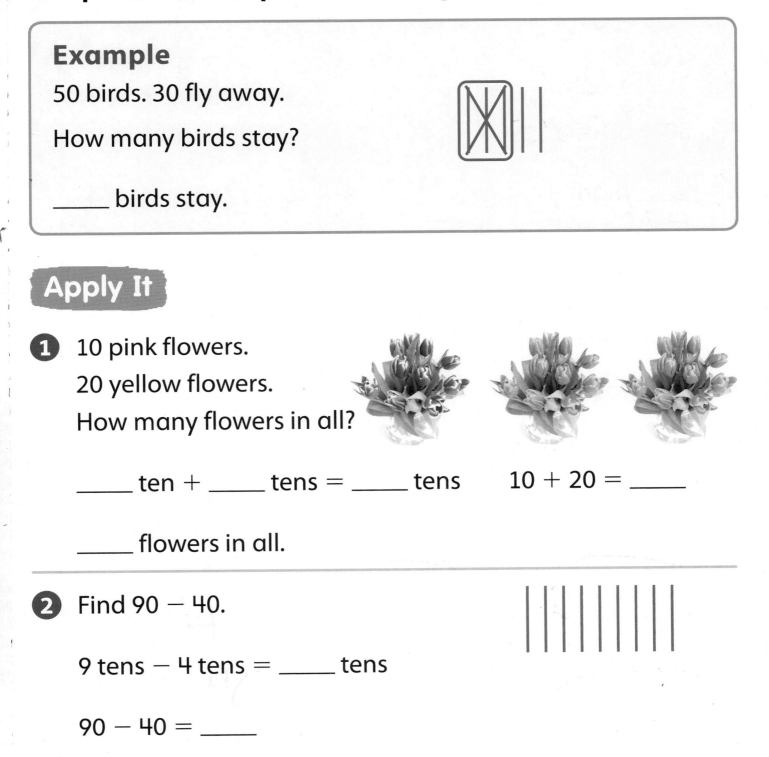

Example

50 birds. 30 fly away.

How many birds stay?

_____ birds stay.

Apply It

1 10 pink flowers.
20 yellow flowers.
How many flowers in all?

_____ ten + _____ tens = _____ tens   10 + 20 = _____

_____ flowers in all.

2 Find 90 − 40.

9 tens − 4 tens = _____ tens

90 − 40 = _____

3 30 red marbles.
50 blue marbles.
How many marbles in all?

30 + 50 = _____

_____ marbles

4 Buzz says 90 − 60 = 3.
Do you agree?
Why or why not?

5 Which has a total of 60? Circle.

Ⓐ 20 + 40

Ⓑ 30 + 20

Ⓒ 40 + 30

Practice Adding and Subtracting Tens

Look at the Example. Then solve problems 1–5.

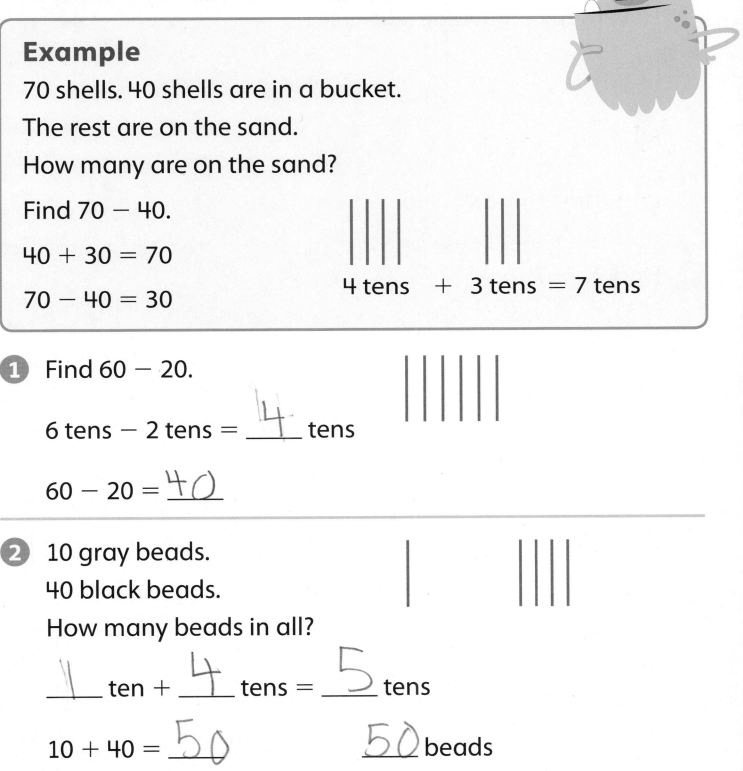

Example

70 shells. 40 shells are in a bucket.

The rest are on the sand.

How many are on the sand?

Find 70 − 40.

40 + 30 = 70

70 − 40 = 30

4 tens   +   3 tens = 7 tens

1   Find 60 − 20.

6 tens − 2 tens = __4__ tens

60 − 20 = __40__

2   10 gray beads.

40 black beads.

How many beads in all?

__1__ ten + __4__ tens = __5__ tens

10 + 40 = __50__   __50__ beads

3 80 blue stickers.

60 green stickers.

How many more blue stickers?

$80 - 60 =$ 20

20 more blue stickers.

4 Find $90 - 70$.

$90 - 70 =$ 20

5 Which have a total of 50? Circle.

Ⓐ $40 + 10$ Ⓑ $20 + 30$

Ⓒ $10 + 30$

Ⓓ $30 + 20$ Ⓔ $40 + 20$

Refine Adding and Subtracting Tens

Apply It

Solve problems 1–6.

1 60 paper clips.

50 are in a box.

How many are not in the box?

60 − 50 = _20_

_20_ not in the box

---

2 30 footballs and 30 basketballs.
What is the total number of balls?

_____ tens + _____ tens = _____ tens

30 + 30 = _____   _____ balls

---

3 Find 80 − 20.

2 + ? = 8

2 tens + _____ tens = 8 tens

20 + _____ = 80   80 − 20 = _____

60 juice boxes.

60 are cold.

How many are not cold?

$60 - 60 =$ _____

_____ are not cold.

---

 40 green markers.

40 black markers.

How many markers in all?

_____ tens + _____ tens = _____ tens

$40 + 40 =$ _____

_____ markers

 Boom says he can use $1 + ? = 5$ to find $50 - 10$.

Do you agree? Why or why not?

Understand 10 More and 10 Less

Dear Family,

This week your child is exploring strategies for finding 10 more and 10 less than a two-digit number.

Learning to quickly find 10 more and 10 less than a number will help your child develop place-value understanding, as well as help your child prepare to add and subtract two-digit numbers.

When 10 is added to a number, the tens digit increases by one. When 10 is subtracted from a number, the tens digit decreases by one.

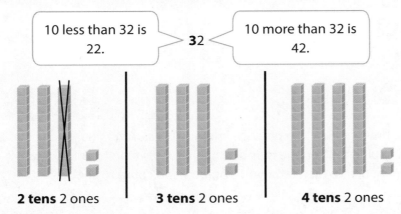

| 10 less than 32 is 22. | **3**2 | 10 more than 32 is 42. |

2 tens 2 ones   **3 tens** 2 ones   **4 tens** 2 ones

On a 120 chart, the number above a given number is 10 less and the number below it is 10 more.

21	22	23	24	25	26	27	28	29	30
31	32	33	34	35	36	37	38	39	40
41	42	43	44	45	46	47	48	49	50

Invite your child to share what he or she knows about finding 10 more and 10 less by doing the following activity together.

Activity · 10 More and 10 Less

Do this activity with your child to find 10 more and 10 less than a number.

Materials a bowl containing 50–80 small objects (such as pennies, paper clips, dried beans, cereal pieces, or pasta shapes), pencil and paper

• Remove a handful of objects from the bowl and place them on the table.

• Have your child count the objects on the table and write how many there are.

• He or she should then tell you the number that is 10 more than the number of objects on the table. For example, if there are 24 objects, your child might say: "10 more than 24 is 34." (If your child needs support, point out that when 10 is added to a number, the tens digit increases by one.)

• Have your child add 10 more objects and count to check.

There are 24 objects.
10 more than 24 is 34.

After repeating the activity several times, adjust it to practice finding 10 less. After your child counts the objects on the table, he or she should tell you the number that is 10 less than the number of objects on the table. Encourage your child to then remove 10 objects and count to check.

Explore 10 More and 10 Less

Learning Target
- Given a two-digit number, mentally find 10 more or 10 less than the number, without having to count; explain the reasoning used.

SMP 1, 2, 3, 4, 5, 6, 7, 8

27 monkeys live at the zoo.

10 more monkeys come to the zoo.

How many monkeys live at the zoo?

Try It

Math Toolkit
- connecting cubes

_____ monkeys live at the zoo.

Connect It

What is 10 more than 31?

10 more than 31 is _____ .

What is 10 less than 31?

10 less than 31 is _____ .

Prepare for Finding 10 More and 10 Less

1 Think about what you know about finding
10 less than a two-digit number. Fill in each box.
Use words, numbers, and pictures. Show as many
ideas as you can.

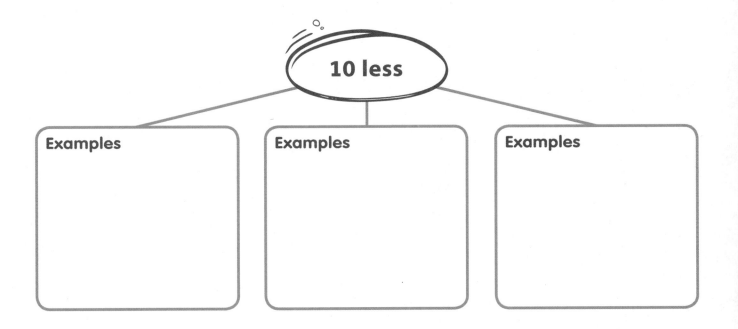

10 less

Examples	Examples	Examples

2 Circle the model that shows 10 less than 35.

10 less than 35 is _____ .

3 Solve the problems. Draw to show your work.

What is 10 more than 36?

10 more than 36 is _____ .

What is 10 less than 36?

10 less than 36 is _____ .

Develop Understanding of 10 More and 10 Less

What is 10 more? What is 10 less?

Start with 48.

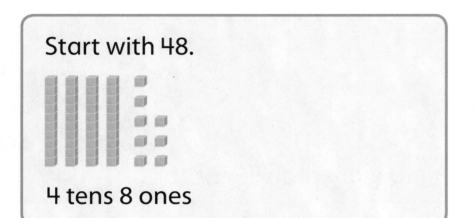

4 tens 8 ones

Math Toolkit
- base-ten blocks
- connecting cubes
- hundred charts

Model It

Show 10 more than 48.

Show 10 less than 48.

DISCUSS IT

What digit changes when you add 10 to a number?

Connect It

Draw another ten or cross out a ten to solve the problem. Fill in the blanks to show the answer.

1 What is 10 more than 45?

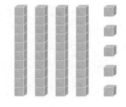

____ tens ____ ones   10 more than 45 is ____.

2 What is 10 less than 74?

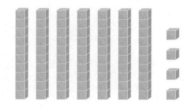

____ tens ____ ones   10 less than 74 is ____.

3 What is 10 less than 58?

____ tens ____ ones

10 less than 58 is ____.

DISCUSS IT

When you find 10 more or 10 less than a number, the ones digit . . .

Practice with 10 More and 10 Less

Look at the Example. Then solve problems 1–4.

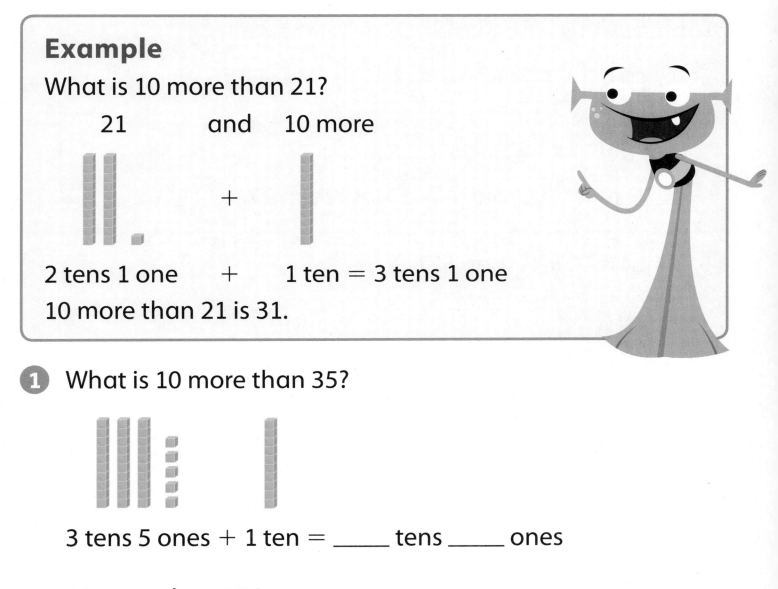

Example

What is 10 more than 21?

21   and   10 more

2 tens 1 one   +   1 ten = 3 tens 1 one

10 more than 21 is 31.

1 What is 10 more than 35?

3 tens 5 ones + 1 ten = _____ tens _____ ones

10 more than 35 is _____ .

Draw another ten or cross out a ten to solve the problem. Fill in the blanks to show the answer.

2 What is 10 less than 32?

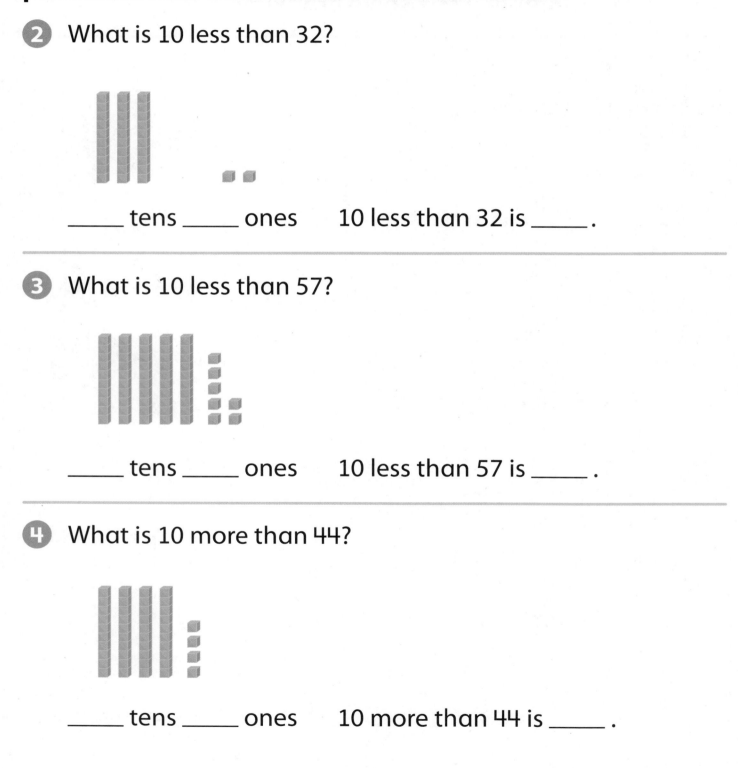

_____ tens _____ ones   10 less than 32 is _____ .

3 What is 10 less than 57?

_____ tens _____ ones   10 less than 57 is _____ .

4 What is 10 more than 44?

_____ tens _____ ones   10 more than 44 is _____ .

Develop Understanding of 10 More and 10 Less

Model It

Find and write the numbers that are 10 less and 10 more than the blue numbers on the chart.

Math Toolkit
- hundred charts
- base-ten blocks
- connecting cubes

31	32	33	34	35	36	37	38	39	40
41	42	43	44	45	46	47	48	49	50
51	52	53	54	55	56	57	58	59	60
61	62	63	64	65	66	67	68	69	70

10 less ☐   10 less ☐   10 less ☐

❶ **Start at 47.**   ❷ **Start at 55.**   ❸ **Start at 42.**

10 more ☐   10 more ☐   10 more ☐

DISCUSS IT

How does the chart help you find 10 less and 10 more than a number?

Connect It

Use the chart to find the numbers.

Color each pair of numbers. Fill in the blanks.

41	42	43	44	45	46	47	48	49	50
51	52	53	54	55	56	57	58	59	60
61	62	63	64	65	66	67	68	69	70
71	72	73	74	75	76	77	78	79	80
81	82	83	84	85	86	87	88	89	90

1 10 less than 83 is _____ .

2 10 more than 45 is _____ .

3 10 less than 78 is _____ .

4 10 less than 90 is _____ .

5 10 more than 52 is _____ .

DISCUSS IT

On the chart, the number that is 10 more is below each number because . . .

Practice with 10 More and 10 Less

Look at the Example. Then solve problems 1–8.

Example

Find 10 less than 86. 10 less than 86 is 76.

Color both numbers.

71	72	73	74	75	76	77	78	79	80
81	82	83	84	85	86	87	88	89	90
91	92	93	94	95	96	97	98	99	100

1 10 more than 48 is _____ .
Color both numbers.

2 10 less than 43 is _____ .
Color both numbers.

31	32	33	34	35	36	37	38	39	40
41	42	43	44	45	46	47	48	49	50
51	52	53	54	55	56	57	58	59	60

41	42	43	44	45	46	47	48	49	50
51	52	53	54	55	56	57	58	59	60
61	62	63	64	65	66	67	68	69	70
71	72	73	74	75	76	77	78	79	80
81	82	83	84	85	86	87	88	89	90
91	92	93	94	95	96	97	98	99	100

3 10 less than 57 is _____ .

4 10 more than 53 is _____ .

5 10 more than 81 is _____ .

6 10 less than 70 is _____ .

7 10 more than 46 is _____ .

8 10 less than 94 is _____ .

Refine Ideas About 10 More and 10 Less

Apply It

1 **Identify** What is 10 more than 82?

71	72	73	74	75	76	77	78	79	80
81	82	83	84	85	86	87	88	89	90
91	92	93	94	95	96	97	98	99	100

10 more than 82 is _____ .

---

2 **Choose** What is the correct number? Draw lines to match.

10 more than 58   48

10 less than 58   68

10 more than 88   98

10 less than 88   78

---

3 **Explain** Buzz says 10 less than 84 is 83.
Do you agree? Why or why not?

Think about 10 more and 10 less.

A: Write a two-digit number.
Find 10 less and 10 more than your number.

[ ] [ ]   10 less than _____ is _____ .

          10 more than _____ is _____ .

Write a different two-digit number.
Find 10 less and 10 more than your number.

[ ] [ ]   10 less than _____ is _____ .

          10 more than _____ is _____ .

B: Find 55 + 10. Tell how you know.

55 + 10 = _____

Add Tens to Any Number

Dear Family,

This week your child is learning to add tens to any two-digit number.

There are many strategies your child can use to add multiples of ten to a two-digit number. Exploring these strategies will help your child recognize that there are many ways to think about and solve problems and will help him or her prepare to add any two-digit numbers with or without regrouping.

Example: Find 26 + 30.

- You can add by breaking apart one of the numbers. You can break apart 26 into tens and ones.

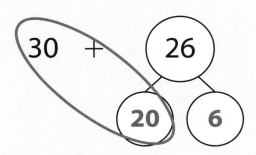

Add the tens first. Then add the ones.

20 + 30 = **50**
50 + 6 = **56**

- You can also make quick drawings to see the tens and ones.

26 + 30 = 50 + 6 = **56**

- You can also count on by tens: 26, 36, 46, **56**.

Invite your child to share what he or she knows about adding tens to any two-digit number by doing the following activity together.

Activity   Adding Tens to Any Number

Do this activity with your child to add tens to any number.

Materials 4 index cards or slips of paper, pencil, and sheet of paper

Help your child practice adding tens to any number by doing the following activity.

- Label the index cards with the numbers 10, 20, 30, and 40. Mix up the cards and place them facedown in a pile.

- Say any two-digit number up to 59.

- Have your child write the number and then turn over the top index card to find the second number for an addition problem. He or she also writes the addition problem. For example, if you say 47 and your child turns over a 20 card, he or she writes "$47 + 20 =$ _____ ."

- Ask your child to solve the problem using any strategy or model.

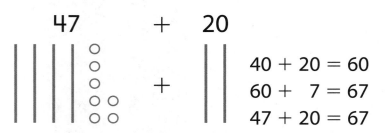

$$40 + 20 = 60$$
$$60 + 7 = 67$$
$$47 + 20 = 67$$

Continue until all four index cards have been used. You can challenge your child to solve each problem using one strategy and then check the answer using a different strategy.

Explore Adding Tens to Any Number

**Jordan has 13 toy cars and
10 toy trucks.
How many toys does Jordan have?**

Learning Target

- Add within 100, including adding a two-digit number and a one-digit number, and adding a two-digit number and a multiple of 10, using concrete models or drawings and strategies based on place value, properties of operations, and/or the relationship between addition and subtraction; relate the strategy to a written method and explain the reasoning used. Understand that in adding two-digit numbers, one adds tens and tens, ones and ones; and sometimes it is necessary to compose a ten.

SMP 1, 2, 3, 4, 5, 6, 7

Try It

🧰 Math Toolkit

- counters
- base-ten blocks
- hundred charts
- place-value charts

_____ + _____ = _____

Jordan has _____ toys.

Connect It

**Maria has 17 shells. She finds 20 more.
How many shells does Maria have now?**

_____ + _____ = _____

Maria has _____ shells.

Prepare for Adding Tens to Any Number

1 Think about what you know about finding 10 more. Fill in each box. Use words, numbers, and pictures. Show as many ideas as you can.

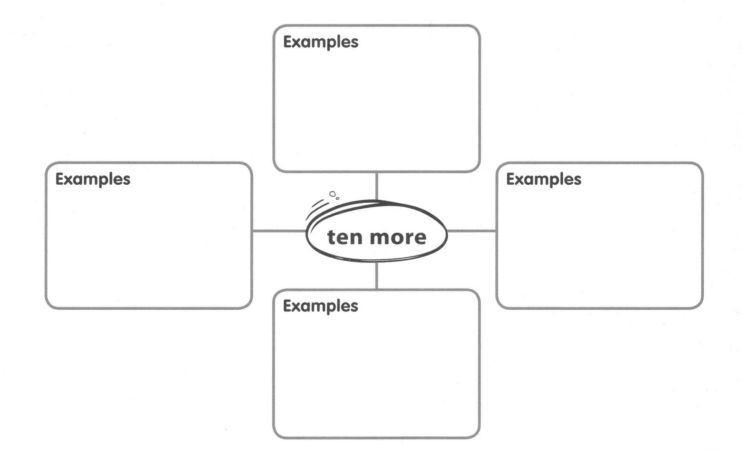

Examples

Examples

ten more

Examples

Examples

2 The blocks show 12. Add 10 more.

The blocks now show _____ .

$12 + 10 =$ _____

3 Solve the problem. Draw to show your work.

Chase has 15 beads. He buys 20 more. How many beads does Chase have now?

_____ + _____ = _____

Chase has _____ beads.

Develop Adding Tens to Any Number

Eli has 16 red fish and 30 yellow fish.
How many fish in all?

Math Toolkit
- base-ten blocks
- hundred charts
- place-value charts

DISCUSS IT

I can use what I know about tens and ones because . . .

Eli has 16 red fish and 30 yellow fish.
How many fish in all?

Model It

Find 16 + 30.

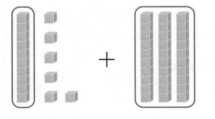

Add the tens.   **10 + 30 =** _____

Then add the 6 ones.   **40 + 6 =** _____

So, 16 + 30 = _____.

There are _____ fish in all.

Connect It

1 How is your way like **Model It**? How is it different?

2 How did using the base-ten blocks help you see how many fish Eli has?

Apply It

3 Rena has 12 pink flowers and 20 purple flowers. How many flowers in all?

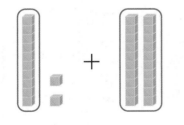

10 + 20 = _____

30 + 2 = _____

So, 12 + 20 = _____.

_____ flowers

4 Find 17 + 10.

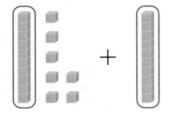

10 + 10 = _____

20 + 7 = _____

17 + 10 = _____

5 Find 46 + 20.

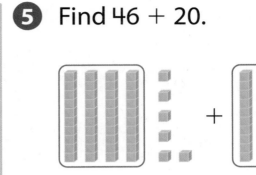

46 + 20 = _____

---

6 Draw lines to show the number of tens in the total.

39 + 50   8

51 + 20   9

64 + 30   7

Practice Adding Tens to Any Number

Look at the Example. Then solve problems 1–4.

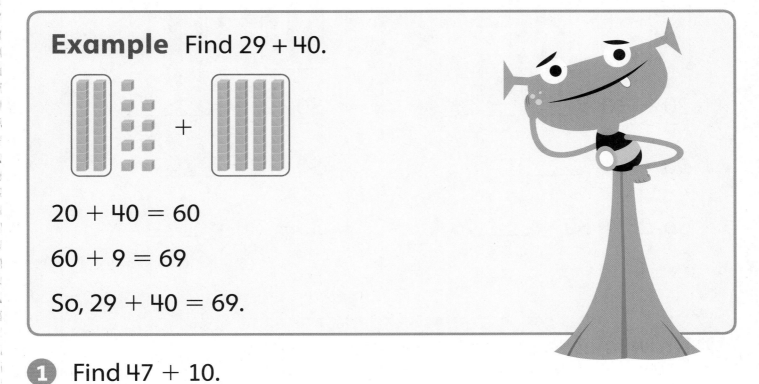

Example   Find $29 + 40$.

$20 + 40 = 60$

$60 + 9 = 69$

So, $29 + 40 = 69$.

1   Find $47 + 10$.

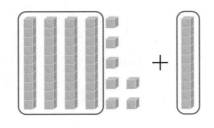

$40 + 10 =$ _____

$50 + 7 =$ _____

$47 + 10 =$ _____

2 Find 25 + 30.

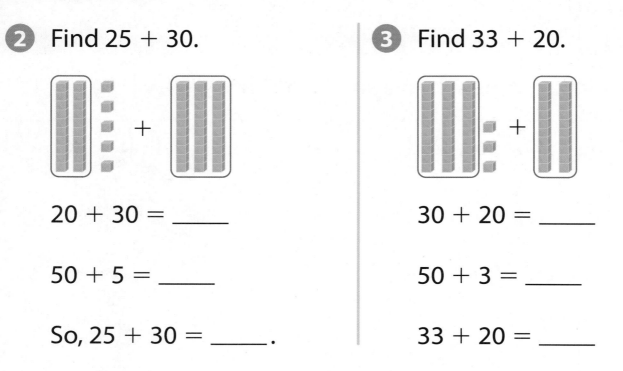

20 + 30 = _____

50 + 5 = _____

So, 25 + 30 = _____ .

3 Find 33 + 20.

30 + 20 = _____

50 + 3 = _____

33 + 20 = _____

---

4 Draw lines to show the number of tens in the total.

38 + 10   7 tens

41 + 20   6 tens

11 + 60   4 tens

©Curriculum Associates, LLC   Copying is not permitted.

Develop Adding Tens to Any Number

50 blue balloons and 13 red balloons.
How many balloons altogether?

Math Toolkit
- base-ten blocks
- hundred charts
- place-value charts
- number bonds

DISCUSS IT
Which number did
you start with?

50 blue balloons and 13 red balloons.
How many balloons altogether?

Model It

Find 50 + 13.

Write the tens and ones.

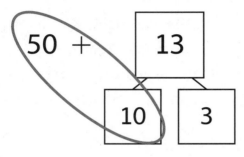

Add the tens.   **50 + 10 = ____**

Then add the 3 ones.   **60 + 3 = ____**

So, 50 + 13 = ____ .

There are ____ balloons altogether.

Connect It

1 How is your way like Model It? How is it different?

2 20 baseballs and 14 footballs.
How many balls?
What is wrong?   2 + 10 + 4 = 16

Show the right way. ____ + ____ + ____ = ____

Apply It

3 Find 30 + 39.

30 + 30 + 9

30 + ____ = 60

So, 60 + ____ = ____ .

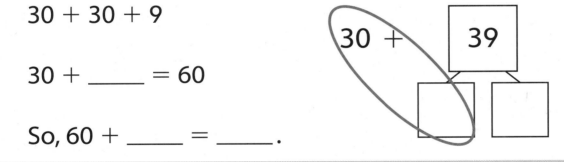

30 + | 39 |

---

4 Find 30 + 15.

30 + 10 + 5

30 + ____ = 40

40 + ____ = 45

So, 30 + 15 = ____ .

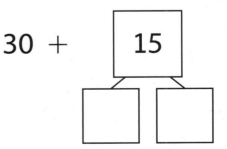

30 + | 15 |

5 50 orange juice boxes and
14 apple juice boxes.
How many juice boxes altogether?

$50 + 10 =$ _____

$50 +$ | 14 |

$60 + 4 =$ _____

$50 + 14 =$ _____

_____ juice boxes

---

6 Which have the same total as $30 + 10 + 2$? Circle.

Ⓐ $30 + 12$

Ⓑ $12 + 30$

Ⓒ $20 + 10 + 2$

Ⓓ $32 + 10$

Practice Adding Tens to Any Number

Look at the Example. Then solve problems 1–4.

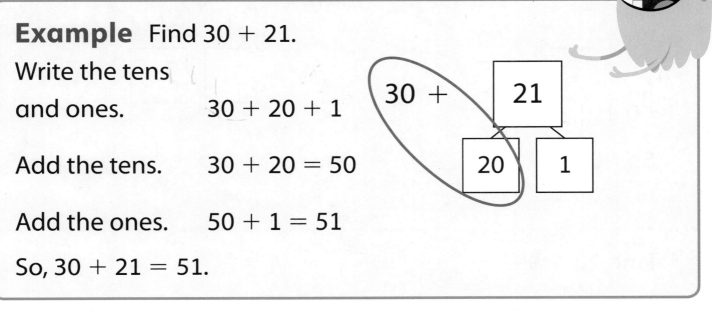

Example Find 30 + 21.

Write the tens
and ones.   30 + 20 + 1

Add the tens.   30 + 20 = 50

Add the ones.   50 + 1 = 51

So, 30 + 21 = 51.

30 +   21
        20   1

1   Find 60 + 15.

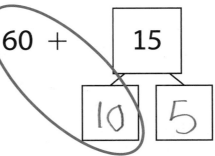

60 + 10 + 5

60 + _10_ = 70

70 + _5_ = 75

So, 60 + 15 = _75_.

60 +   15
        10   5

2 Find $40 + 49$.

$40 + 40 + 9$

$40 + \underline{40} = 80$

$80 + \underline{9} = \underline{89}$

So, $40 + 49 = \underline{89}$.

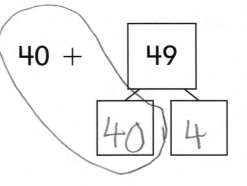

3 Find $20 + 44$.

$20 + 40 = \underline{60}$

$60 + 4 = \underline{64}$

So, $20 + 44 = \underline{64}$.

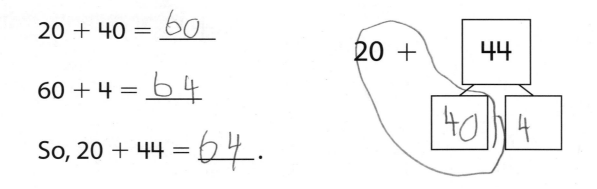

4 Which have the same total as $20 + 18$? Circle.

Ⓐ $18 + 20$

Ⓑ $28 + 10$ 38

Ⓒ $20 + 10 + 8$ 18

Ⓓ $10 + 10 + 8$

Refine Adding Tens to Any Number

Complete the Example. Then solve problems 1–4.

Example

10 blue marbles and 19 green marbles.
How many marbles in all?

10 + 10 = __**20**__

20 + 9 = __**29**__

10 + 19 = _29_

_29_ marbles

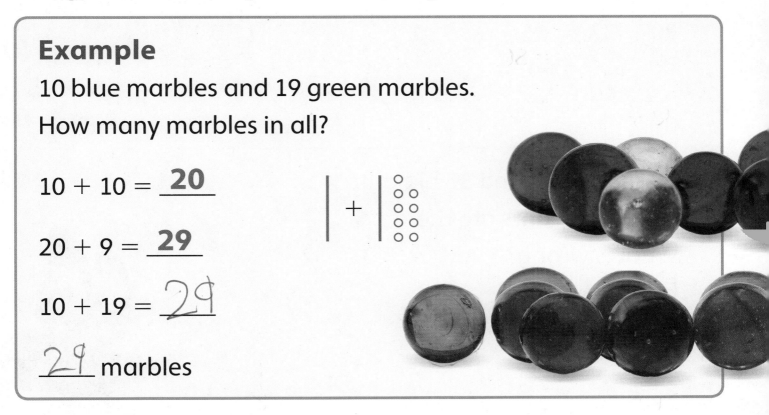

 Apply It

1 Find 52 + 20.

50 + 20 = _60_

70 + 2 = _72_

52 + 20 = _27_

2 20 black cars and 32 white cars.
What is the total number of cars?

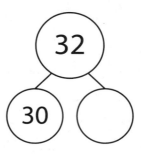

20 + 32 = _____

_____ cars

---

3 29 small ants and 30 big ants.
How many ants are there?
What is wrong?   20 + 9 + 3 = 32
Explain.

---

4 25 blue butterflies and 50 brown butterflies.
How many butterflies in all?

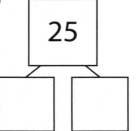

_____ = 25 + 50

_____ butterflies

Practice Adding Tens to Any Number

Look at the Example. Then solve problems 1–5.

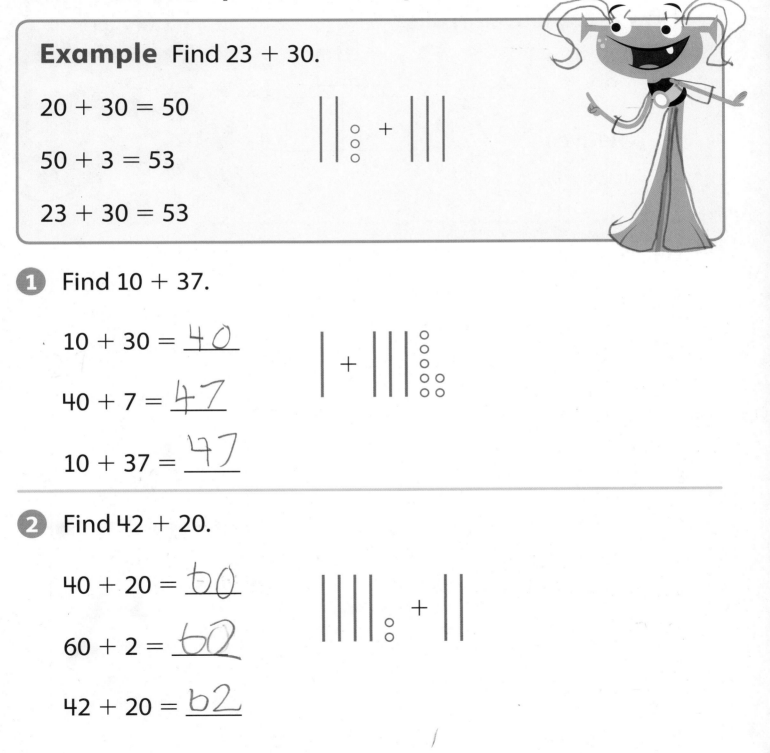

Example Find 23 + 30.

20 + 30 = 50

50 + 3 = 53

23 + 30 = 53

1 Find 10 + 37.

10 + 30 = 40

40 + 7 = 47

10 + 37 = 47

2 Find 42 + 20.

40 + 20 = 60

60 + 2 = 62

42 + 20 = 62

Fill in the blanks. Complete the number bonds.

3 18 yellow leaves and 80 red leaves.
How many leaves in all?

18 + 80 = _88_

_88_ leaves

```
┌──────┐
│  18  │
└──┬─┬─┘
┌──┘ └──┐
│ 98 │ 8 │
└────┴───┘
```

4 34 big rocks and 50 small rocks.
How many rocks in all?

34 + 50 = _84_

_84_ rocks

```
┌──────┐   ┌───┐
│  34  │───│ 4 │
└──────┘   └───┘
       └───┌───┐
           │ 8 │
           └───┘
```

5 Ruby picks 20 apples. Kim picks 35 apples.
How many apples altogether?

_25_ = 20 + 35

_25_ apples

Refine Adding Tens to Any Number

Apply It

Solve problems 1–6.

1 70 small paper clips and 14 big paper clips.
How many paper clips in all?

_____ = 70 + 14

_____ paper clips

2 40 green frogs and 25 yellow frogs.
How many frogs in all?

40 + 25 = _____

_____ frogs

3 17 triangles and 20 squares.
How many shapes in all? Show your work.

17 + 20 = _____

_____ shapes

4 19 red buttons and 60 blue buttons.
How many buttons in all?

Ⓐ 69 buttons

Ⓑ 79 buttons

Ⓒ 89 buttons

---

5 Boom says 20 + 12 is the same as 20 + 10 + 2.
Is he right? How do you know?

---

6 Kyra plants 24 sunflowers.
Nic plants 30 sunflowers.
How many sunflowers altogether?

_____ sunflowers

Add Two-Digit and One-Digit Numbers

Dear Family,

This week your child is learning to add a two-digit number and a one-digit number, making a new ten when necessary.

When adding a two-digit number and a one-digit number, you can break up the two-digit number into tens and ones. All the ones can be added and then combined with the tens.

Your child will begin by solving problems in which the ones total up to 9 or less, such as 23 + 5 and 34 + 2.

Example: Find 34 + 2.

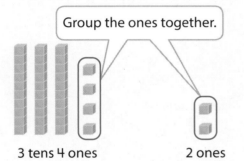

Group the ones together.

3 tens 4 ones   2 ones

$$\begin{array}{r} 3 \text{ tens } 4 \text{ ones} \\ + \qquad 2 \text{ ones} \\ \hline 3 \text{ tens } 6 \text{ ones} = 36 \end{array}$$

They will then move on to problems that require them to make a new 10 when there are more than 9 ones, such as 13 + 8 and 65 + 6.

Example: Find 13 + 8.

Group the ones together.

1 ten 3 ones   8 ones

$$\begin{array}{r} 1 \text{ ten } 3 \text{ ones} \\ + \qquad 8 \text{ ones} \\ \hline 1 \text{ ten } 11 \text{ ones} \end{array}$$

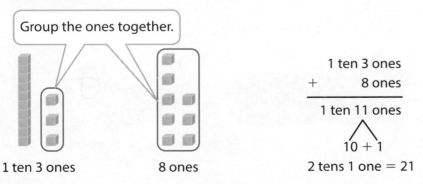

10 + 1

2 tens 1 one = 21

Invite your child to share what he or she knows about adding a two-digit and a one-digit number by doing the following activity together.

Adding Two-Digit and One-Digit Numbers

Do this activity with your child to practice adding two-digit and one-digit numbers.

Materials pencil and paper

Tell your child that you are going to work together to solve the addition problems listed below.

- Have your child write the two-digit number in the problem as tens and ones.

- Underneath what your child has written, you write the number of ones you are adding. Then draw a line under the numbers and a plus sign to the left.

- Your child adds the ones, combines them with the tens, and writes the total.

- Talk about how your child knows when it is possible to make another ten from the ones.

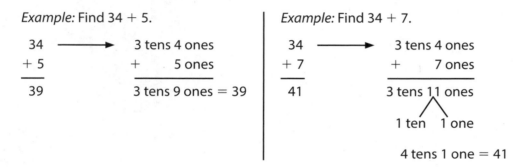

Example: Find 34 + 5.

$$\begin{array}{r} 34 \\ + 5 \\ \hline 39 \end{array}$$ → 3 tens 4 ones
+ 5 ones
———————
3 tens 9 ones = 39

Example: Find 34 + 7.

$$\begin{array}{r} 34 \\ + 7 \\ \hline 41 \end{array}$$ → 3 tens 4 ones
+ 7 ones
———————
3 tens 11 ones

1 ten   1 one

4 tens 1 one = 41

- Repeat the activity above to solve the problems below.

45 + 7 = _____   84 + 6 = _____

22 + 6 = _____   32 + 7 = _____

91 + 3 = _____   18 + 8 = _____

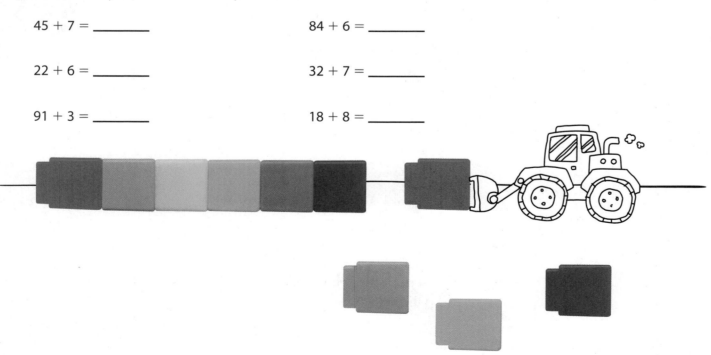

Explore Adding Two-Digit and One-Digit Numbers

Learning Target

- Add within 100, including adding a two-digit number and a one-digit number, and adding a two-digit number and a multiple of 10, using concrete models or drawings and strategies based on place value, properties of operations, and/or the relationship between addition and subtraction; relate the strategy to a written method and explain the reasoning used. Understand that in adding two-digit numbers, one adds tens and tens, ones and ones; and sometimes it is necessary to compose a ten.

SMP 1, 2, 3, 4, 5, 6, 7

Blake collects 23 seashells.

He finds 4 more.

How many seashells does he have now?

Try It

Math Toolkit
- counters
- hundred charts

23 and 4 more is _____.

Blake has _____ seashells.

Connect It

35 children are at Jada's party.
4 more children come to the party.
How many children are at Jada's party?

1	2	3	4	5	6	7	8	9	10
11	12	13	14	15	16	17	18	19	20
21	22	23	24	25	26	27	28	29	30
31	32	33	34	35	36	37	38	39	40
41	42	43	44	45	46	47	48	49	50

$35 + 4 = $ _____

There are _____ children at Jada's party.

Prepare for Adding 2- and 1-Digit Numbers

1 Think about what you know about ones. Fill in each box. Use words, numbers, and pictures. Show as many ideas as you can.

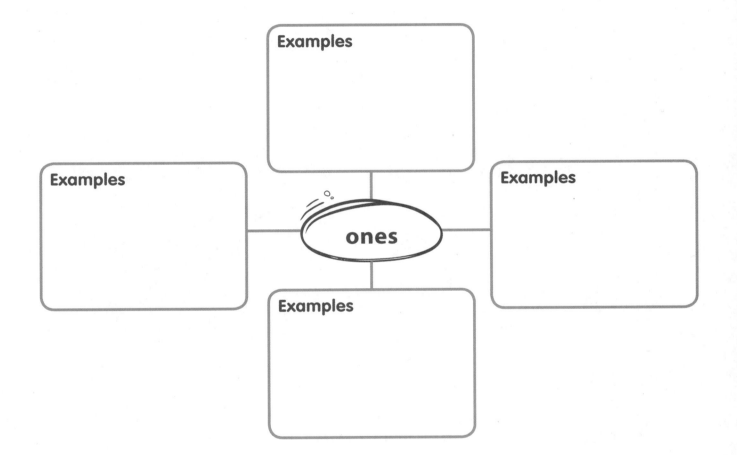

Examples

Examples

Examples

ones

Examples

2 Jack says 24 has 2 tens and 4 ones. Maya says 24 has 24 ones. Who is right? Why?

Lesson 28 Add Two-Digit and One-Digit Numbers   **641**

3 Solve the problem. Show your work.

21 children are on a bus.

5 more children get on the bus.

How many children are on the bus?

1	2	3	4	5	6	7	8	9	10
11	12	13	14	15	16	17	18	19	20
21	22	23	24	25	26	27	28	29	30
31	32	33	34	35	36	37	38	39	40
41	42	43	44	45	46	47	48	49	50

$21 + 5 =$ _____

There are _____ children on the bus.

Develop Adding Two-Digit and One-Digit Numbers

Lou has 18 blue buttons
and 7 red buttons.
How many buttons in all?

 **Try It**

 **Math Toolkit**
- base-ten blocks
- counters
- 10-frames
- hundred charts

DISCUSS IT
I found the total
number of buttons
by . . .

Lou has 18 blue buttons
and 7 red buttons.
How many buttons in all?

Model It

Find 18 + 7.
Make the next ten.

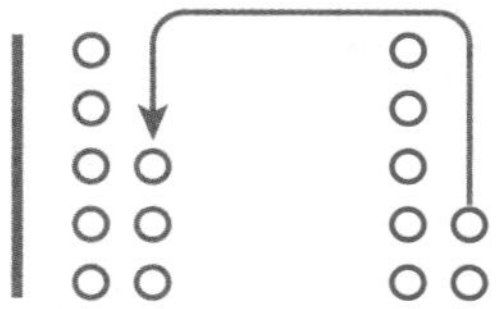

18   +   7

Then add the tens and ones.

18 + 2 + 5

20 + 5 = _____

So, 18 + 7 = _____.

20   +   5

There are _____ buttons in all.

Connect It

1 How is your way like **Model It**? How is it different?

2 How does making a ten help you add these numbers?

Apply It

3 Shanna makes 41 snack bags.
Alicia makes 7 snack bags.
How many snack bags in all?

40 + 1 + _____ = _____

_____ snack bags

Lesson 28 Add Two-Digit and One-Digit Numbers

4 Find 67 + 5.

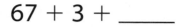

67 + 3 + _____

_____ + 2 = _____

67 + 5 = _____

---

5 Tessa counts 23 penguins.
Then she counts 6 more penguins.
How many penguins does she count?

23 + _____ = _____

_____ penguins

---

6 Find 54 + 8.

54 + 8 = _____

Practice Adding 2- and 1-Digit Numbers

Look at the Example. Then solve problems 1–5.

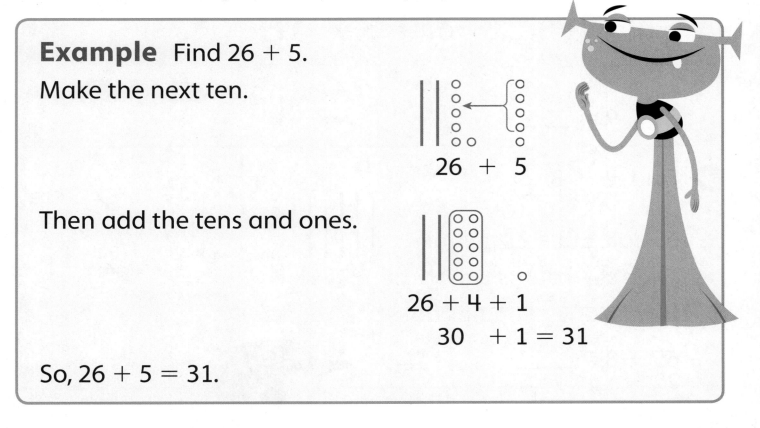

Example Find $26 + 5$.

Make the next ten.

$26 + 5$

Then add the tens and ones.

$26 + 4 + 1$

$30 \quad + 1 = 31$

So, $26 + 5 = 31$.

1 Find $33 + 6$.

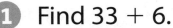
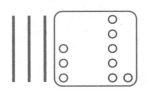

$30 + 3 + 6 =$ _____

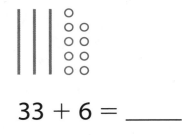

$33 + 6 =$ _____

2 Find 19 + 9.

19 + 1 + 8 = _____

20 + _____ = _____

19 + 9 = _____

3 Find 65 + 8.

65 + 5 + 3 = _____

70 + _____ = _____

65 + 8 = _____

4 Find 22 + 6.

_____ + _____ = _____

5 34 crows. 5 jays.

How many birds altogether?

34 + 5 = _____   _____ birds

Develop Adding Two-Digit and One-Digit Numbers

Malia picks 47 apples from the tree.
She gets 5 apples from the ground.
How many apples does Malia have?

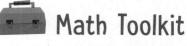 **Math Toolkit**
- base-ten blocks
- counters
- 10-frames
- hundred charts

DISCUSS IT

How can an addition equation show the problem?

Malia picks 47 apples from the tree.
She gets 5 apples from the ground.
How many apples does Malia have?

Model It

Find 47 + 5.
Add the tens.
Add the ones.

```
  4 tens   7 ones
+          5 ones
_____
  4 tens  12 ones
```

40 + 12 = _____

So, 47 + 5 = _____ .

Malia has _____ apples.

Connect It

1 How is your way like **Model It**? How is it different?

2 Buzz says $39 + 2$ is the same as $40 + 1$.
Is he right? How do you know?

Apply It

3 Find $73 + 6$.

$$\begin{array}{r} 7 \text{ tens} \quad 3 \text{ ones} \\ + \qquad\qquad 6 \text{ ones} \\ \hline \underline{} \text{ tens } \underline{} \text{ ones} \end{array}$$

$70 + \underline{} = \underline{}$

So, $73 + 6 = \underline{}$.

4 Find $37 + 7$.

$$\begin{array}{r} 3 \text{ tens} \quad 7 \text{ ones} \\ + \qquad\qquad 7 \text{ ones} \\ \hline \underline{} \text{ tens } \underline{} \text{ ones} \end{array}$$

$30 + 14 = \underline{}$

So, $37 + 7 = \underline{}$.

5 Find 38 + 5.

_____ tens _____ ones

\+   _____ ones

_____ tens _____ ones

30 + _____ = _____

So, 38 + 5 = _____ .

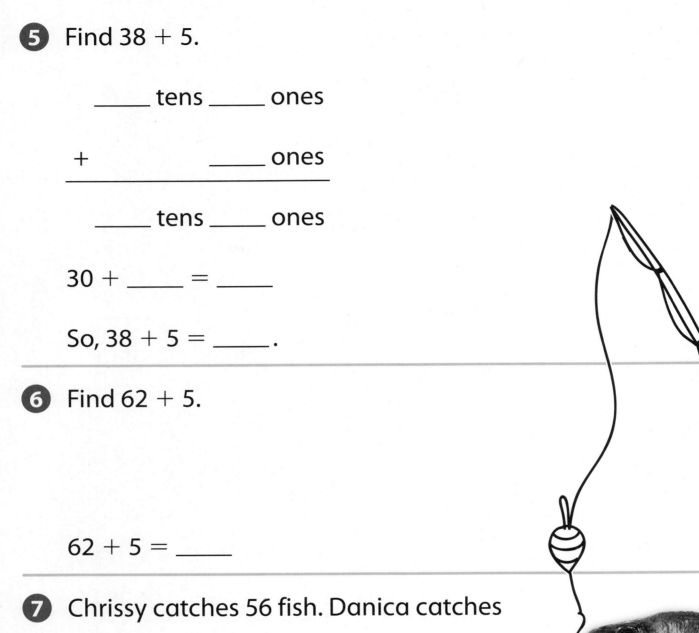

6 Find 62 + 5.

62 + 5 = _____

7 Chrissy catches 56 fish. Danica catches 7 fish. How many fish altogether?

56 + 7 = _____   _____ fish

Practice Adding 2- and 1-Digit Numbers

Look at the Example. Then solve problems 1–4.

Example

Mary hits the ball 34 times. Tim hits the ball 7 times. How many hits in all?

3 tens 4 ones

+   7 ones
_____

3 tens 11 ones

$30 + 11 = 41$

So, $34 + 7 = 41$.

41 hits in all.

1 Find $45 + 4$.

      4 tens   5 ones

+   4 ones
_____

_____ tens _____ ones

$40 +$ _____ $=$ _____

So, $45 + 4 =$ _____.

2 22 birds sit on a fence.

7 more birds fly to the fence.

How many birds on the fence?

22 + _____ = ?

22 + 7 = _____

_____ birds

3 Find 66 + 8.

_____ tens _____ ones

+   _____ ones
_____

_____ tens _____ ones

60 + _____ = _____

So, 66 + 8 = _____ .

4 Find 83 + 9.

83 + 9 = _____

Refine Adding Two-Digit and One-Digit Numbers

Complete the Example. Then solve problems 1–4.

Example Find 36 + 8.

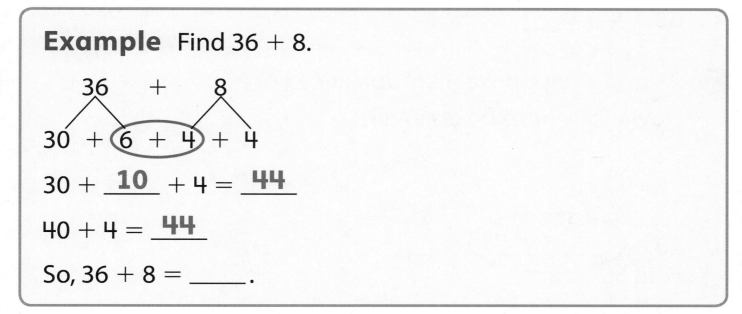

30 + $\underline{\textbf{10}}$ + 4 = $\underline{\textbf{44}}$

40 + 4 = $\underline{\textbf{44}}$

So, 36 + 8 = _____.

Apply It

1 Find 21 + 8.

2 tens 1 one

+   8 ones
_____

20 + _____ = _____

So, 21 + 8 = _____.

2 Find 67 + 4.

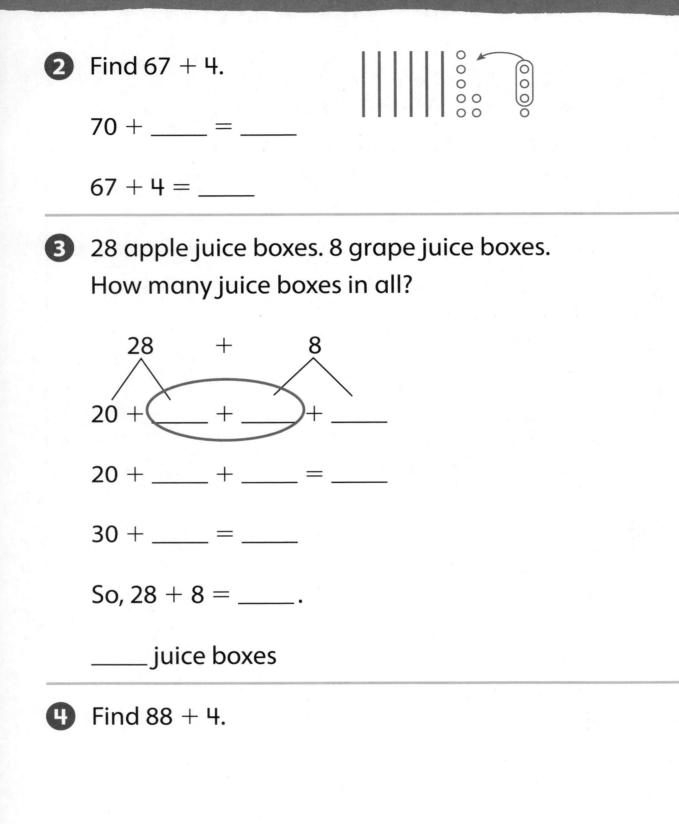

70 + _____ = _____

67 + 4 = _____

---

3 28 apple juice boxes. 8 grape juice boxes.
How many juice boxes in all?

28   +   8

20 + (_____ + _____) + _____

20 + _____ + _____ = _____

30 + _____ = _____

So, 28 + 8 = _____ .

_____ juice boxes

---

4 Find 88 + 4.

88 + 4 = _____

Practice Adding 2- and 1-Digit Numbers

Look at the Example. Then solve problems 1–6.

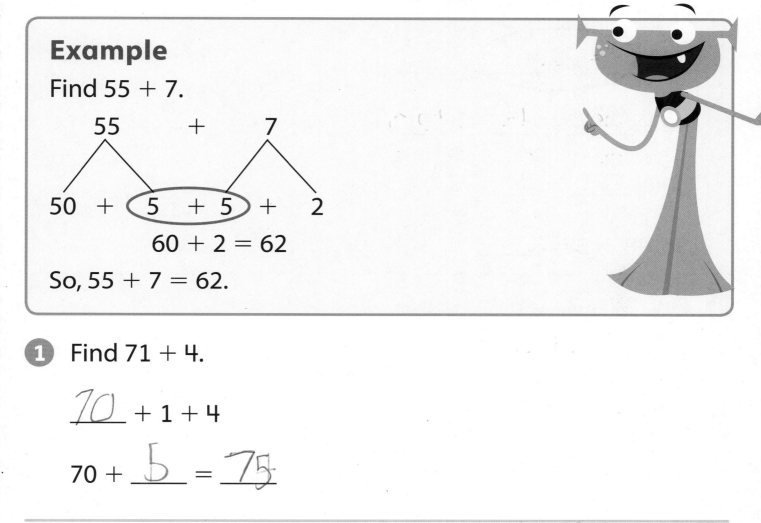

Example

Find 55 + 7.

$$55 \qquad + \qquad 7$$

$$50 \: + \: \boxed{5 \: + \: 5} \: + \: 2$$

$$60 + 2 = 62$$

So, 55 + 7 = 62.

1 Find 71 + 4.

$\underline{70} + 1 + 4$

$70 + \underline{5} = \underline{75}$

2 Julia reads 26 pages before lunch.
   She reads 6 pages after lunch.
   How many pages does Julia read?

   $26 + 6 = \underline{32}$ $\underline{32}$ pages

3 Find 48 + 5.

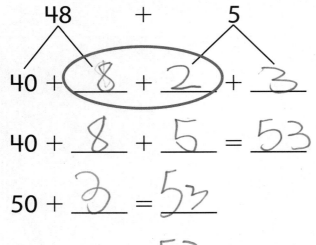

48   +   5

40 + (8 + 2) + 3

40 + 8 + 5 = 53

50 + 3 = 52

So, 48 + 5 = 53 .

4 Find 37 + 3.

37 + 3 = 40

5 Find 59 + 4.

59 + 4 = 63

6 Find 76 + 7.

76 + 7 = 83

Refine Adding Two-Digit and One-Digit Numbers

Apply It

Solve problems 1–6.

1 Sofia pins 58 pictures on the board.

Mr. Rico pins 4 pictures on the board.

How many pictures in all?

$58 + 4 = $ _62_

_62_ pictures

---

2 Hamal picks 52 strawberries.

Umi picks 9 strawberries.

How many strawberries in all?

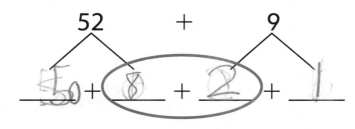

_31_ strawberries

3 Find 24 + 7.

$$2 \text{ tens } 4 \text{ ones}$$
$$+ \qquad 7 \text{ ones}$$

$$24 + 7 = \underline{31}$$

4 Find 65 + 3.

$$65 + 3 = \underline{68}$$

5 Find 43 + 6.

Ⓐ 46

Ⓑ 48

Ⓒ 49

6 Boom says 35 + 7 is the same as 40 + 5.
Is he right? How do you know?

42

Add Two-Digit Numbers

Dear Family,

This week your child is learning to add two-digit numbers, making a new ten when necessary.

One strategy for adding two-digit numbers is to add the tens to the tens and add the ones to the ones. If adding the ones to the ones results in a total of 10 or more, your child will see how to combine 10 ones to make 1 ten.

Example: Find 25 + 14.

There are fewer than 10 ones. You do not need to make a new ten.

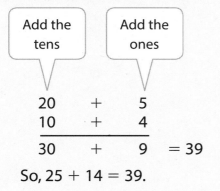

Add the tens		Add the ones
20	+	5
10	+	4
30	+	9 = 39

So, 25 + 14 = 39.

Example: Find 38 + 17.

There are more than 10 ones. You can make a new ten.

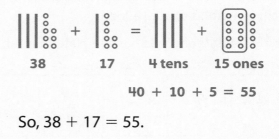

| 38 | 17 | 4 tens | 15 ones |

40 + 10 + 5 = 55

So, 38 + 17 = 55.

Learning to make a ten in this way will help your child add two-digit numbers and will prepare your child to use other addition and subtraction strategies.

Invite your child to share what he or she knows about adding two-digit numbers by doing the following activity together.

Activity Adding Two-Digit Numbers

Do this activity with your child to practice adding two-digit numbers.

Materials 2 number cubes, pencil, and paper

Tell your child you will be practicing adding two-digit numbers and that sometimes it will be necessary to make a new ten.

- Have your child roll two 1–6 number cubes to form a two-digit number. For example, for a roll of 3 and 5, he or she can make 35 or 53. Write this number in the first column of the table below.

- Ask your child to add 27 to the number and record the answer below. This may or may not require making a new ten.

- Ask your child how he or she can tell whether a new ten will be made when looking at the numbers being added.

- Have your child make quick drawings like the Example on the previous page to model the numbers being added.

- Repeat this activity until your child has completed the table.

35	+	27	=	62
	+	27	=	
	+	27	=	
	+	27	=	
	+	27	=	
	+	27	=	
	+	27	=	

Explore Adding Two-Digit Numbers

Learning Target

- Add within 100, including adding a two-digit number and a one-digit number, and adding a two-digit number and a multiple of 10, using concrete models or drawings and strategies based on place value, properties of operations, and/or the relationship between addition and subtraction; relate the strategy to a written method and explain the reasoning used. Understand that in adding two-digit numbers, one adds tens and tens, ones and ones; and sometimes it is necessary to compose a ten.

SMP 1, 2, 3, 4, 5, 6, 7, 8

Juliana has 15 pennies.

Nico has 23 pennies.

How many pennies in all?

 Try It

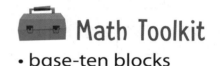 **Math Toolkit**

- base-ten blocks

15 + 23 = _____

They have _____ pennies in all.

Connect It

22 children play on the hill.

38 children play in the field.

How many children are playing?

1	2	3	4	5	6	7	8	9	10
11	12	13	14	15	16	17	18	19	20
21	22	23	24	25	26	27	28	29	30
31	32	33	34	35	36	37	38	39	40
41	42	43	44	45	46	47	48	49	50
51	52	53	54	55	56	57	58	59	60
61	62	63	64	65	66	67	68	69	70
71	72	73	74	75	76	77	78	79	80
81	82	83	84	85	86	87	88	89	90
91	92	93	94	95	96	97	98	99	100

$22 + 38 = $ _____

_____ children are playing.

Prepare for Adding Two-Digit Numbers

1 Think about what you know about tens.
Fill in each box. Use words, numbers, and
pictures. Show as many ideas as you can.

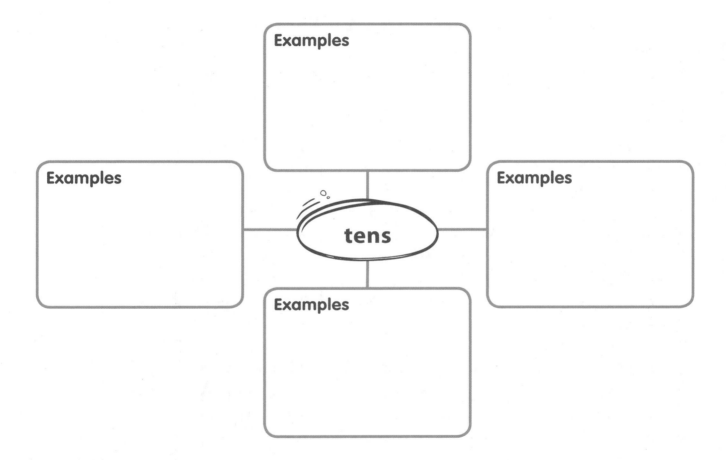

Examples

Examples

tens

Examples

Examples

2 Celia and Jamal made drawings
to show 32. Which drawing is right?
Explain.

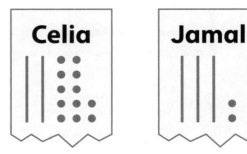

3 Solve the problem. Use two colors to count on by tens and ones from the starting number.

26 children swim in the pool.
44 children swim in the lake.
How many children are swimming?

1	2	3	4	5	6	7	8	9	10
11	12	13	14	15	16	17	18	19	20
21	22	23	24	25	26	27	28	29	30
31	32	33	34	35	36	37	38	39	40
41	42	43	44	45	46	47	48	49	50
51	52	53	54	55	56	57	58	59	60
61	62	63	64	65	66	67	68	69	70
71	72	73	74	75	76	77	78	79	80
81	82	83	84	85	86	87	88	89	90
91	92	93	94	95	96	97	98	99	100

$26 + 44 =$ _____

_____ children are swimming.

Develop Adding Two-Digit Numbers

How many marbles in all?

35 marbles   **27 marbles**

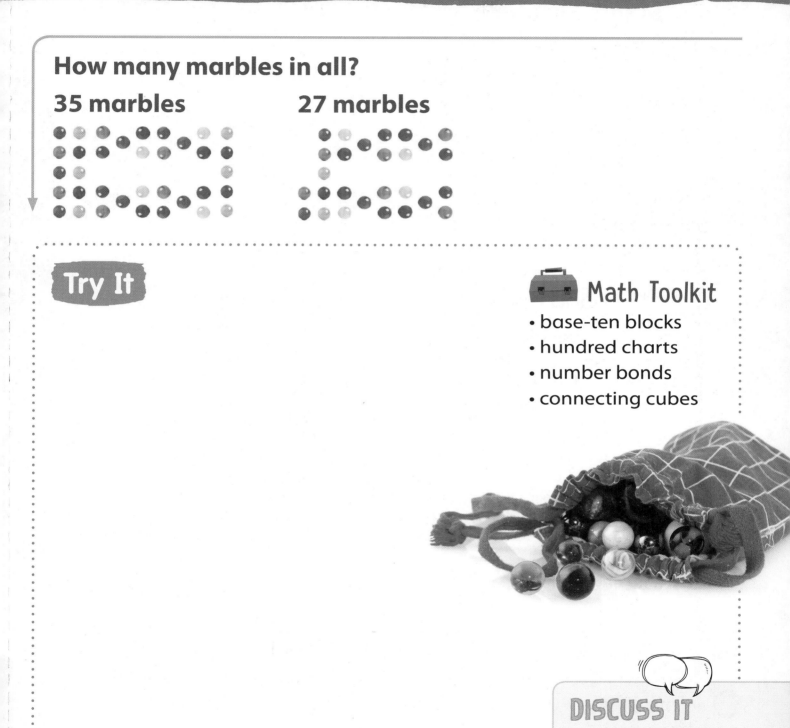

Try It

🧰 **Math Toolkit**
- base-ten blocks
- hundred charts
- number bonds
- connecting cubes

DISCUSS IT

To find the number of marbles, I started by . . .

How many marbles in all?

35 marbles   **27 marbles**

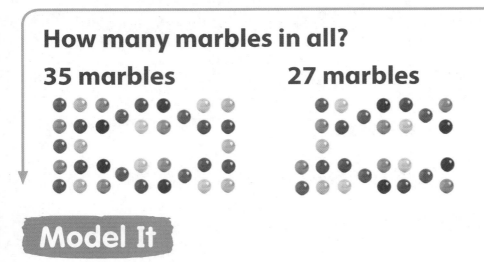

Model It

Find 35 + 27.

Add the tens and ones.

5 tens   12 ones

50   +   12   = _____

35 + 27 = _____

_____ marbles in all.

Connect It

1 How is your way like **Model It**? How is it different?

2 Who is right? How do you know?

Boom: 25 + 16 = 31

Buzz: 25 + 16 = 41

3 Find 35 + 28.
Add the tens and ones.

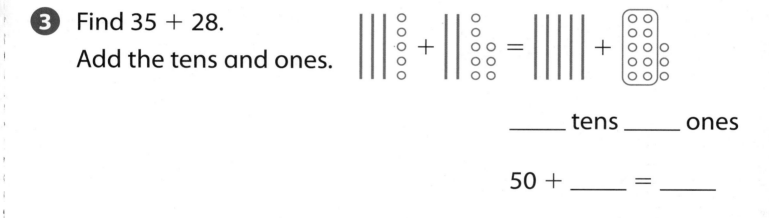

_____ tens _____ ones

50 + _____ = _____

35 + 28 = _____

4 Find 24 + 25.
Add the tens and ones.

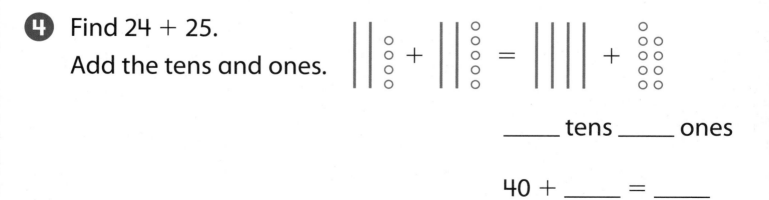

_____ tens _____ ones

40 + _____ = _____

24 + 25 = _____

5 Find 56 + 28.

7 tens _____ ones

_____ + _____ = _____

56 + 28 = _____

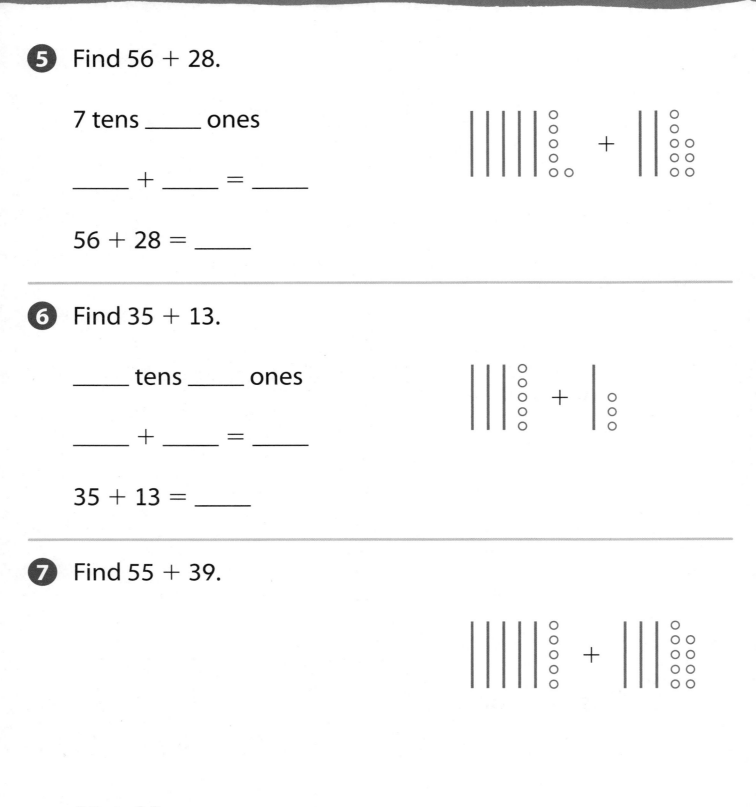

6 Find 35 + 13.

_____ tens _____ ones

_____ + _____ = _____

35 + 13 = _____

7 Find 55 + 39.

55 + 39 = _____

Practice Adding Two-Digit Numbers

Look at the Example. Then solve problems 1–4.

Example Find 29 + 16.
Add the tens and ones.

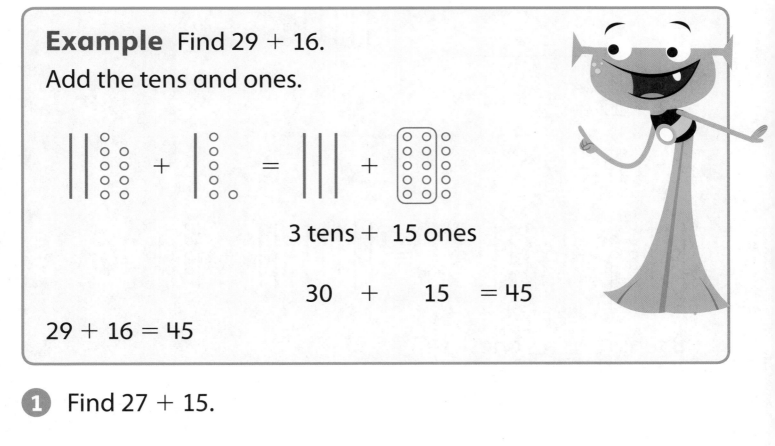

3 tens + 15 ones

30 + 15 = 45

29 + 16 = 45

1 Find 27 + 15.

2 tens   7 ones

+ 1 ten   5 ones
_____

_____ tens _____ ones

30 + _____ = _____

27 + 15 = _____

2 Find 52 + 17.

_____ tens _____ ones

60 + _____ = _____

52 + 17 = _____

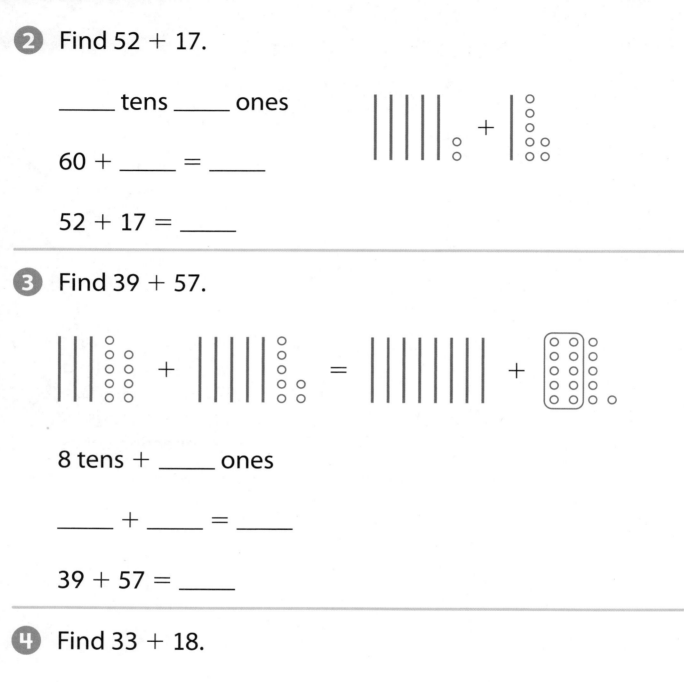

3 Find 39 + 57.

8 tens + _____ ones

_____ + _____ = _____

39 + 57 = _____

4 Find 33 + 18.

33 + 18 = _____

Develop Adding Two-Digit Numbers

How many shells in all?

24 shells   **58 shells**

Try It

 **Math Toolkit**
- base-ten blocks
- hundred charts
- number bonds
- connecting cubes

DISCUSS IT
Which addition
strategy could
help?

How many shells in all?   **24 shells**   **58 shells**

Model It

Find 24 + 58.

Add the tens.
Then add the ones.

2 tens	**4 ones**
+ 5 tens	**8 ones**
7 tens	**12 ones**
1 ten	**2 ones**

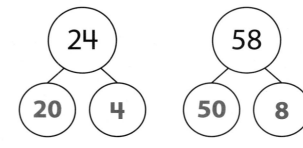

_____ tens _____ ones

So, 24 + 58 = _____.

_____ shells in all.

Connect It

1 How is your way like **Model It**? How is it different?

2 How is adding 24 + 58 like adding 24 + 8?

Apply It

3 Manny has 43 cards.

Mark has 17 cards.

How many cards in all?

Complete the number bonds and fill in the blanks.

4 tens   3 ones

+ 1 ten   7 ones
_____

_____ tens _____ ones

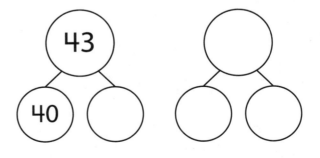

_____ + _____ = _____

_____ cards

4 Find 35 + 43.

Complete the number bonds
and fill in the blanks.

30 + _____

40 + _____
_____

_____ + _____ = _____

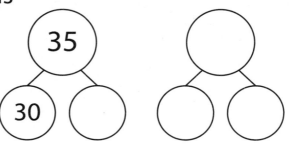

35 + 43 = _____

---

5 55 carrots grow in Asha's garden.
38 pumpkins grow in her garden.
How many plants in all?

50 + 5

30 + 8
_____

_____ + _____ = _____   _____ plants

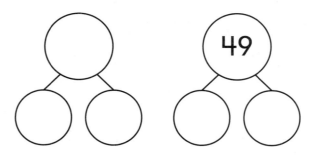

---

6 Find 14 + 49.

_____ = 14 + 49

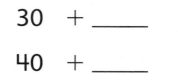

Practice Adding Two-Digit Numbers

Look at the Example. Then solve problems 1–5.

Example Find $47 + 35$.

$$
\begin{array}{rr}
& 4 \text{ tens} \quad 7 \text{ ones} \\
+ & 3 \text{ tens} \quad 5 \text{ ones} \\
\hline
& 7 \text{ tens} \ 12 \text{ ones}
\end{array}
$$

$47 + 35 = 82$ $70 + 10 + 2 = 82$

1 Find $26 + 27$.

$$
\begin{array}{rr}
& 2 \text{ tens} \quad 6 \text{ ones} \\
+ & 2 \text{ tens} \quad 7 \text{ ones} \\
\hline
\end{array}
$$

_____ tens _____ ones = _____

$26 + 27 =$ _____

2 18 big spoons and 31 small spoons. How many spoons in all?

$$
\begin{array}{r}
10 + 8 \\
30 + 1 \\
\hline
\end{array}
$$

_____ + _____ = _____

_____ spoons $18 + 31 =$ _____

Lesson 29 Add Two-Digit Numbers   **677**

3 Find 56 + 28.

50 + _____

_____ + 8
_____

_____ + _____ = _____

56 + 28 = _____

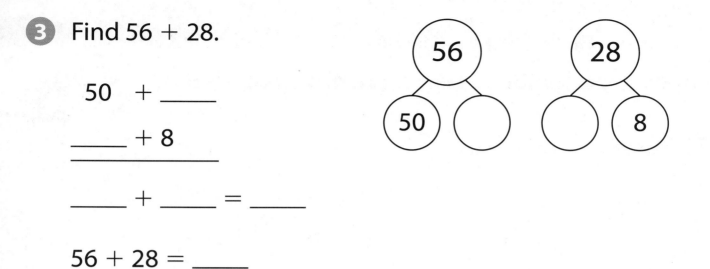

_____

4 47 green hats and 28 blue hats.
How many hats altogether?

_____ + 7

20 + _____
_____

_____ + _____ = _____

47 + 28 = _____

_____ hats

5 Find 62 + 18.

62 + 18 = _____

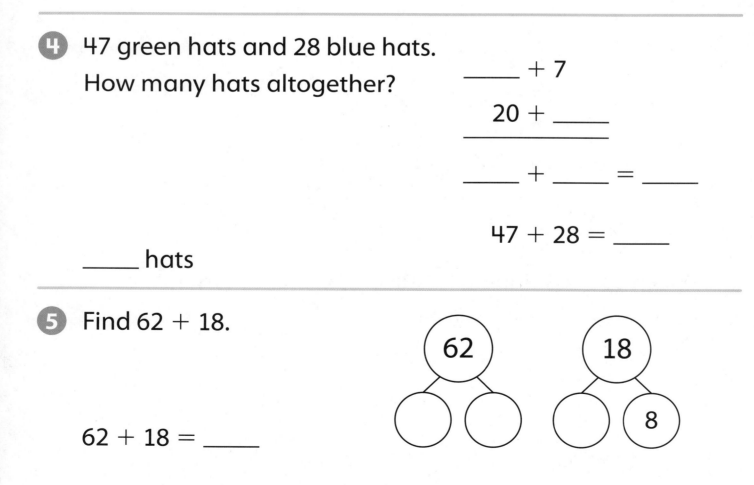

Refine Adding Two-Digit Numbers

Complete the Example. Then solve problems 1–4.

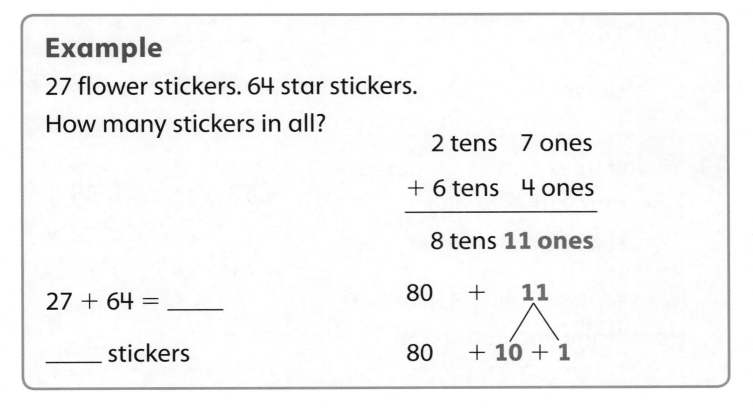

Example

27 flower stickers. 64 star stickers.

How many stickers in all?

$$\begin{array}{r} 2 \text{ tens} \quad 7 \text{ ones} \\ + \ 6 \text{ tens} \quad 4 \text{ ones} \\ \hline 8 \text{ tens } \mathbf{11 \text{ ones}} \end{array}$$

27 + 64 = _____

80   +   **11**

_____ stickers

80   + **10 + 1**

Apply It

1 38 soccer balls and 46 kickballs.

How many balls in all?

38 + 46 = _____

_____ balls

2 17 yellow flowers and 28 white flowers.
How many flowers altogether?

$$17 + 28 = \underline{\hphantom{000}}$$

____ flowers

	1 ten	7 ones
+	2 tens	8 ones

____ tens ____ ones

---

3 52 oak trees and 35 pine trees.
How many trees in all?

$$52 + 35 = \underline{\hphantom{000}}$$

____ trees

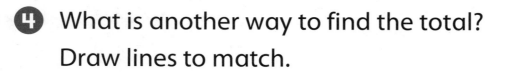

---

4 What is another way to find the total?
Draw lines to match.

    1 ten   5 ones   20 + 2
+ 3 tens 7 ones   50 + 4

    6 tens 3 ones   10 + 5
+ 1 ten   9 ones   30 + 7

    2 tens 2 ones   60 + 3
+ 5 tens 4 ones   10 + 9

Practice Adding Two-Digit Numbers

Look at the Example. Then solve problems 1–4.

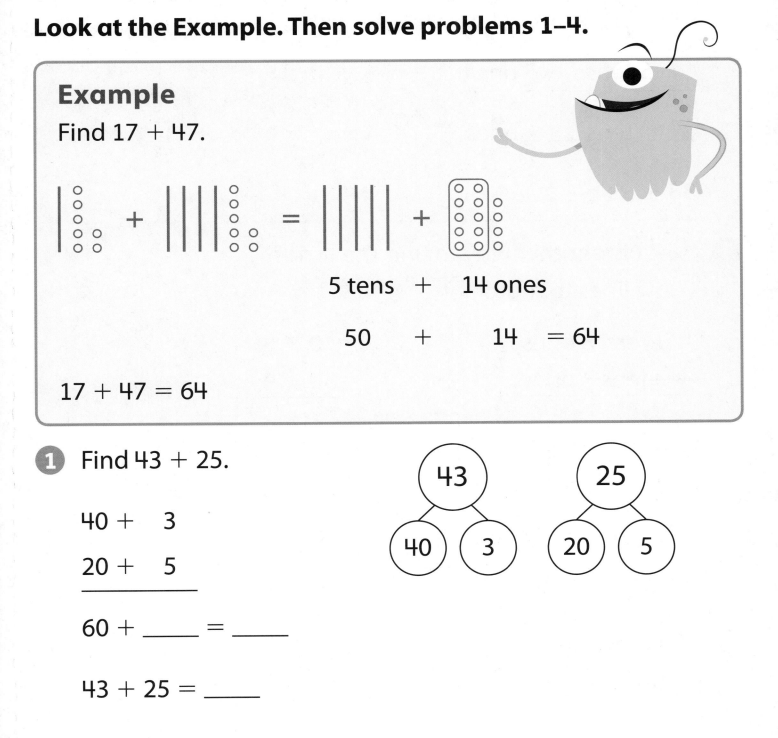

Example

Find 17 + 47.

5 tens   +   14 ones

50   +   14   = 64

17 + 47 = 64

1 Find 43 + 25.

43

40   3

25

20   5

40 +   3

20 +   5
_____

60 + _____ = _____

43 + 25 = _____

2 Find 38 + 53.

$$
\begin{array}{rl}
& 3 \text{ tens} \quad 8 \text{ ones} \\
+ & 5 \text{ tens} \quad 3 \text{ ones} \\
\hline
\end{array}
$$

_____ tens _____ ones

38 + 53 = _____

3 What is another way to find the total?
Draw lines to match.

$$
\begin{array}{l}
 1 \text{ ten } \; 8 \text{ ones} \\
+ 3 \text{ tens } 4 \text{ ones} \\
\hline
\end{array}
\qquad
\begin{array}{l}
10 + 8 \\
30 + 4 \\
\hline
\end{array}
$$

$$
\begin{array}{l}
 2 \text{ tens } 6 \text{ ones} \\
+ 4 \text{ tens } 2 \text{ ones} \\
\hline
\end{array}
\qquad
\begin{array}{l}
70 + 9 \\
10 + 3 \\
\hline
\end{array}
$$

$$
\begin{array}{l}
 7 \text{ tens } 9 \text{ ones} \\
+ 1 \text{ ten } \; 3 \text{ ones} \\
\hline
\end{array}
\qquad
\begin{array}{l}
20 + 6 \\
40 + 2 \\
\hline
\end{array}
$$

4 39 road bikes and 39 trail bikes.
How many bikes in all?

_____ = 39 + 39   _____ bikes

Refine Adding Two-Digit Numbers

Apply It

Solve problems 1–6.

1 33 math books and 27 reading books. What is the total number of books?

33 + 27 = _____

_____ books

2 Find 72 + 22.

Ⓐ 74

Ⓑ 84

Ⓒ 94

3 17 gold stars and 29 silver stars. How many stars in all?

17 + 29 = _____

_____ stars

4 Find 13 + 65.

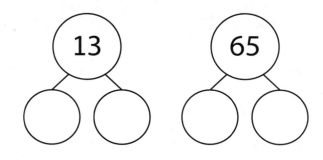

13 + 65 = _____

---

5 48 circles and 35 squares.
How many shapes in all?
What is wrong? Explain.

$$
\begin{array}{ll}
\text{4 tens} & \text{8 ones} \\
+\ \text{3 tens} & \text{5 ones} \\
\hline
\text{7 tens} & \text{13 ones} = 73
\end{array}
$$

---

6 Find 65 + 18.

65 + 18 = _____

Self Reflection

In this unit you learned to . . .

Skill	Lesson
Add and subtract tens.	25
Add or subtract 10 from any number.	26
Add tens to any number.	27
Add one-digit and two-digit numbers.	28
Add 2 two-digit numbers.	29

Think about what you learned.

Use words, numbers, and drawings.

1 I worked hardest to learn how to . . .

2 One thing I still need to work on is . . .

Solve the problems.

1 Draw lines to match the numbers.

10 more than 78   38

10 less than 78   58

10 more than 48   68

                                88

2 There are 27 circles.

There are 7 squares.

How many shapes? Circle.

Ⓐ   24 shapes

Ⓑ   34 shapes

Ⓒ   97 shapes

3 Find 60 − 30.

Draw or write how base-ten blocks can help.

60 − 30 = _____

4 Find $34 + 4$.

$34 + 4 = $ _____

5 Find $50 - 20$.

$2 + ? = 5$

2 tens $+$ _____ tens $= 5$ tens

$20 + $ _____ $= $ _____

$50 - 20 = $ _____

6 Find $25 + 34$.

$25 + 34 = $ _____

7 Jo has 20 stamps.
Bo has 70 stamps.
How many stamps in all?

$20 + 70 = $ _____

_____ stamps

Put It Together

8 Draw 5, 6, 7, 8, or 9 tens.
Complete the problem using your number.

There are _____ shapes.

30 of them are squares.

The rest are circles.

How many are circles?

Show your work.

_____ shapes are circles.

Draw or write to show math words in the unit.

My Word: _____

_____

_____

_____

My Example

My Word: _____

_____

_____

_____

My Example

My Word: _____

_____

_____

_____

My Example

My Word: _____

_____

_____

_____

My Example

My Word: _____

_____

_____

_____

My Example

My Word: _____

_____

_____

_____

My Example

My Word: _____

_____

_____

_____

My Example

My Word: _____

_____

_____

_____

My Example

Length
Comparing, Ordering, and Measuring

☑ **Self Check**

Before starting this unit, check off the skills you know below. As you complete each lesson, see how many more skills you can check off!

I can . . .	Before	After
Order objects by length.	☐	☐
Compare lengths of objects.	☐	☐
Measure lengths of objects.	☐	☐

Build Your Vocabulary

My Math Words
Work with a partner to compare the rods.

1 The blue rod is _____ than the red rod.

2 The orange rod is _____ than the red rod.

3 We are comparing the _____ of the rods.

My Academic Words
Use the academic words to complete the sentences.

☐ arrange   ☐ observe   ☐ process

1 When I _____ birds, I watch what they do.

2 My brother helped me _____ my books. We put them in order from shortest to tallest.

3 Our teacher explained the _____ she used to solve the problem. The steps she took made sense.

Order Objects by Length

Dear Family,

This week your child is learning to order objects by length.

Your child will line up three objects at one end to compare the **lengths** and then order the objects by length. For example, the three pencils below are ordered from longest to shortest.

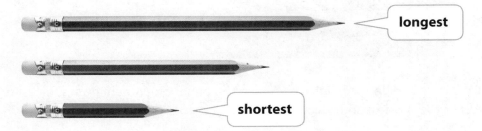

longest

shortest

The brown pencil is **shorter** than the yellow pencil but **longer** than the red pencil.

Your child will also compare the heights of three objects and order them by height.

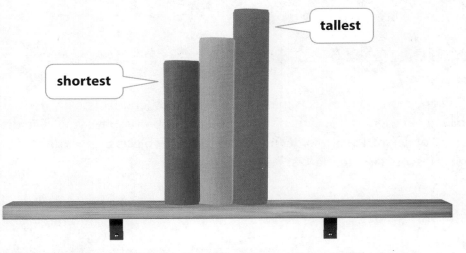

tallest

shortest

The green book is **taller** than the red book but shorter than the blue book. Learning to compare and order objects by length and height will help your child develop measurement concepts and connect these concepts to real-world situations.

Invite your child to share what he or she knows about ordering objects by length by doing the following activity together.

Activity Ordering Objects by Length

Do this activity with your child to practice ordering objects by length.

Materials 3 crayons of different lengths, 3 cups of different heights, 3 other household objects whose lengths or heights can be compared.

- Give your child 3 crayons of different lengths and have him or her order the crayons from shortest to longest. Remind your child to line up the crayons at one end to compare their lengths. Ask your child which crayon is the shortest and which crayon is the longest.

- Then give your child 3 cups of different heights and have him or her order them from shortest to tallest. Ask which cup is the shortest and which cup is the tallest.

- Help your child find one more set of objects that can be ordered by length or height. For example, your child might suggest hair clips, ribbons, trophies, or books. Have your child order the objects by length or height. Practice ordering different sets of objects by reversing the order to be longest to shortest or tallest to shortest.

Explore Ordering Objects by Length

Each cube train is a different length.

Draw the cube trains.

Circle the shortest.

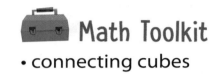 **Math Toolkit**
• connecting cubes

Connect It

Draw the straws. Circle the tallest.

Prepare for Ordering Objects by Length

1 Think about what you know about length.
Fill in each box. Use words, numbers, and pictures.
Show as many ideas as you can.

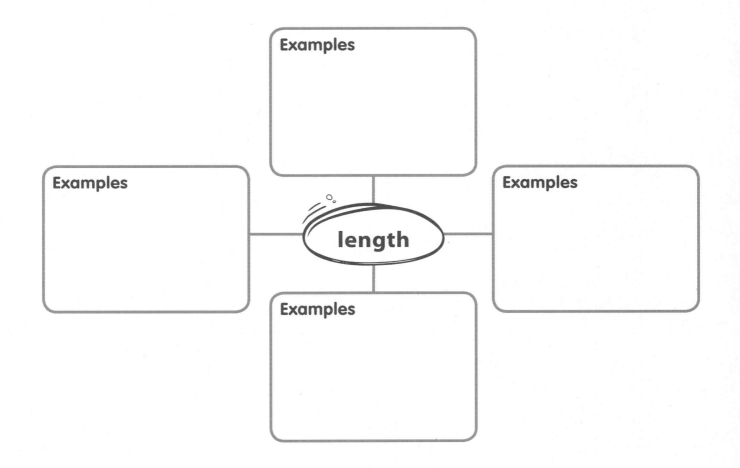

Examples

Examples

length

Examples

Examples

2 Draw a line the same length as the crayon.

Lesson 30 Order Objects by Length   **697**

3 Solve the problem. Draw to show your work.

Draw 3 crayons of different lengths.
Circle the longest.

Develop Ordering Objects by Length

Put your pencils in order from shortest to longest.
Which is the shortest? Which is the longest?

Math Toolkit
• connecting cubes

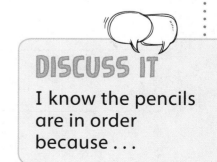

DISCUSS IT

I know the pencils
are in order
because . . .

Lesson 30 Order Objects by Length   **699**

Put your pencils in order from shortest to longest.
Which is the shortest? Which is the longest?

Model It

Find the shortest and longest pencils.
Lay the pencils on the table.
Line up the ends.
Put them in order from shortest to longest.

The _____ pencil is the shortest.

The _____ pencil is the longest.

Connect It

1 How is your way like **Model It**? How is it different?

2 Why is it important to line up one end when you order objects by length?

Apply It

3 Order the spoons by length. Complete the sentences.

The _____ spoon is the shortest.

The _____ spoon is the longest.

4 Order the combs by length. Complete the sentences.

The <u>red</u> comb is the shortest.

The <u>orange</u> comb is the longest.

5 Circle the group of pencils that shows them in order from longest to shortest.

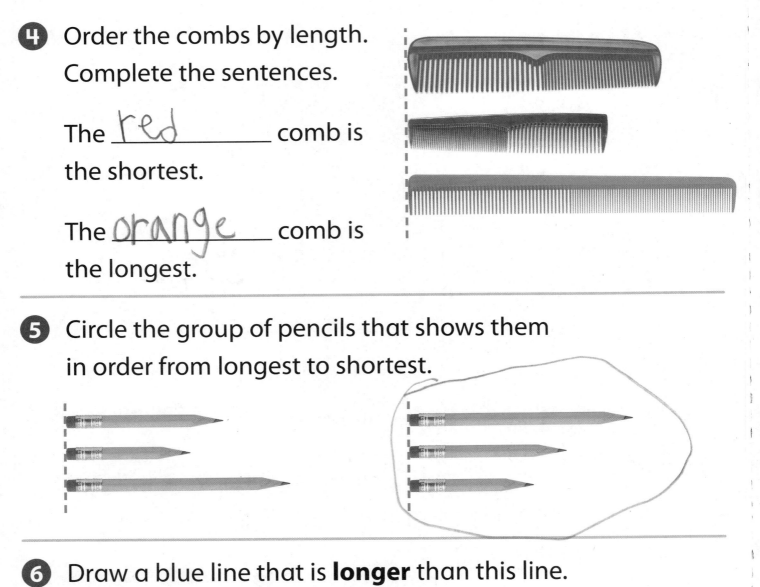

6 Draw a blue line that is **longer** than this line.
Draw a red line that is **shorter** than this line.

Practice Ordering Objects by Length

Look at the Example. Then solve problems 1–5.

Example

The pencils are lined up at one end.

They are ordered by length.

The green pencil is the shortest.

The red pencil is the longest.

1

The _black_ dog is the shortest.

The _white_ dog is the longest.

2

The _yellow_ ribbon is the shortest.

The _blue_ ribbon is the longest.

3

The _green_ paintbrush is the longest.

The _purple_ paintbrush is the shortest.

4

The _blue_ paint streak is the longest.

The _yellow_ paint streak is the shortest.

5 Draw a red line that is longer than this line.
Draw a blue line that is shorter than this line.

Develop Ordering Objects by Length

Ron has 3 books. He puts them on a shelf in order from shortest to tallest.

How might Ron's books look on the shelf?

 **Try It**

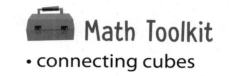 **Math Toolkit**
• connecting cubes

DISCUSS IT

How did you know how tall to draw the last book?

Ron has 3 books. He puts them on a shelf in order from shortest to tallest.

How might Ron's books look on the shelf?

Model It

Order the books from shortest to tallest.
Line up the bottom edges.
Circle the shortest.
Put an X on the tallest.

The _____ book is the shortest.

The _____ book is the tallest.

Connect It

1 How is your way like **Model It**? How is it different?

2 Buzz says the red flower is the shortest.
Do you agree? Why or why not?

3 Circle the shortest plant. Put an X on the tallest plant.

4 Complete the sentences.

The ___blue___ pencil is **taller** than the green pencil.

The ___yellow___ pencil is shorter than the green pencil.

5 Circle the group of animals that shows them in order from tallest to shortest.

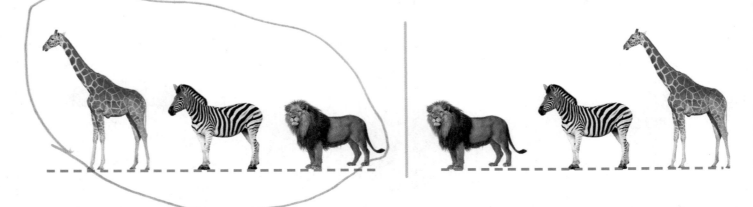

6 Circle the shortest pin.
Put an X on the tallest pin.

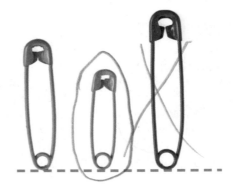

©Curriculum Associates, LLC   Copying is not permitted.

Practice Ordering Objects by Length

Look at the Example. Then solve problems 1–5.

> ### Example
> The bats are ordered from shortest
> to tallest.
> A circle is around the shortest bat.
> An X is on the tallest bat.

1 Circle the shortest plant.
Put an X on the tallest plant.

2 Circle the shortest flower.
Put an X on the tallest flower.

3 Circle the shortest rectangle.
Put an X on the tallest rectangle.

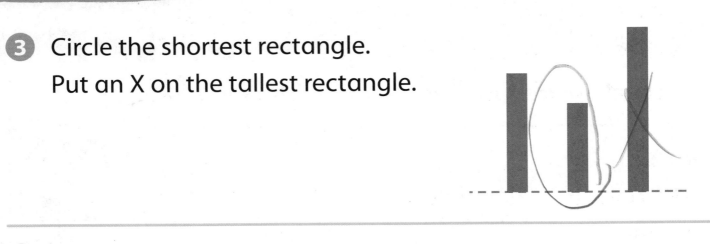

4 Circle the group of pencils that shows them in order from tallest to shortest.

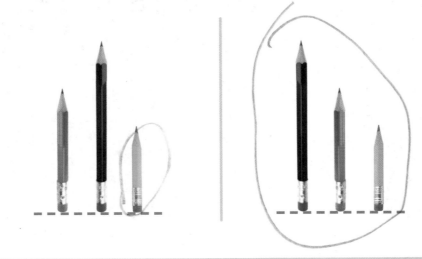

5 Buzz says the black ribbon is the shortest.
Boom says the blue ribbon is the shortest.

Who is right? Circle.

Buzz   Boom

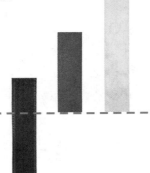

Refine Ordering Objects by Length

Complete the Example. Then solve problems 1–5.

Example

Read the clues. Then color the strips.

The green strip is longest.

The yellow strip is shorter than
the red strip.

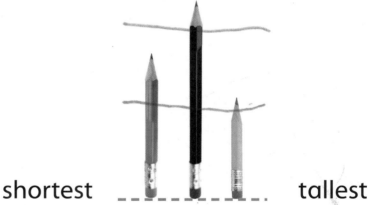

Apply It

1 Draw lines to show
which pencil is tallest
and which is shortest.

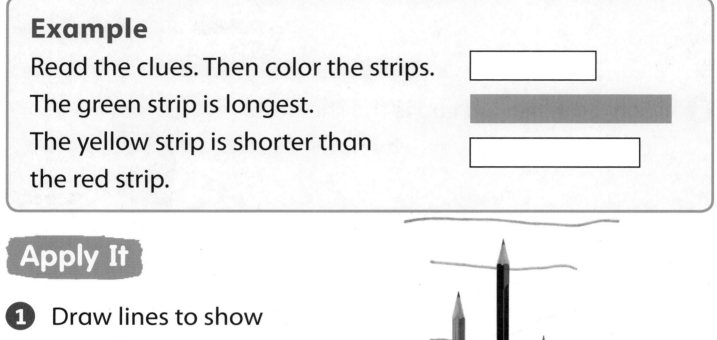

shortest _ _ _ _ _ _ _ _ _ _ _ tallest

2 Read the clues.
Then color the dogs.

The red dog is longest.
The blue dog is shorter
than the yellow dog.

3 Circle the shortest one.
Put an X on the longest one.

4 Boom says the red cup is the shortest.
Do you agree? Why or why not?

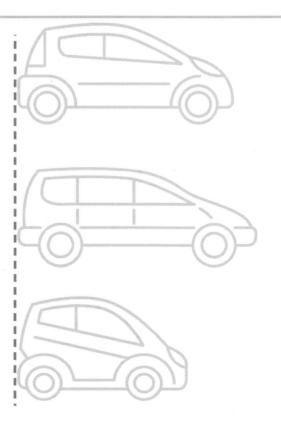

5 Read the clues.
Color the cars.

The blue car is shortest.
The red car is longer than
the yellow car.

Practice Ordering Objects by Length

Look at the Example. Then solve problems 1–5.

Example

Read the clues. Then color the crayons to match.

The blue crayon is shortest.

The yellow crayon is longer than the red crayon.

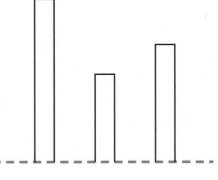

1 Color the tallest rectangle red.
Color the shortest rectangle blue.

2 Circle the shortest paintbrush. Put an X on the longest paintbrush.

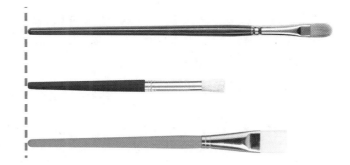

3 Draw lines to show which book is tallest and which is shortest.

tallest

shortest

4 Draw lines to show which fork is longest and which is shortest.

shortest

longest

5 Read the clues. Then color the boats.

The blue boat is shortest.
The red boat is longer than the yellow boat.

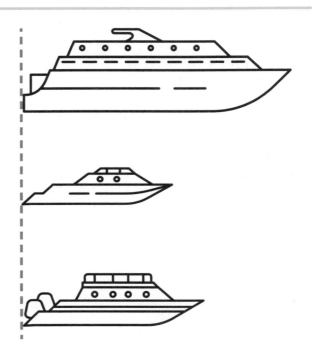

Refine Ordering Objects by Length

Apply It

Solve problems 1–6.

1 Read the clues.
Then color the bats.

The green bat is shortest.
The purple bat is longer than
the blue bat.

---

2 Circle the word that makes the sentence
true. Put an X on the other word.

The green balloon is shorter/longer
than the orange balloon.

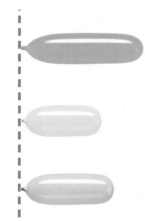

---

3 Draw a line that is taller than
both rectangles.

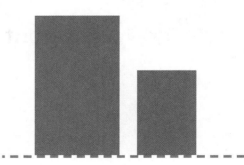

4 Boom says the red ribbon is the longest.
Buzz says that Boom is wrong.
How does Buzz know?

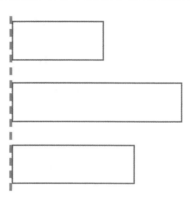

---

5 Read the clues.
Color the rectangles.

The red rectangle is shortest.
The purple rectangle is longer
than the blue rectangle.

---

6 Circle the word that makes the sentence true.
Put an X on the other word.
The blue mug is taller/shorter than the yellow mug.

©Curriculum Associates, LLC   Copying is not permitted.

Compare Lengths

Dear Family,

This week your child is learning to compare the lengths of two objects by comparing each object to a third object.

Sometimes the lengths of two objects cannot be directly compared. For example, you may not be able to easily move two tables side-by-side to see which is longer. To find which table is longer, you can compare each table to a reference (third) object, such as a piece of string. If only one table is shorter than the string, it is the shorter table. If only one table is longer than the string, it is the longer table.

Compare the string to one table.

Then compare the same string to the other table.

This method can also be used with smaller objects. In class your child will practice using a reference object, such as a piece of string or strip of paper, to compare the lengths of two objects. This concept will help prepare your child for using standard measuring tools such as rulers.

Invite your child to share what he or she knows about using a third object to compare the lengths of two objects by doing the following activity together.

Activity Comparing Lengths

Do this activity with your child to practice comparing lengths.

Materials yarn, string, or ribbon; large household objects to compare, such as a table and a dresser or a sofa and a kitchen counter; smaller household objects

- Help your child select two large objects in your home whose lengths cannot be easily compared, either because the objects are in different rooms or because you cannot tell which is longer or shorter simply by looking. For example, you and your child may choose to compare the lengths of a table and a dresser.

- Cut a piece of yarn (or string/ribbon) that is the same length as one of the objects. Help your child use the yarn to compare the lengths of the two objects. Ask your child which of the two objects is longer and why.

- Then cut the yarn to about 6 inches and ask your child to find one object that is shorter than the piece of yarn and one object that is longer. Have your child tell which object is shorter and why.

The comb is shorter than the yarn, and the spoon is longer than the yarn. So, the comb is shorter than the spoon.

©Curriculum Associates, LLC   Copying is not permitted.

Explore Comparing Lengths

Learning Target
- Order three objects by length; compare the lengths of two objects indirectly by using a third object.

SMP 1, 2, 3, 4, 5, 6

Trace your strip next to the strip of paper below. Is it taller, shorter, or the same? Circle the word.

Try It

🧰 **Math Toolkit**
- connecting cubes

My strip is:　　taller　　　　shorter　　　　the same

Connect It

Draw a line that is shorter than the yellow pencil.

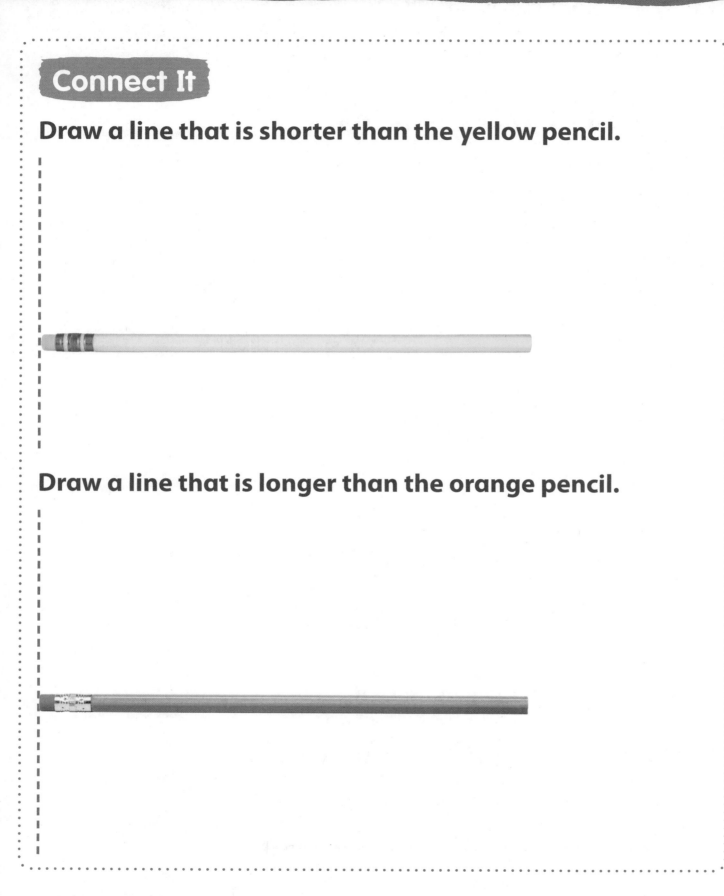

Draw a line that is longer than the orange pencil.

Prepare for Comparing Lengths

1 Think about what you know about length and the word longer. Fill in each box. Use words, numbers, and pictures. Show as many ideas as you can.

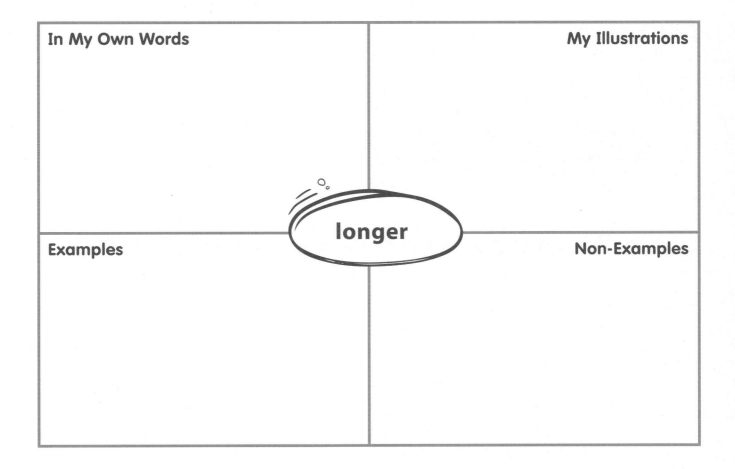

In My Own Words	My Illustrations
Examples	Non-Examples

longer

2 Draw an X on the longer arrow.

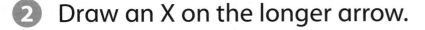

3 Solve the problem. Draw to show your work.

Draw a line that is shorter than the orange crayon.

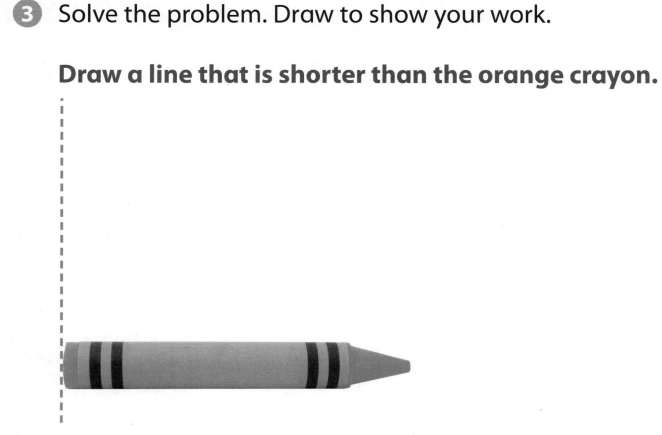

Draw a line that is longer than the green crayon.

Develop Comparing Lengths

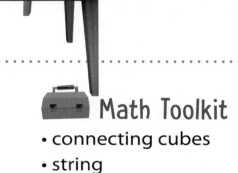

How can you find which table is longer without putting them next to each other?

 Try It

Math Toolkit
• connecting cubes
• string

DISCUSS IT
What did you use to help?

How can you find which table is longer without putting them next to each other?

Model It

Find which table is longer.

Use another object, such as a piece of string.

Compare it to the length of each table.

The red table is longer than the string.

The brown table is _____ than the string.

So, the red table is _____ than the brown table.

Connect It

1 How is your way like **Model It**? How is it different?

2 How would using a piece of string help you compare the lengths of the tables?

Apply It

3 Compare each comb to the same piece of string. Which comb is longer?

The blue comb is longer than the string.

The pink comb is _____ than the string.

So, the blue comb is _____ than the pink comb.

Lesson 31 Compare Lengths   **725**

4 Which dresser is shorter?

The blue dresser is _Shorter_ than the string.

The pink dresser is _longer_ than the string.

So, the blue dresser is _Shorter_ than the pink dresser.

5 Which animal is longer?

The lizard is _Shorter_ than the string.

The cat is _longer_ than the string.

So, the cat is _longer_ than the lizard.

Practice Comparing Lengths

Look at the Example. Then solve problems 1–3.

Example

Which desk is longer?

Use a piece of string.

Compare it to the length of each desk.

The blue desk is shorter than the string.

The pink desk is longer than the string.

So, the pink desk is longer than the blue desk.

1 Compare each bench to the same piece of string.
Which bench is longer?

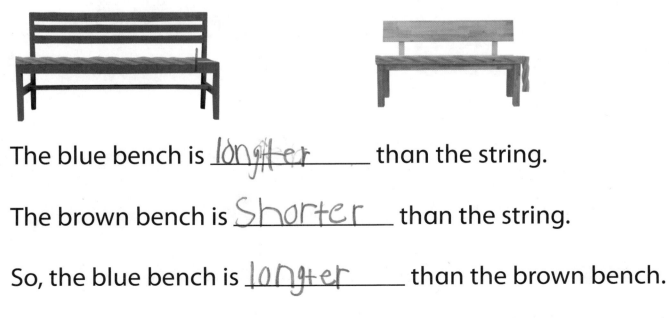

The blue bench is _longer_ than the string.

The brown bench is _shorter_ than the string.

So, the blue bench is _longer_ than the brown bench.

2 Which bookshelf is shorter?

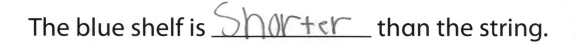

The blue shelf is _Shorter_ than the string.

The green shelf is _longer_ than the string.

So, the blue shelf is _Shorter_ than the green shelf.

---

3 Boom measured the two desks with the same piece of string.

Buzz says the green desk is longer.
Boom says the purple desk is longer.
Who is right? Circle.

Buzz   (Boom)

©Curriculum Associates, LLC   Copying is not permitted.

Develop Comparing Lengths

This shoe is shorter than a strip of paper.

This spoon is longer than the same strip of paper.

Is the shoe longer or shorter than the spoon?

How do you know?

 Math Toolkit
• connecting cubes

DISCUSS IT

Can you explain your thinking to me?

This shoe is shorter than a strip of paper.

This spoon is longer than the same strip of paper.

Is the shoe longer or shorter than the spoon?

How do you know?

Model It

Use a paper strip.

Compare each object to the paper.

Fill in the blanks.

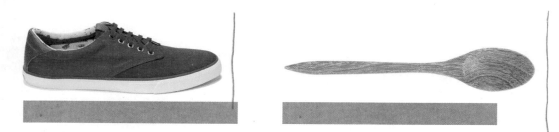

The shoe is ___SAMe___ than the spoon.

The spoon is ___longer___ than the shoe.

Connect It

1 How is your way like **Model It**? How is it different?

2 Chris is shorter than Amy.
Ray is taller than Amy.
Boom says Chris is shorter than Ray.

Do you agree? Why or why not?

Apply It

3 Compare each object to the paper.
Fill in the blanks.

The pin is _____ than the pencil.

The pencil is _____ than the pin.

4 Compare each object to the paper.
Fill in the blanks.

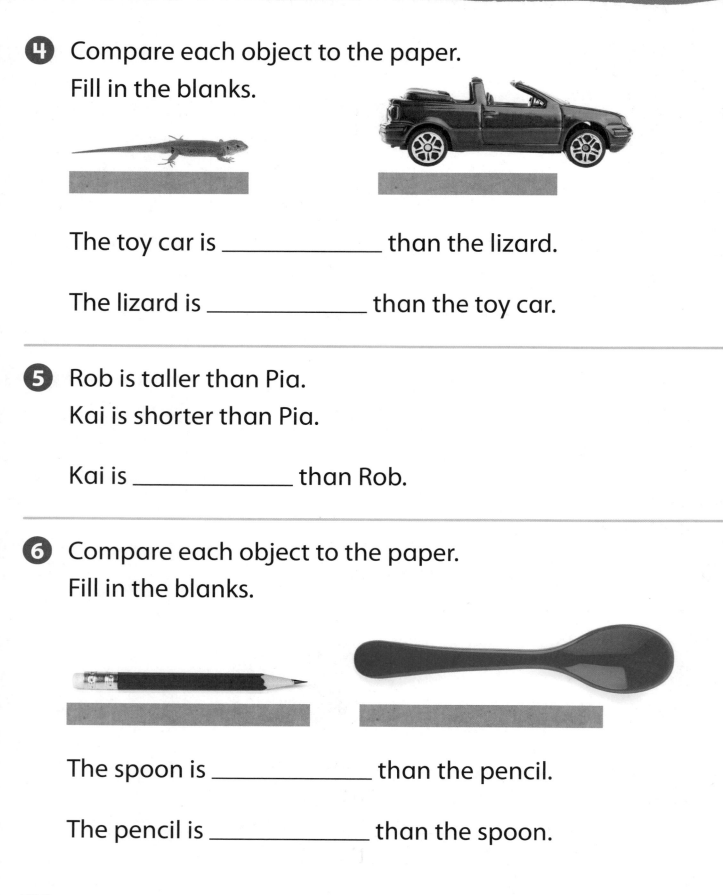

The toy car is _____ than the lizard.

The lizard is _____ than the toy car.

---

5 Rob is taller than Pia.
Kai is shorter than Pia.

Kai is _____ than Rob.

---

6 Compare each object to the paper.
Fill in the blanks.

The spoon is _____ than the pencil.

The pencil is _____ than the spoon.

Practice Comparing Lengths

Look at the Example. Then solve problems 1–4.

Example

Compare each object to the paper.

Fill in the blanks.

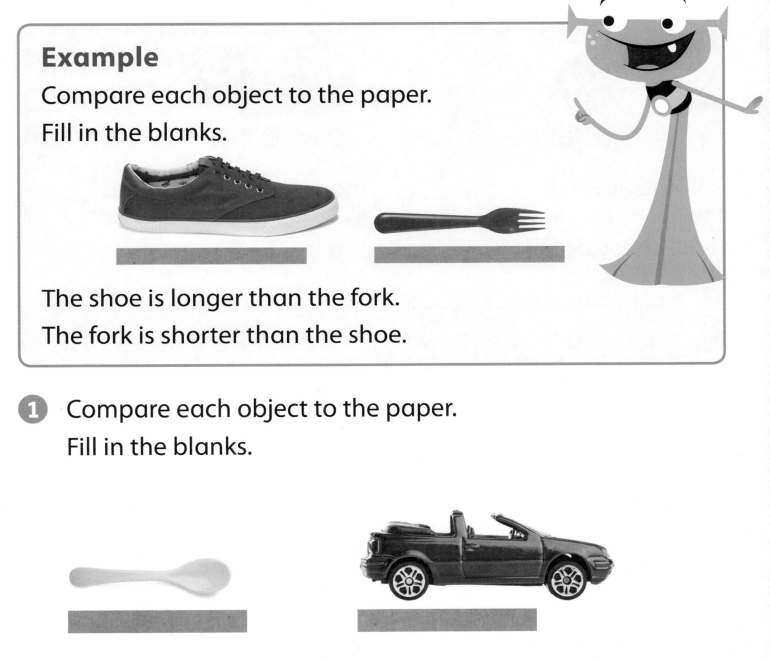

The shoe is longer than the fork.

The fork is shorter than the shoe.

① Compare each object to the paper.
   Fill in the blanks.

The spoon is _____ than the toy car.

The toy car is _____ than the spoon.

2 Compare each object to the paper.
Fill in the blanks.

The flower is _____ than the toy boat.

The toy boat is _____ than the flower.

---

3 Carla is taller than Steve.
Yuki is shorter than Steve.
Boom says Steve is the shortest.
Buzz says Yuki is the shortest.
Who is right? Circle.

Buzz   Boom

---

4 Look at problem 3. Write the names in order from
the shortest to the tallest.

_____   _____   _____

Refine Comparing Lengths

Complete the Example. Then solve problems 1–5.

Example

The red bar is longer
than the blue bar.
The blue bar is longer
than the green bar.

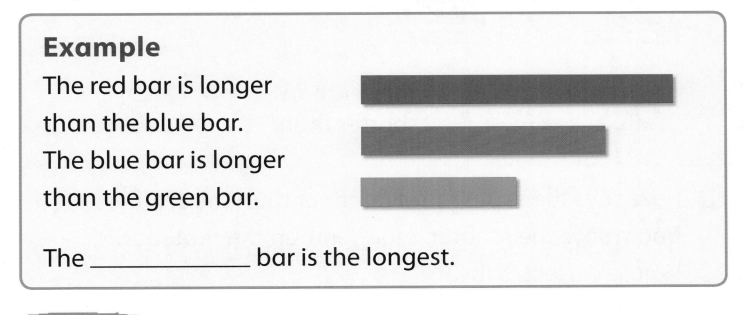

The _____ bar is the longest.

Apply It

1 Draw a line that is longer than the pencil.
Circle the shortest object.

2 The crayon is shorter than the pencil.
The pencil is shorter than the notebook.

The crayon is _____ than the notebook.

3 Compare lengths. Then circle the correct words.

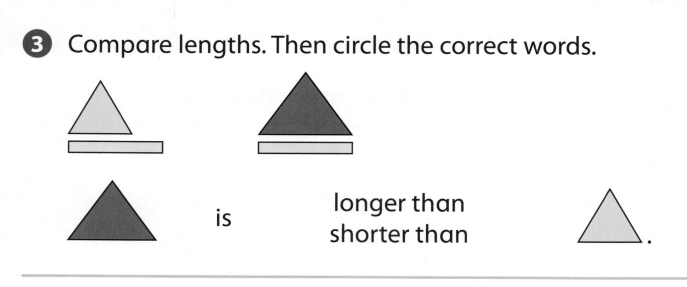

is   longer than
       shorter than

4 Buzz says the skateboard is longer than the scooter.
Boom says the scooter is longer than the skateboard.
Who is correct? Why?

scooter

skateboard

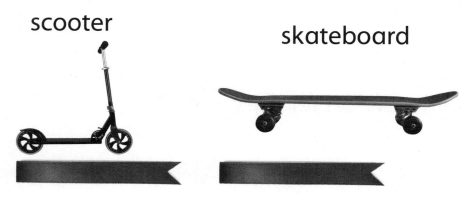

5 The cat is longer than the lizard.
The dog is longer than the cat.

The lizard is _____ than the dog.

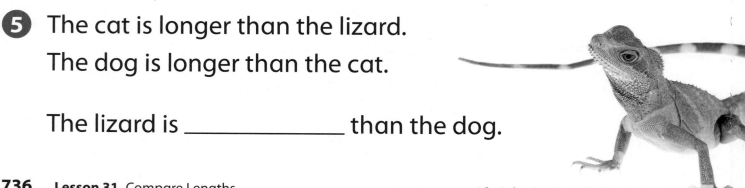

Practice Comparing Lengths

Look at the Example. Then solve problems 1–5.

Example

The yellow ribbon is shorter than the red ribbon.

The red ribbon is shorter than the blue ribbon.

The yellow ribbon is the shortest.

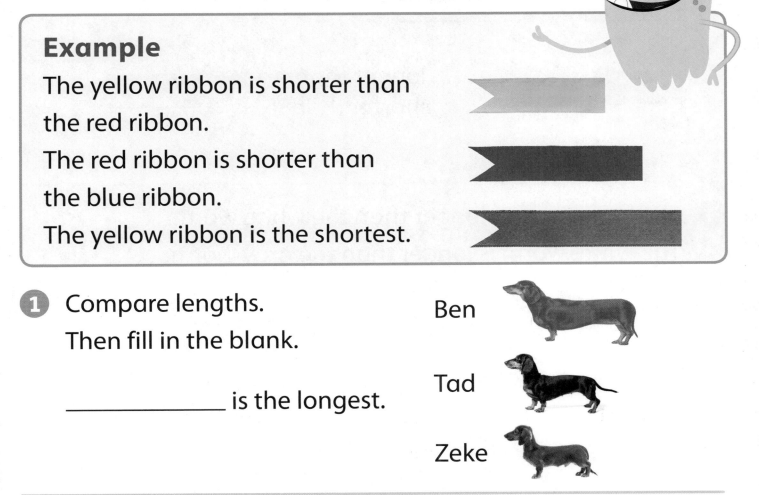

1 Compare lengths.
Then fill in the blank.

_____ is the longest.

Ben

Tad

Zeke

2 Draw a line that is shorter than the pencil.
Circle the longest object.

3 Compare lengths. Then circle the correct words.

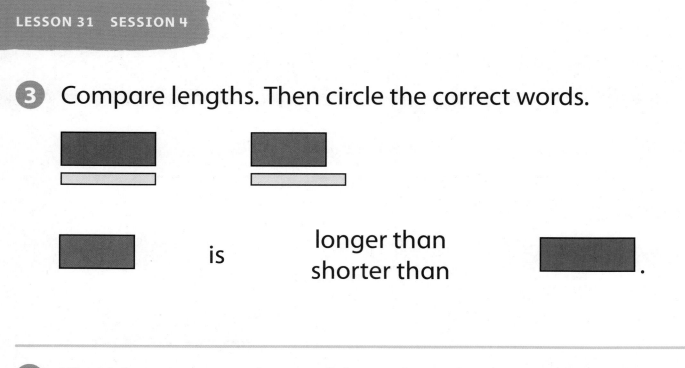

is

longer than
shorter than

———

4 The blue worm is longer than the white worm.
The white worm is longer than the gray worm.

The blue worm is _____ than the gray worm.

———

5 The red crayon is shorter than the green crayon.
The green crayon is shorter than the blue crayon.

The red crayon is _____ than the blue crayon.

Refine Comparing Lengths

Apply It

Solve problems 1–6.

1 Compare lengths.

Then circle the shorter object.

---

2 Draw a line that is shorter than the yellow rectangle.
Circle the longest shape.

---

3 The bee is longer than the ant.
The worm is longer than the bee.

The ant is _____ than the worm.

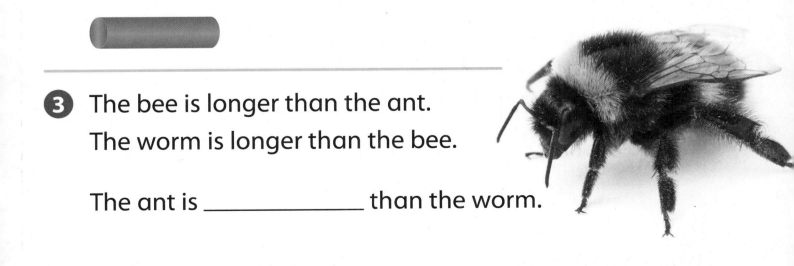

4 Compare lengths. Then circle the correct words.

 is

longer than

shorter than

.

5 Draw a line that is shorter than the spoon.
Circle the longest object.

6 The pen is longer than the marker.
The pencil is longer than the pen.
Buzz says the marker is shorter than the pencil.
Do you agree? Why or why not?

Understand Length Measurement

Dear Family,

This week your child is exploring measuring length with nonstandard units.

Your child will **measure** the length of objects using a known **unit**. Before measuring with standard units such as inches or centimeters, it is helpful for children to first practice measuring with nonstandard units—any same-sized units that are repeated. For example, your child can use toothpicks, small square blocks, and paper clips to measure the length of objects. By placing multiple same-sized paper clips in a row under a crayon, your child may find that the crayon is about 4 paper clips long. He or she will learn to line up the objects when measuring this way, and why there should be no gaps or overlaps.

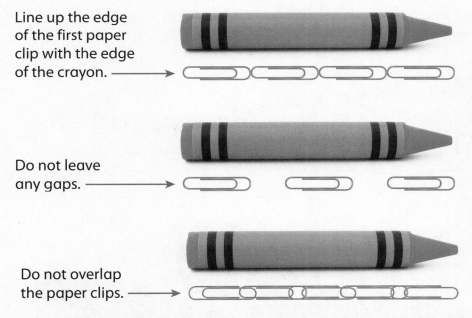

Line up the edge of the first paper clip with the edge of the crayon. ——→

Do not leave any gaps. ——→

Do not overlap the paper clips. ——→

Your child will also measure objects that may not line up exactly with the end of a nonstandard unit. Your child will count the number of units to the nearest whole unit and use the word *about* to describe the length.

Measuring length with nonstandard units will help prepare your child to measure with standard units in later grades.

Invite your child to share what he or she knows about measuring length with nonstandard units by doing the following activity together.

Activity Measuring Length

Do this activity with your child to understand measuring the length of an object.

Materials measuring units (same-sized objects to measure with, such as crackers, paper clips, or mini pretzel sticks), paper, pencil, 5 objects to measure such as a toothbrush, bandage, crayon, cup, and fork

Tell your child you are going on a measuring adventure together.

- Make a list of 5 objects from around your home that your child can find the length of using measuring units.

- Help your child find each object on the list. Give your child the measuring units. (The objects to measure with must all be the same size.)

- Have your child lay the units from one end of the object to the other end, ensuring there are no gaps and no overlapping.

- Count how many objects were used to measure the length.

- Remind your child that if the other end of the object does not reach a whole measuring unit, they should use the word *about*. For example: *The toothbrush is about 4 paper clips long.*

©Curriculum Associates, LLC   Copying is not permitted.

Explore Length Measurement

Try It

Find the length of a book using toothpicks. Write the length.

Learning Target
- Express the length of an object as a whole number of length units, by laying multiple copies of a shorter object (the length unit) end to end; understand that the length measurement of an object is the number of same-size length units that span it with no gaps or overlaps.

SMP 1, 2, 3, 4, 5, 6

_____ is about

_____ toothpicks long.

Find the length of a different book using toothpicks. Write the length.

 **Math Toolkit**
- books
- toothpicks

_____ is about

_____ toothpicks long.

Which book is longer? _____

Connect It

Find the length of the string using toothpicks. Draw the toothpicks. Write the length.

about _____ toothpicks long

Find the length of an object in the classroom using toothpicks. Draw the object. Write the length.

about _____ toothpicks long

Prepare for Measuring Length

1 Think about what you know about length.
Fill in each box. Use words, numbers and pictures.
Show as many ideas as you can.

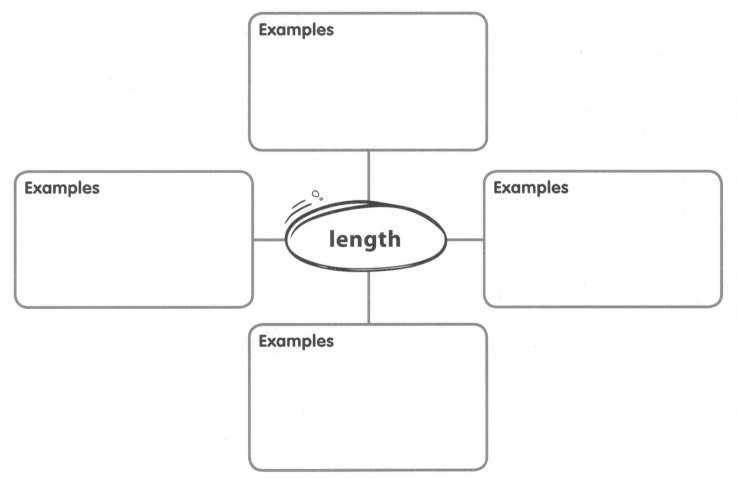

Examples

Examples

Examples

length

Examples

2 Buzz uses toothpicks to find the length of an object. He says that it does not matter that some of the toothpicks are broken. Do you agree? Why or why not?

3 Solve the problem. Draw to show your work.

Find the length of each object using toothpicks. Write the length.

about _____ toothpicks long

about _____ toothpick long

Develop Understanding of Length Measurement

How do you **measure** length?

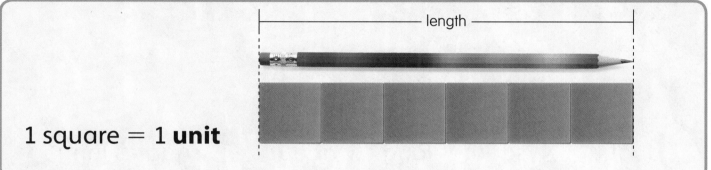

length

1 square = 1 **unit**

Model It

1 What is the length in squares?

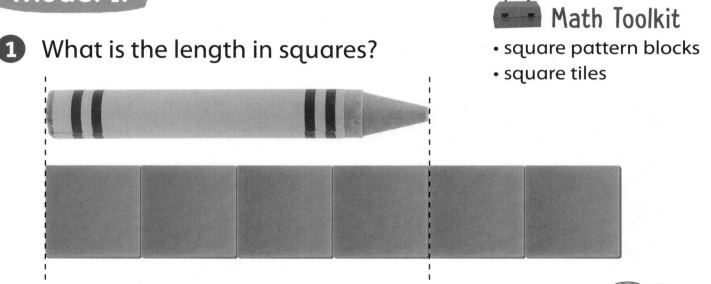

about _____ squares long

Math Toolkit
- square pattern blocks
- square tiles

DISCUSS IT

I found the length of the crayon by . . .

Connect It

Measure length using squares.

2

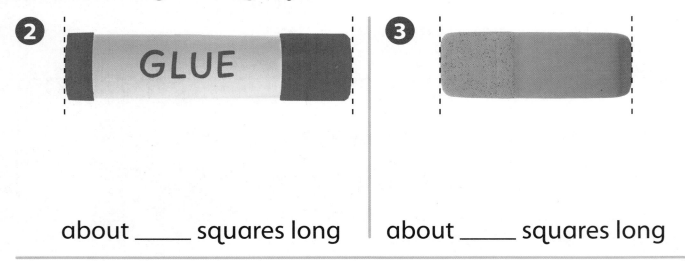

about _____ squares long   │   about _____ squares long

4   Boom uses 4 squares to measure a ribbon.
Did Boom measure the right way?
Why or why not?

3

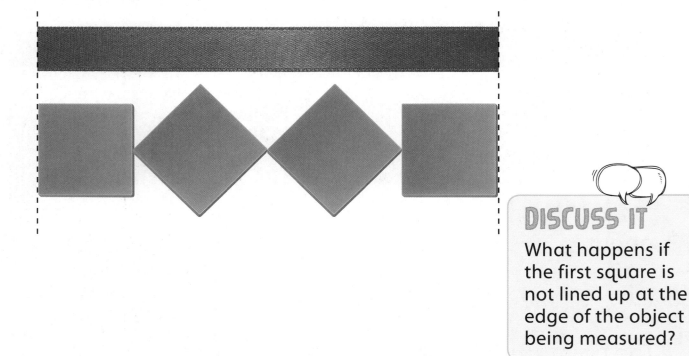

> **DISCUSS IT**
> What happens if the first square is not lined up at the edge of the object being measured?

Practice Measuring Length

Look at the Example. Then solve problems 1–5.

Example

Measure length with squares.

How long is this pencil?

The pencil is about 5 squares long.

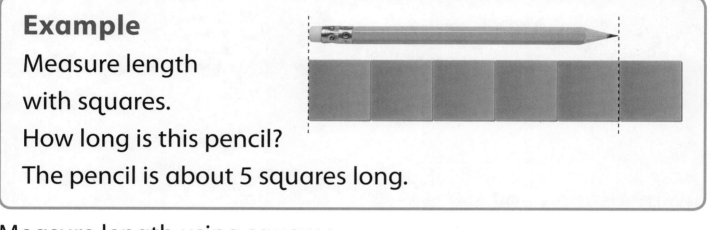

Measure length using squares.

1

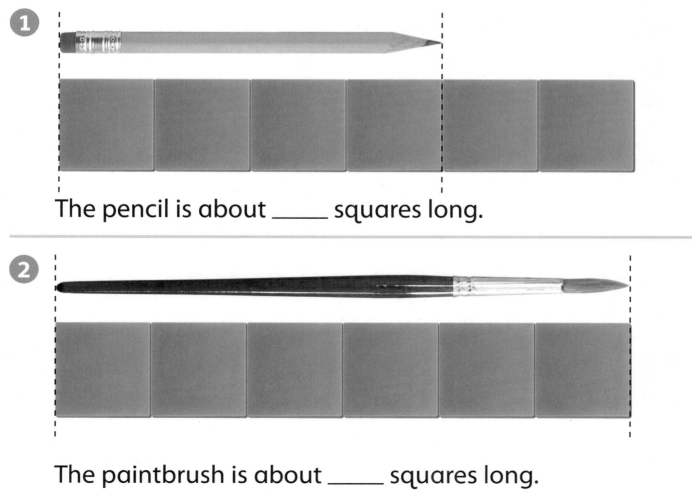

The pencil is about _____ squares long.

2

The paintbrush is about _____ squares long.

Lesson 32 Understand Length Measurement   **749**

Choose a measuring unit to find the length of the fork and the ribbon. Draw to show your work.

3

measuring unit _____

The fork is about _____ _____ long.

4

measuring unit _____

The ribbon is about _____ _____ long.

5 Boom says that his leaf is 4 paper clips long.

Do you agree? Why or why not?

Develop Understanding of Length Measurement

Model It

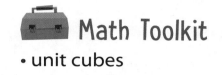 **Math Toolkit**
• unit cubes

1 Use unit cubes to measure the lengths of two objects. Draw the objects you measure. Complete the sentences.

This _____ is

about _____ unit cubes long.

This _____ is

about _____ unit cubes long.

DISCUSS IT

How do you know where to put the first unit cube to measure length?

Connect It

Use unit cubes to measure for problems 2 and 3.

2

The comb is about _____ unit cubes long.

3

The carrot is about _____ unit cubes long.

4 Buzz says that the crayon is 4 paper clips long.
Do you agree? Why or why not?

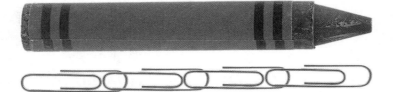

DISCUSS IT
It makes sense to measure the length of the objects with unit cubes because . . .

Practice Measuring Length

Look at the Example. Then solve problems 1–5.

Example

Use paper clips to measure the length of the brush. Line up the edge of the first paper clip with the edge of the brush.

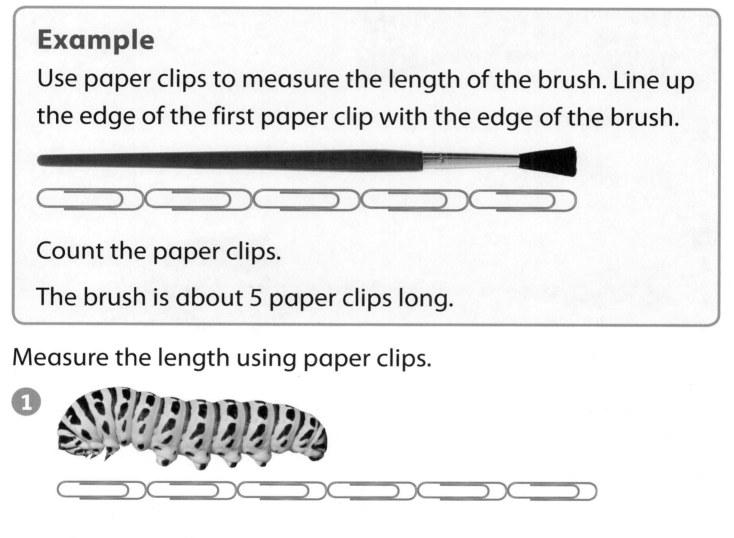

Count the paper clips.

The brush is about 5 paper clips long.

Measure the length using paper clips.

1

The caterpillar is about _____ paper clips long.

2

The pencil is about _____ paper clips long.

Choose a measuring unit to find the length of the bone and the spoon. Draw to show your work.

3

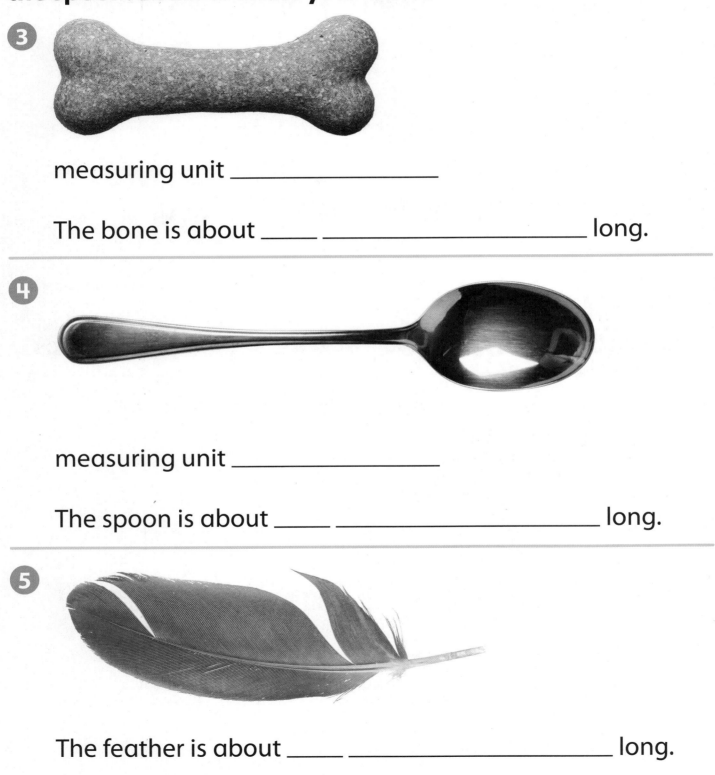

measuring unit _____

The bone is about _____ _____ long.

4

measuring unit _____

The spoon is about _____ _____ long.

5

The feather is about _____ _____ long.

Refine Ideas About Length Measurement

Apply It

1 **Identify** What is the length of the watch?

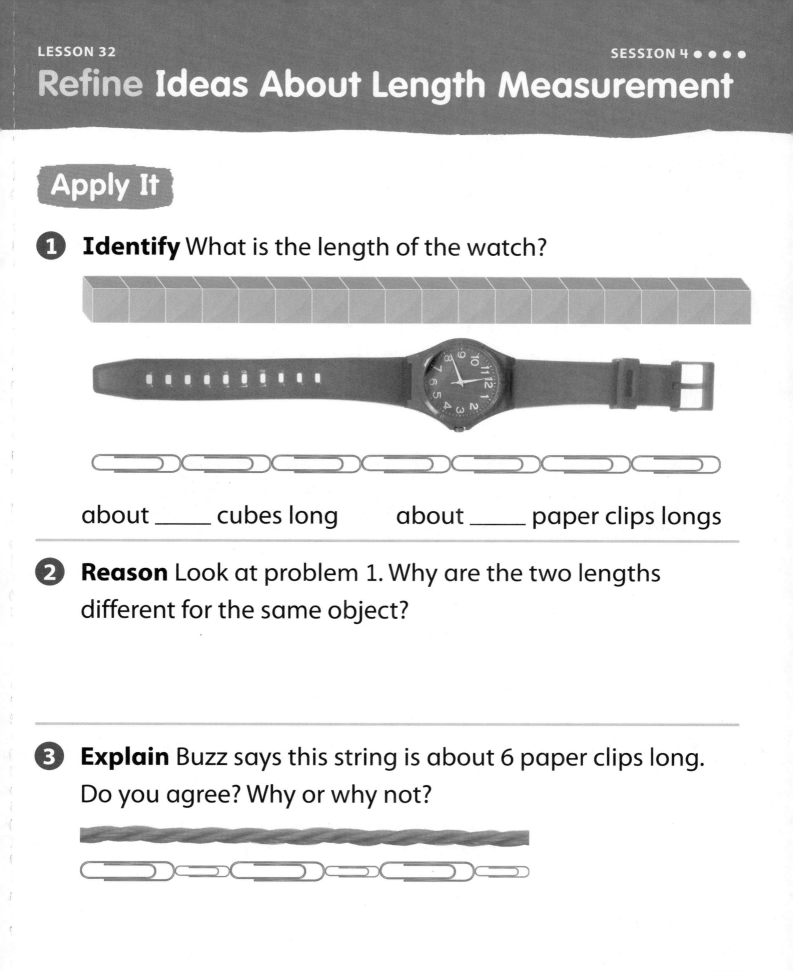

about _____ cubes long   about _____ paper clips longs

2 **Reason** Look at problem 1. Why are the two lengths different for the same object?

3 **Explain** Buzz says this string is about 6 paper clips long. Do you agree? Why or why not?

Show your work.

4 Think about measuring length.

A: Use squares to measure.

The scissors are about _____ squares long.

Show how you measured.

B: Draw an object that is about 1 square shorter than the scissors.

In this unit you learned to . . .

Skill	Lesson
Order objects by length.	30
Compare lengths of objects.	31
Measure lengths of objects.	32

Think about what you learned.

Use words, numbers, and drawings.

1 A mistake I made that helped me learn was . . .

2 A question I still have is . . .

Solve the problems.

1 Draw lines from the words to show which belt is longest and which is shortest.

Shortest

Longest

2 What is the length of the pencil in squares?

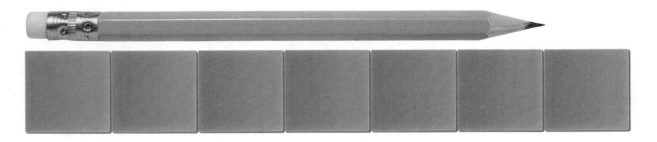

about _____ squares long

3 Circle the right way to measure the beads.

Ⓐ

Ⓑ

4 Compare lengths. Then circle the correct words.

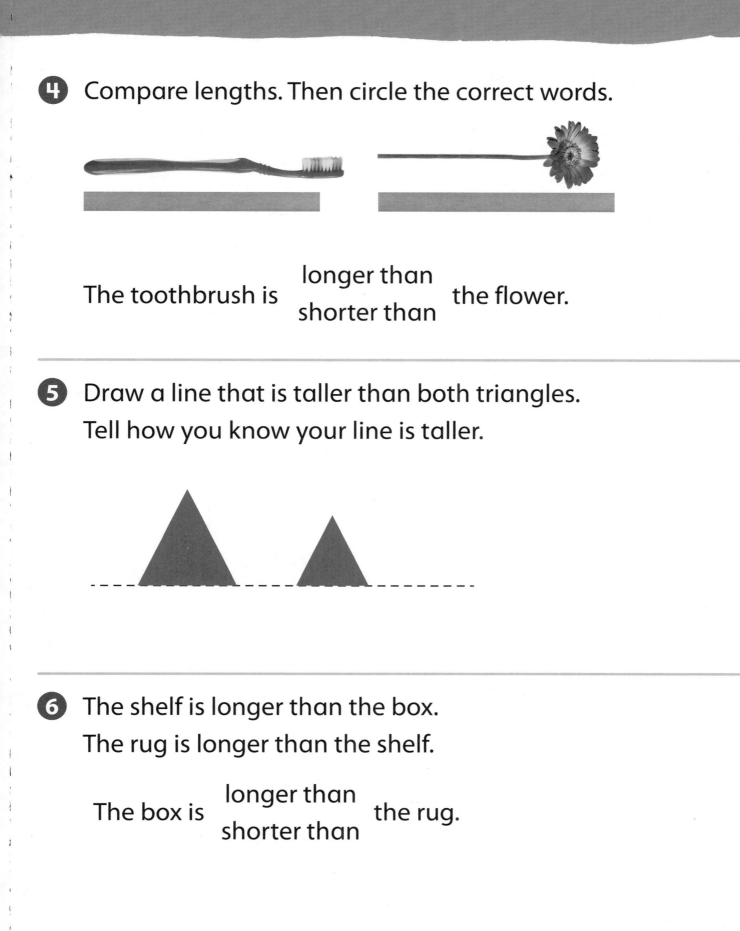

The toothbrush is   longer than / shorter than   the flower.

---

5 Draw a line that is taller than both triangles.
Tell how you know your line is taller.

---

6 The shelf is longer than the box.
The rug is longer than the shelf.

The box is   longer than / shorter than   the rug.

Put It Together

7 Color the longest pencil red.
Color the shortest pencil blue.

Measure the length of the longest pencil.
Use unit cubes.

Length of longest pencil:
about _____ unit cubes long

Draw or write examples for each word. Then draw or write to show other math words in the unit.

length how long something is.

My Example

longer greater in length.

My Example

longest greatest in length.

My Example

measure to find length, height, or weight using a known unit.

My Example

shorter lesser in length or height.

My Example

shortest least in length or height.

My Example

taller greater in height.

My Example

tallest greatest in height.

My Example

unit a part that is used to measure. Each part for one kind of unit has the same length.

My Example

My Word: _____

_____

_____

_____

My Example

My Word: _____

_____

_____

My Example

My Word: _____

_____

_____

My Example

My Word: _____

_____

_____

_____

My Example

My Word: _____

_____

_____

_____

My Example

My Word: _____

_____

_____

_____

My Example

My Word: _____

_____

_____

_____

My Example

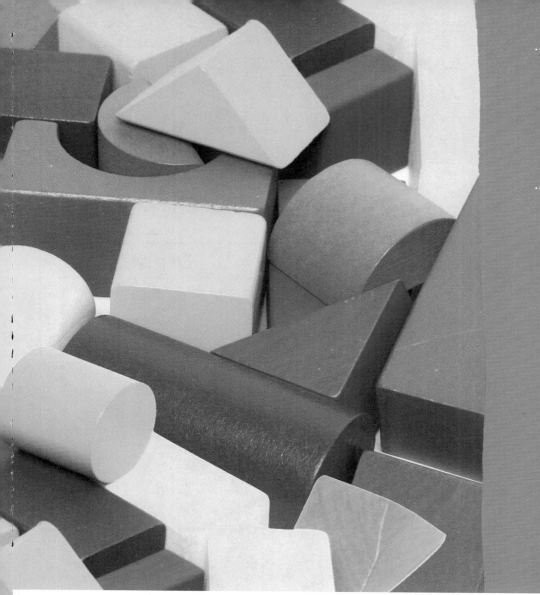

☑ Self Check

Before starting this unit, check off the skills you know below. As you complete each lesson, see how many more skills you can check off!

I can ...	Before	After
Use sides and corners to name shapes.	☐	☐
Put shapes together to make new shapes.	☐	☐
Break shapes into halves.	☐	☐
Break shapes into fourths.	☐	☐

Build Your Vocabulary

Review
circle
corner
rectangle
side
triangle

My Math Words

Work with a partner to complete the table.

Shape	Sides	Corners	Draw It
		3	
circle			

My Academic Words

Use the academic words to complete the sentences.

☐ describe   ☐ in common   ☐ reason

1 The _____ I think this shape is a triangle is because it has three sides.

2 A square and a rectangle have things _____. Each has four sides and four corners.

3 Can you _____ a shape you see?

Shapes

Dear Family,

This week your child is learning to name and describe shapes.

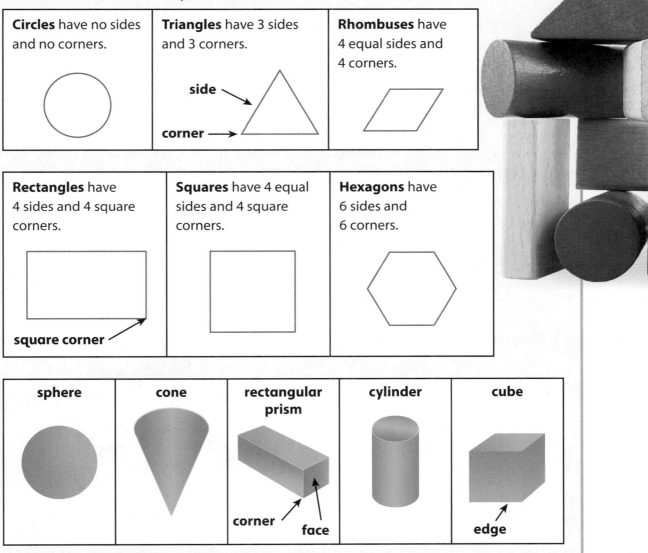

Circles have no sides and no corners.

Triangles have 3 sides and 3 corners.

side
corner

Rhombuses have 4 equal sides and 4 corners.

Rectangles have 4 sides and 4 square corners.

square corner

Squares have 4 equal sides and 4 square corners.

Hexagons have 6 sides and 6 corners.

sphere	cone	rectangular prism	cylinder	cube

corner   face

edge

Learning to name and describe shapes based on their sides, corners, faces, and edges will help your child recognize and classify both familiar and unfamiliar shapes in school and in real life.

Invite your child to share what he or she knows about naming and describing shapes by doing the following activity together.

Activity Naming and Describing Shapes

Do this activity with your child to practice naming shapes.

Materials household items of various shapes, paper and pencil

Tell your child that you are going on a shape hunt.

- Together, look around your home and neighborhood for objects shaped like triangles, rectangles, squares, hexagons, and rhombuses. You can refer to these as *flat shapes*.

- Make a list of these shapes, and write the name of each object you find next to the appropriate shape name. See how many objects you can find for each shape.

- Each time you add an object to the list, have your child explain how he or she knows what shape it is. For example, if your child is explaining that a picture frame is a rectangle, he or she might say, "A rectangle has four sides and four square corners."

- Make another list of *solid shapes* that includes sphere, cone, rectangular prism, cylinder, and cube. See how many objects you can find for each of these shapes. Your child may notice that some of the solid shapes have flat shapes as their faces.

- In addition to looking for objects around your home and neighborhood, you may also look for pictures of shapes in magazines, in picture books, and on packaged food items.

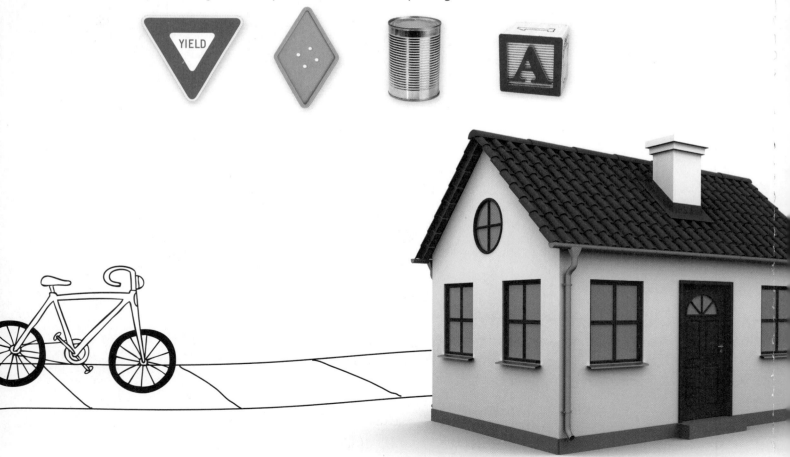

Explore Sorting Shapes

How can you sort the shapes?

Learning Target
• Distinguish between defining attributes versus non-defining attributes; build and draw shapes to possess defining attributes.
SMP 1, 2, 3, 4, 5, 6

Try It

Math Toolkit
• flat shapes

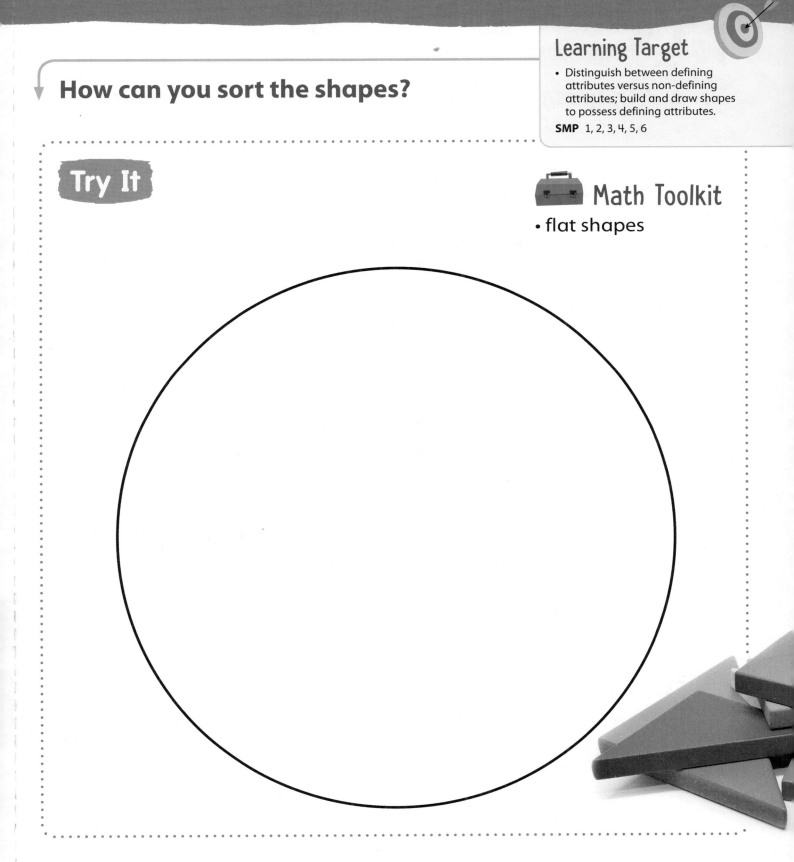

Connect It

Draw 3 shapes that have straight sides and 4 corners.

Prepare for Naming and Describing Shapes

1 Think about what you know about the corners of shapes. Fill in each box. Use words, numbers, and pictures. Show as many ideas as you can.

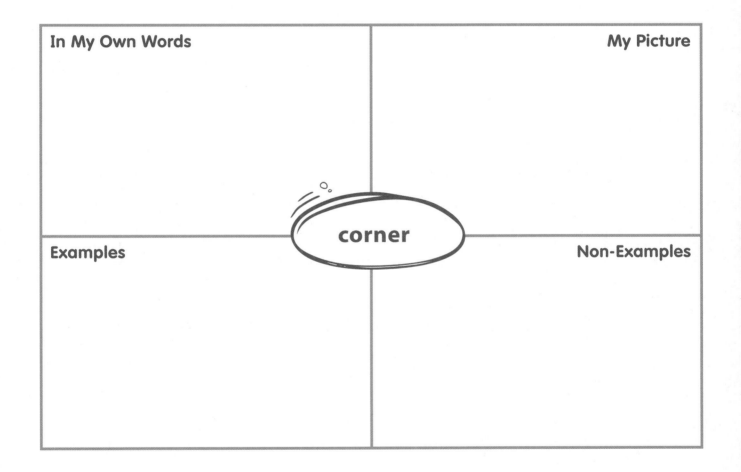

In My Own Words	My Picture

corner

Examples	Non-Examples

2 Circle the corners on the shapes.

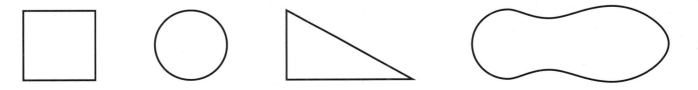

3 Solve the problem.

Draw 3 shapes that are closed and have straight sides.

Develop Naming and Describing Two-Dimensional Shapes

Sophie says the shapes in each group are the same in some way. How are they the same?

Group A | Group B | Group C

Try It

Math Toolkit
• flat shapes

DISCUSS IT
What are some ways to sort shapes?

Sophie says the shapes in each group are the same in some way. How are they the same?

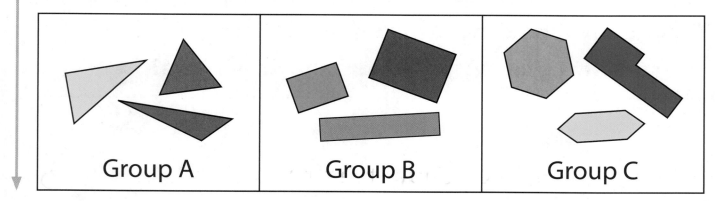

Group A | Group B | Group C

Model It

The number of sides and corners tells the shape name.

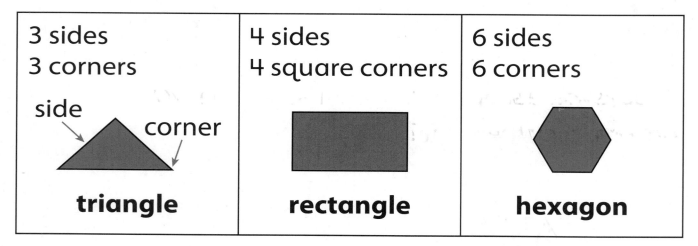

| 3 sides
3 corners

side ➔ corner
triangle | 4 sides
4 square corners

rectangle | 6 sides
6 corners

hexagon |

_____ have 3 sides and 3 corners.

Rectangles have _____ sides and _____ square corners.

Hexagons have _____ sides and _____ corners.

Connect It

1 How is your way like **Model It**?
How is it different?

2 Why can shapes that have the same name look different?

Apply It

3 Ali says these shapes are the same in some way.
How are they the same?

They have _____ sides and _____ square corners.

The shapes are _____.

Lesson 33 Shapes   **775**

4 June says these shapes are the same in some way. How are they the same?

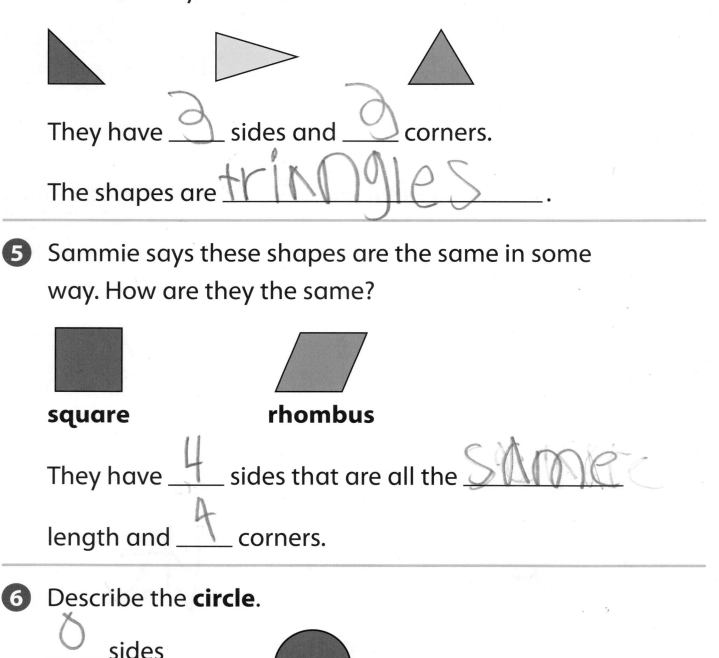

They have __3__ sides and __3__ corners.

The shapes are __trinngles__.

5 Sammie says these shapes are the same in some way. How are they the same?

square   **rhombus**

They have __4__ sides that are all the __same__

length and __4__ corners.

6 Describe the **circle**.

__0__ sides

__0__ corners

Practice Naming and Describing Shapes

Look at the Example. Then solve problems 1–6.

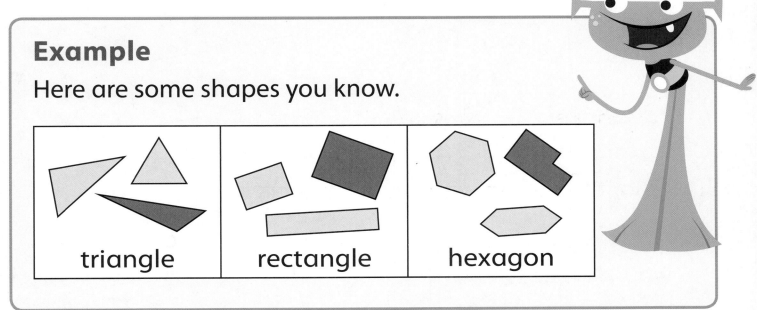

Example

Here are some shapes you know.

triangle	rectangle	hexagon

Count sides and corners.

Name the shape.

1 4 sides
4 square corners

_____

2 ___ sides
___ corners

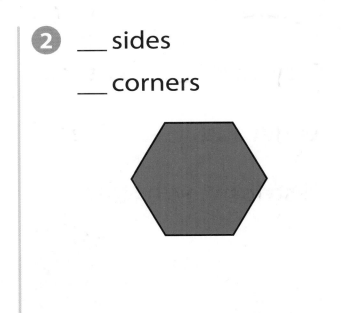

_____

3 Color the triangle green. Color the rectangle red. Color the hexagon yellow.

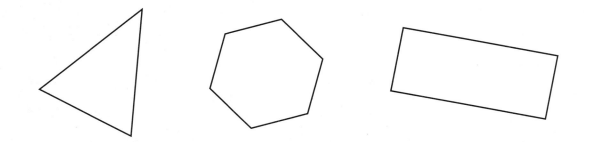

4 Color the shapes with square corners blue.

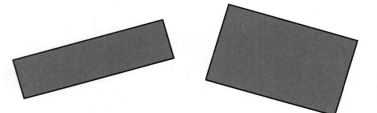

5 Circle the shape that has 6 sides and 6 corners.

6 What is the same about these two shapes? Circle.

square corners

number of corners

Develop Naming and Describing Three-Dimensional Shapes

How are these shapes the same?

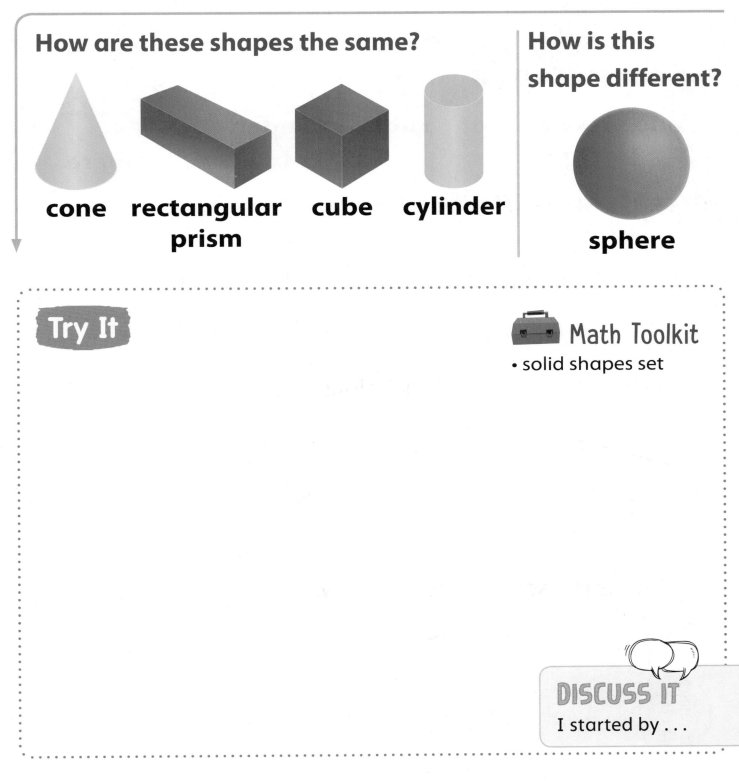

cone — rectangular prism — cube — cylinder

How is this shape different?

sphere

Try It

Math Toolkit
• solid shapes set

DISCUSS IT
I started by . . .

How are these shapes the same?

cone   **rectangular prism**   **cube**   **cylinder**

How is this shape different?

sphere

Model It

Make a ✓ if true. Make an X if not true.

A cylinder has:

_____ 2 circle **faces**

_____ 2 straight **edges**

A cube has:

_____ 0 straight edges

_____ 6 square faces

A cone has 1 circle _____ .

A rectangular prism has _____ faces.

A sphere has _____ faces.

Connect It

1 How is your way like **Model It**? How is it different?

2 Boom says he can make a cube with 6 faces.
Buzz says he can make a sphere with 2 faces.

Who is right? How do you know?

Apply It

3 Make a ✔ if true. Make an X if not true.

Describe this rectangular prism.

_____ 12 straight edges

_____ 6 corners

_____ 4 square faces

_____ cannot roll

Describe this cone.

_____ 0 sides

_____ 0 straight edges

_____ 1 circle face

_____ 1 triangle face

4 Describe this cube. Make a ✓ if true.
Make an X if not true.

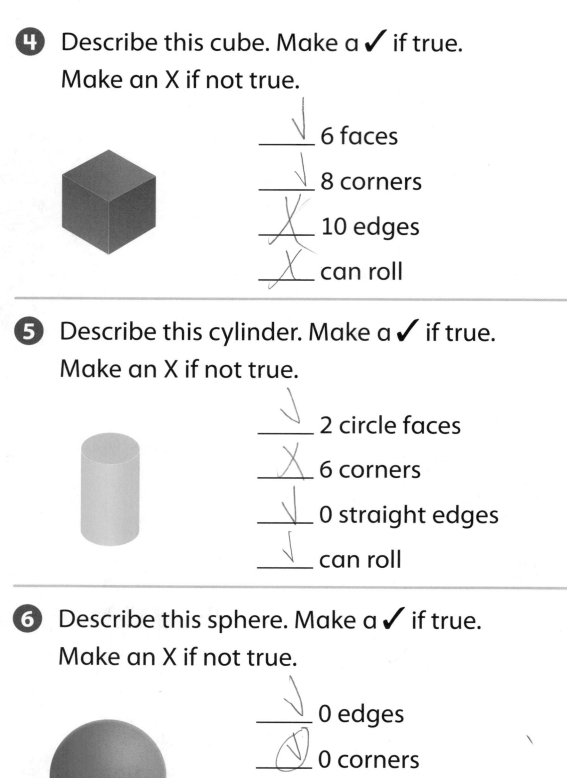

_____ ✓ 6 faces

_____ ✓ 8 corners

_____ X 10 edges

_____ X can roll

5 Describe this cylinder. Make a ✓ if true.
Make an X if not true.

_____ ✓ 2 circle faces

_____ X 6 corners

_____ ✓ 0 straight edges

_____ ✓ can roll

6 Describe this sphere. Make a ✓ if true.
Make an X if not true.

_____ ✓ 0 edges

_____ ✓ 0 corners

_____ 2 faces

_____ can roll

Practice Naming and Describing Shapes

Look at the Example. Then solve problems 1–5.

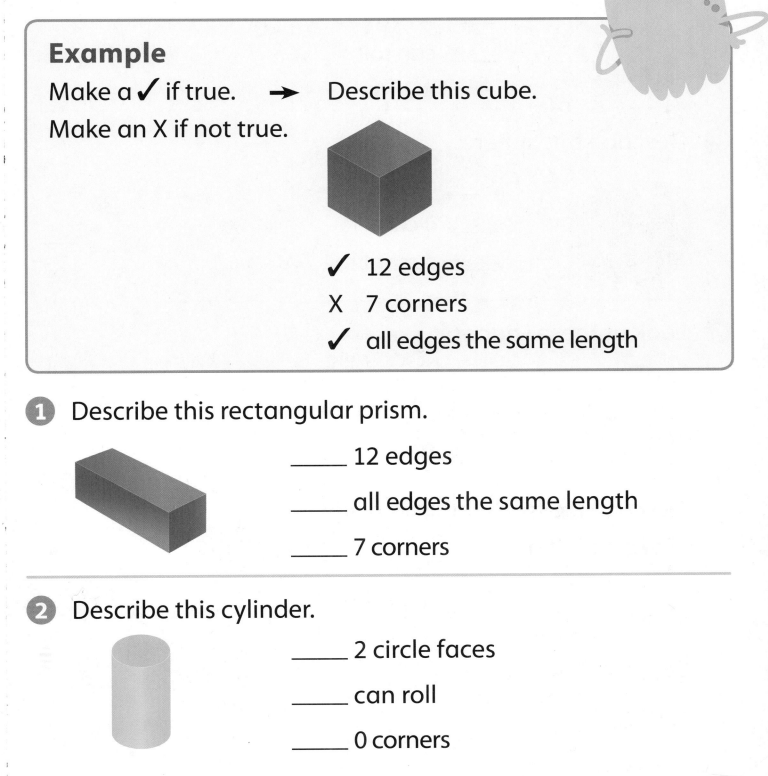

Example

Make a ✓ if true.   →   Describe this cube.

Make an X if not true.

✓ 12 edges

X   7 corners

✓ all edges the same length

1   Describe this rectangular prism.

_____ 12 edges

_____ all edges the same length

_____ 7 corners

2   Describe this cylinder.

_____ 2 circle faces

_____ can roll

_____ 0 corners

3 Describe this cone.

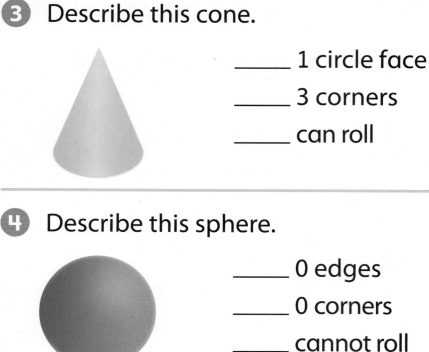

_____ 1 circle face

_____ 3 corners

_____ can roll

4 Describe this sphere.

_____ 0 edges

_____ 0 corners

_____ cannot roll

5 Look at these shapes.

Circle all the ways they are alike.

Ⓐ 12 edges

Ⓑ 8 corners

Ⓒ all square faces

Ⓓ 6 faces

Refine Naming and Describing Shapes

Complete the Example. Then solve problems 1–5.

Example Draw the shape named in each box.

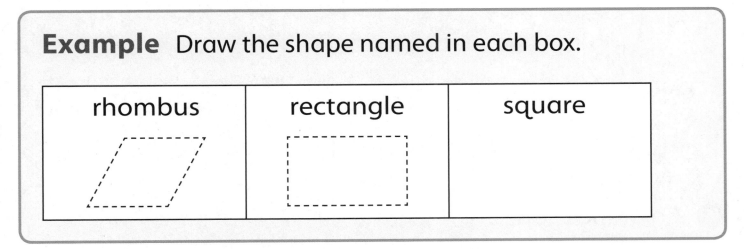

| rhombus | rectangle | square |

Apply It

1 Color the shapes.

triangles ■ hexagons ▨ rectangles ■ rhombuses ▨

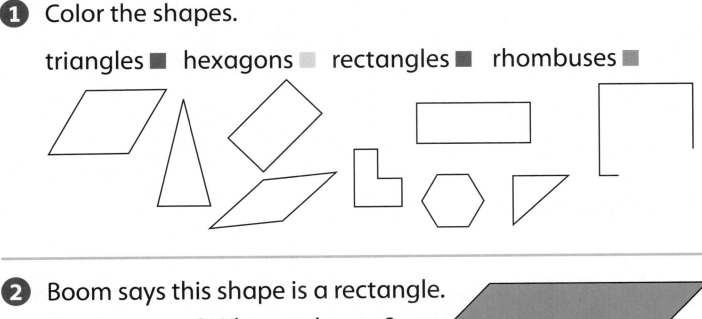

2 Boom says this shape is a rectangle.
Do you agree? Why or why not?

3 Draw each shape.

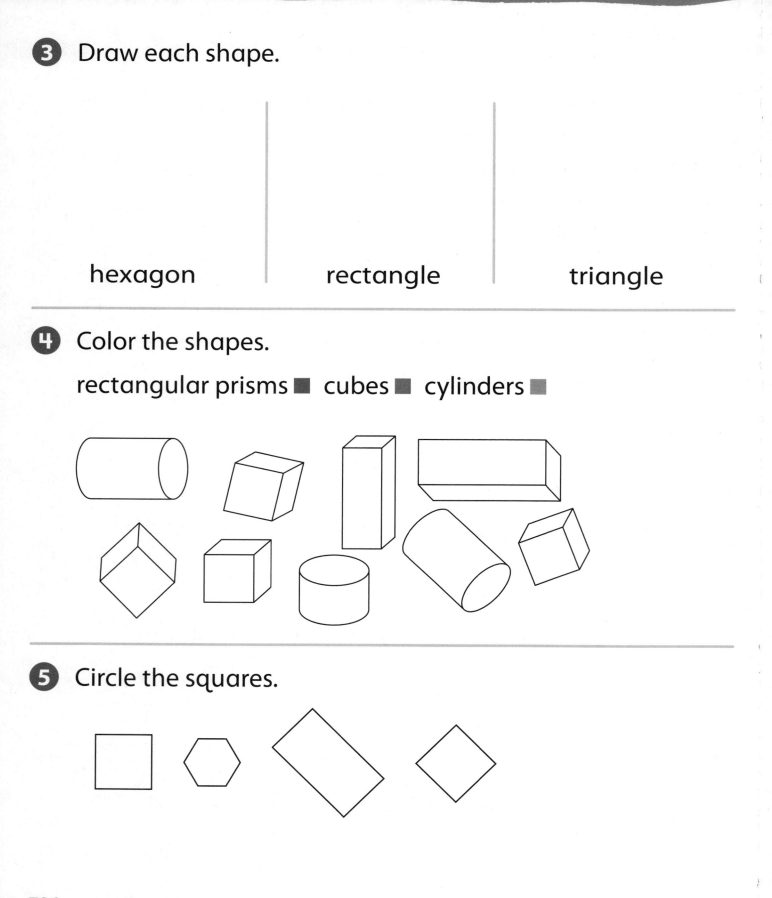

hexagon   rectangle   triangle

4 Color the shapes.

rectangular prisms ■ cubes ■ cylinders ■

5 Circle the squares.

Practice Naming and Describing Shapes

Look at the Example. Then solve problems 1–5.

Example Draw each shape.

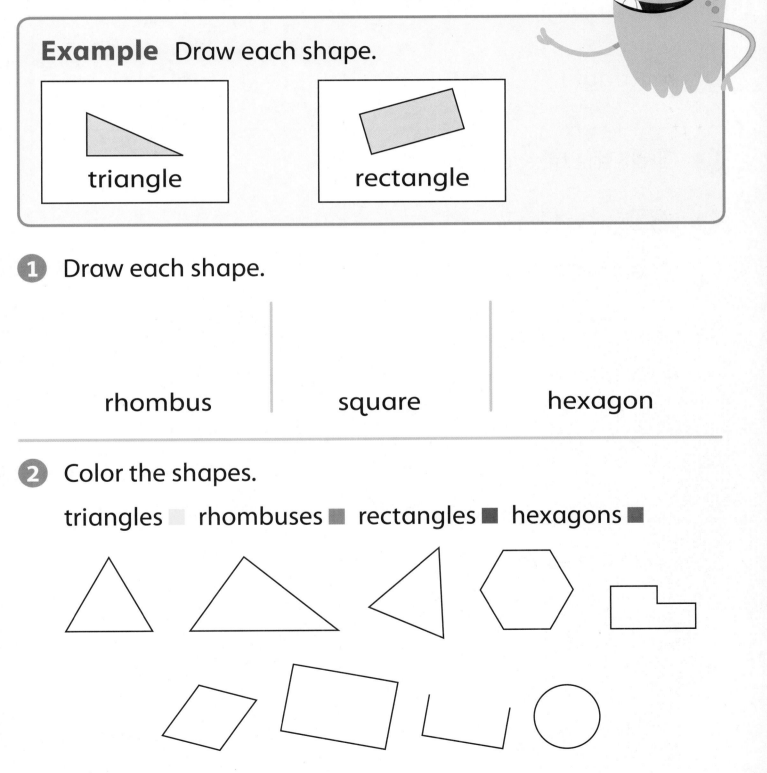

triangle   rectangle

1 Draw each shape.

rhombus   square   hexagon

2 Color the shapes.

triangles ▢ rhombuses ■ rectangles ■ hexagons ■

3 Draw each shape.

rectangle   triangle

4 Circle the hexagons.

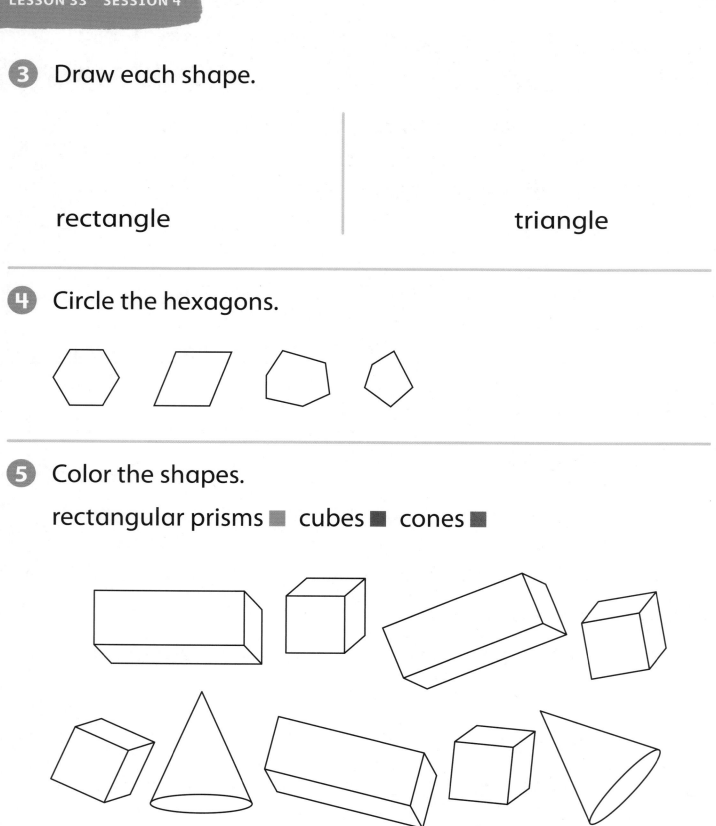

5 Color the shapes.

rectangular prisms ▨ cubes ▨ cones ▨

Apply It

Solve problems 1–5.

1 Make the same shape in different ways.

Choose a shape to draw. Circle its name.

hexagon	triangle	rectangle
rhombus	square	

Draw your shape 3 different ways.

2 How are your shapes different? How are they alike?

3 Circle all the reasons this shape is a rectangle.

Ⓐ It has 4 sides.

Ⓑ It is bigger than a square.

Ⓒ It has 4 square corners.

Ⓓ It is red.

---

4 Circle all the reasons this shape is a cube.

Ⓐ It has 12 edges.

Ⓑ It has all square faces.

Ⓒ It is purple.

Ⓓ It has 8 corners.

---

5 Draw each shape.

| rhombus | triangle | hexagon |

Putting Shapes Together

Dear Family,

This week your child is learning to put shapes together to make other shapes.

The hexagons below are made by putting together other shapes.

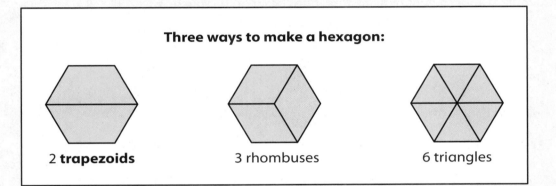

Three ways to make a hexagon:

2 **trapezoids**   3 rhombuses   6 triangles

The rectangular prisms below are also made by putting together other shapes.

Two ways to make a rectangular prism:

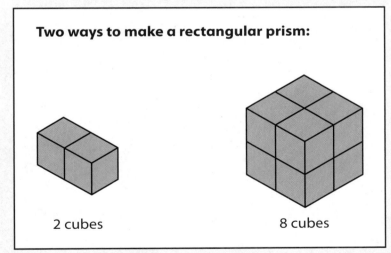

2 cubes   8 cubes

Composing shapes in this way will help your child understand patterns and practice identifying shapes. It will also help prepare your child to learn about equal parts and fractions.

Invite your child to share what he or she knows about putting shapes together to make other shapes by doing the following activity together.

Activity Putting Shapes Together

Do this activity with your child to explore putting shapes together.

Materials paper and pencil, crayons or markers (optional)

To prepare for this activity, trace each of the shapes below twice.

- On one set of shapes, ask your child draw a line to show how the shape can be made by putting together two other shapes.

- Ask your child to name or describe the two shapes that make the larger shape. For example, if your child drew a line from one corner of the square to the opposite corner, he or she should tell you that two triangles make the square.

- Then on the second set of shapes, ask your child to draw more than one line on each shape to show how it can be made from more than two other shapes.

- Again, ask your child to name the shapes that make each larger shape.

- Your child may wish to create designs by coloring the shapes that make each larger shape.

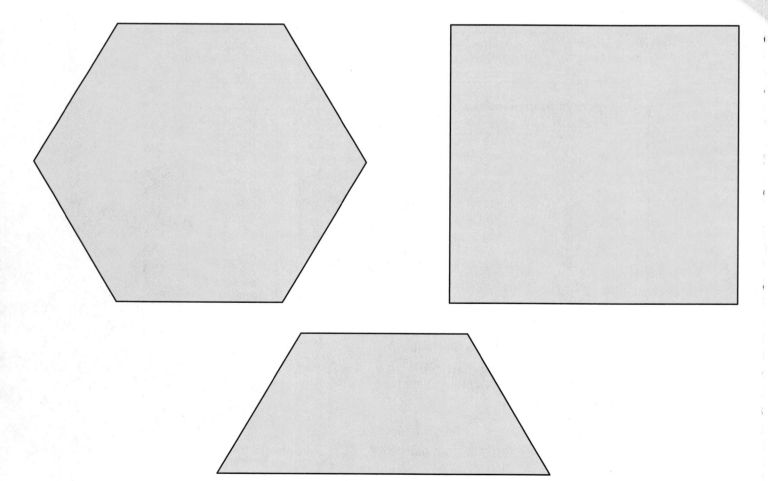

Explore Putting Shapes Together

Learning Target
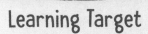
- Compose two-dimensional shapes or three-dimensional shapes to create a composite shape, and compose new shapes from the composite shape.

SMP 1, 2, 3, 4, 5, 6, 7

What shapes are the faces of these solid shapes?

Try It

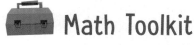 **Math Toolkit**
- solid shapes set

Draw 1 face of a cube.

Draw 1 face of a cone.

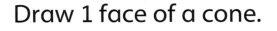

Draw 1 face of a rectangular prism.

Connect It

What shapes are these faces?

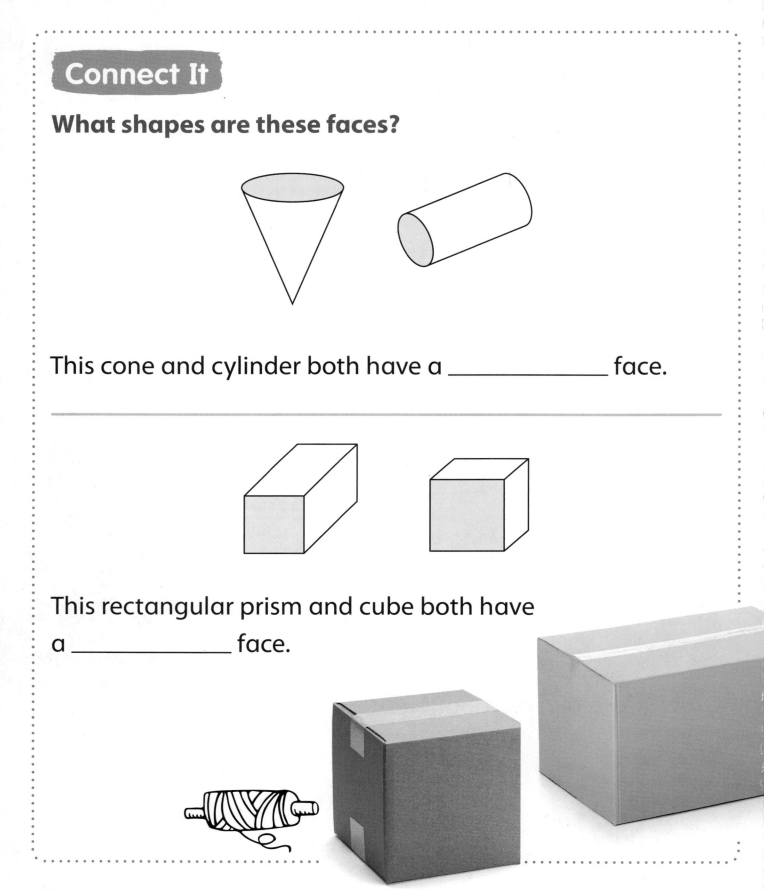

This cone and cylinder both have a _____ face.

This rectangular prism and cube both have a _____ face.

Prepare for Putting Shapes Together

1 Think about what you know about circles. Fill in
each box. Use words, numbers, and pictures.
Show as many ideas as you can.

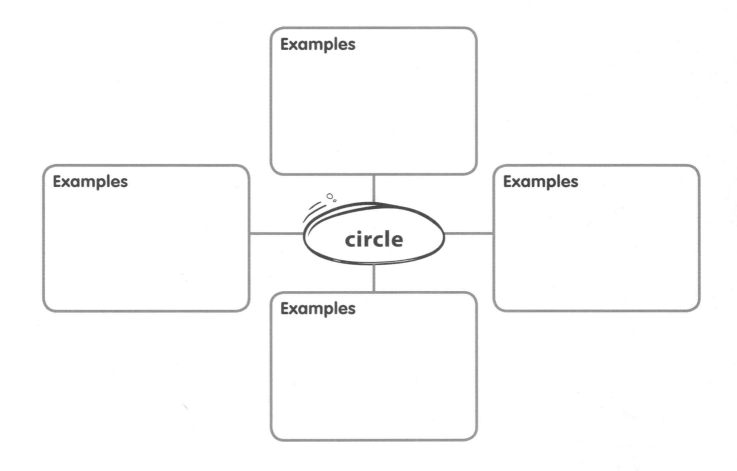

Examples

Examples

circle

Examples

Examples

2 Color the parts of the two shapes that are circles.

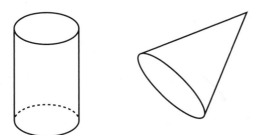

Name: _____

3 Solve the problem. Show your work.

Draw 1 face of a cylinder.

_____

Draw 1 face of a cone.

_____

Draw 1 face of a rectangular prism.

Use pattern blocks to make a hexagon.

Trace or draw how you made it.

Color the shapes to match the blocks.

Math Toolkit
• pattern blocks

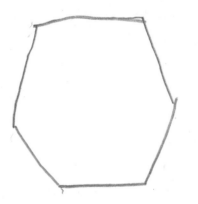

DISCUSS IT

How can thinking about parts of shapes help?

Use pattern blocks to make a hexagon.
Trace or draw how you made it.
Color the shapes to match the blocks.

Model It

You can make the same shape in different ways.

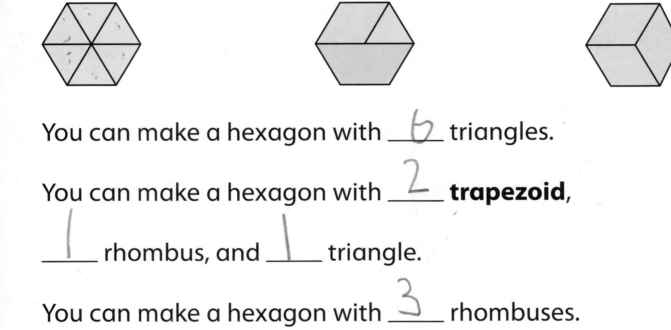

You can make a hexagon with __6__ triangles.

You can make a hexagon with __2__ **trapezoid**,

__1__ rhombus, and __1__ triangle.

You can make a hexagon with __3__ rhombuses.

©Curriculum Associates, LLC   Copying is not permitted.

Connect It

1 How is your way like **Model It**?
How is it different?

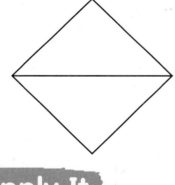

2 Buzz says the two triangles make a square.
Boom says the shape is not a square.

Who is right? How do you know?

Apply It

3 Draw lines and color to show how to make this
trapezoid using 3 pattern blocks.

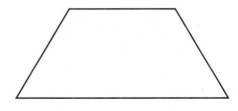

What shapes did you use? _____

4 Draw lines and color to show 2 ways to make this shape using pattern blocks.

5 Color to show how to make this hexagon.

Use 3 shapes.

Use 4 shapes.

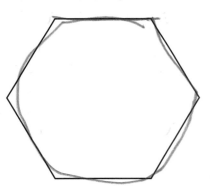

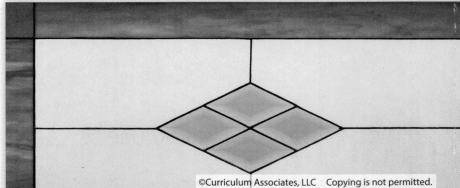

Practice Putting Shapes Together

Look at the Example. Then solve problems 1–3.

Example

You can put shapes together to make new shapes.

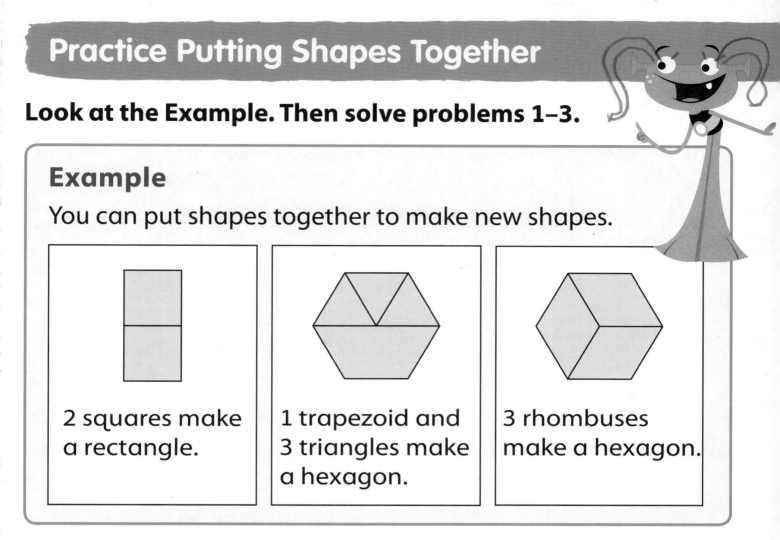

2 squares make a rectangle.

1 trapezoid and 3 triangles make a hexagon.

3 rhombuses make a hexagon.

Use shapes like those shown above to make new shapes.

1 Show two ways to put together shapes to make a trapezoid.

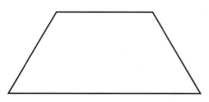　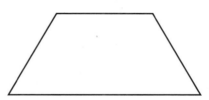

Name: _____

2 Show different ways to make a hexagon.

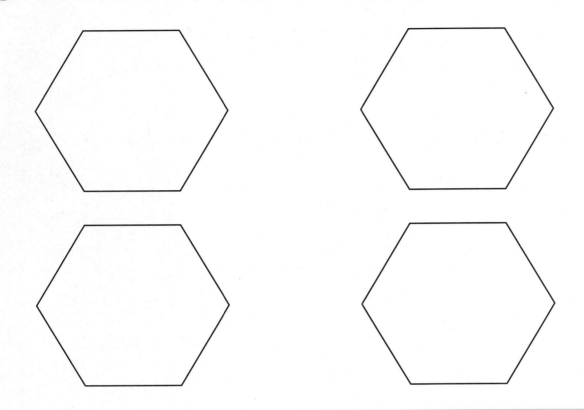

3 Buzz and Boom each have 3 rhombuses. Buzz says he can put them together to make a trapezoid. Boom says he can put them together to make a hexagon. Draw to show who is right.

Buzz   Boom

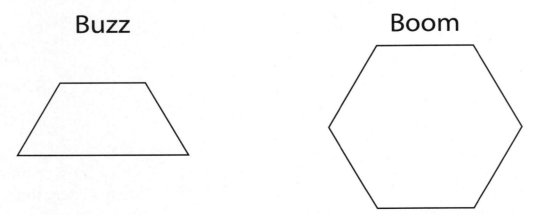

Develop Putting Shapes Together

Put some cubes together to make a new shape.

Tell how many faces it has.

 Try It

 Math Toolkit

• connecting cubes

DISCUSS IT

The faces on my shape look like . . .

Lesson 34 Putting Shapes Together   **803**

Put some cubes together to make a new shape.
Tell how many faces it has.

Model It

You can make larger shapes from smaller shapes in different ways.

You can make a larger rectangular prism using _____.

Connect It

 1 How is your way like **Model It**? How is it different?

2 How can you tell the name of the new shape?

Apply It

3 How many cubes make up this shape?

There are _____ cubes that make up the shape.

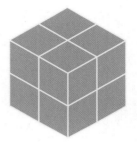

---

4 Circle the shape you could make with 2 cylinders and 2 cubes.

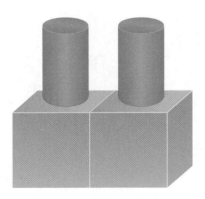

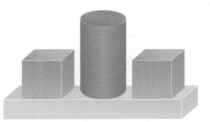

Draw a line to match each set of shapes with the larger shape you could make with them.

5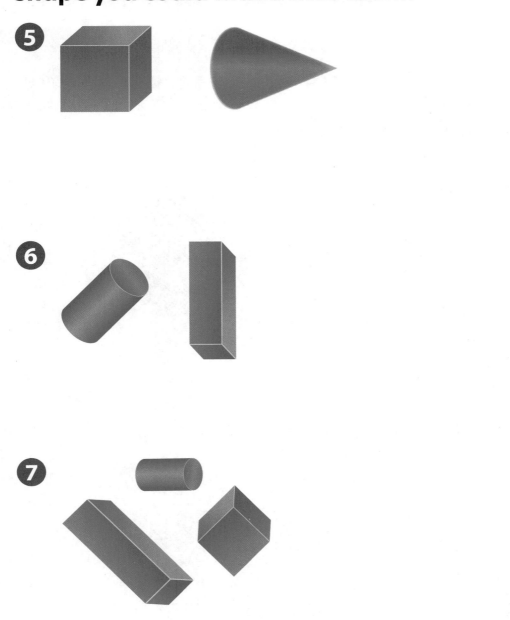

6

7

©Curriculum Associates, LLC   Copying is not permitted.

Practice Putting Shapes Together

Look at the Example. Then solve problems 1–4.

Example

Circle the shapes that go together to make this shape.

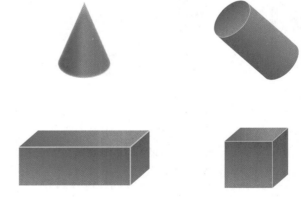

1 Circle the shapes that go together to make this shape.

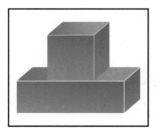

2 Circle the shapes that go together to make this shape.

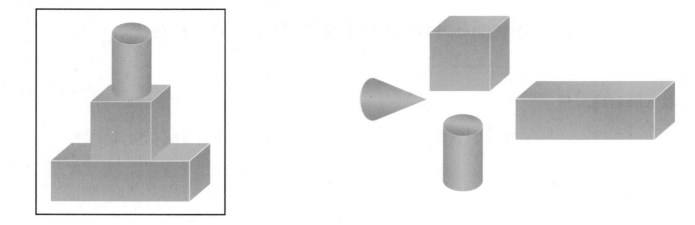

3 Circle the shape you can make if you put these two shapes together.

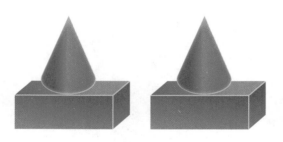

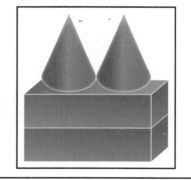

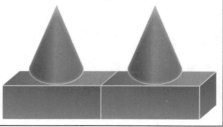

4 How many cubes make this shape?

_____ cubes make the shape.

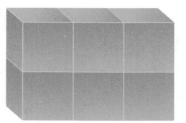

Refine Putting Shapes Together

Complete the Example. Then solve problems 1–5.

Example

What shapes do you see shaded purple here?

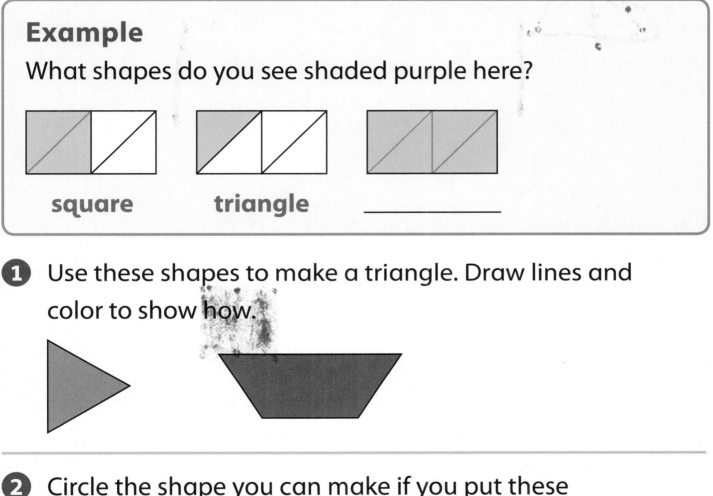

square   triangle   _____

1 Use these shapes to make a triangle. Draw lines and color to show how.

2 Circle the shape you can make if you put these two shapes together.

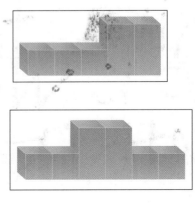

3 Draw lines and color to show 2 different ways to make this shape with pattern blocks.

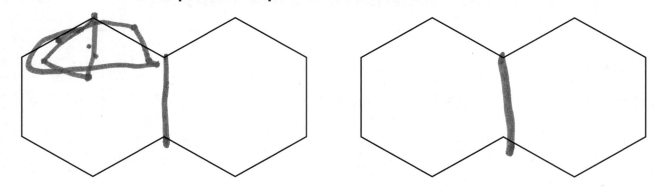

4 Which shows a square made with 2 rectangles? Circle it.

5 Buzz says any even number of squares can be used to make a larger square.
Is he right? How do you know?

I thik that
Bass is writ Buss
I oso thik that is thic
ing

Practice Putting Shapes Together

Look at the Example. Then solve problems 1–3.

Example

Draw lines to match the picture with the number of shapes that make it.

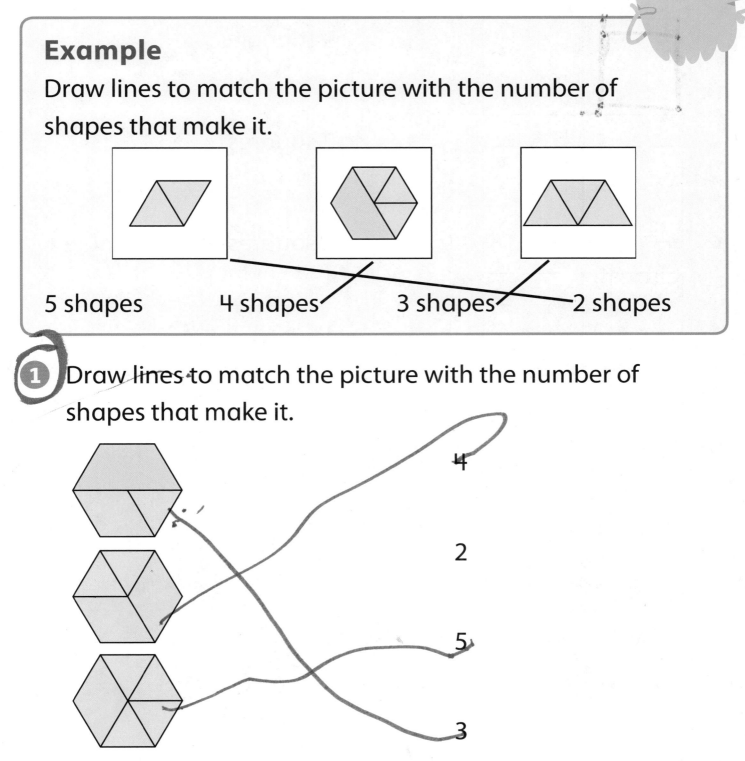

5 shapes   4 shapes   3 shapes   2 shapes

1. Draw lines to match the picture with the number of shapes that make it.

4

2

5

3

Name:  Valerie

2 Draw lines to match each picture with the shapes that make it.

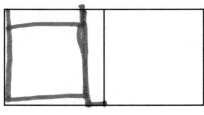

4 triangles

2 squares

2 squares and 1 triangle

1 square and 2 triangles

3 Circle the shapes you could use to make this shape.

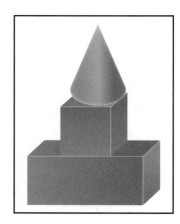

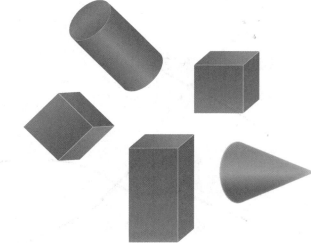

Refine Putting Shapes Together

Apply It

Solve problems 1–4.

1 Use 4 or more pattern block shapes to make 2 new shapes. Draw them.

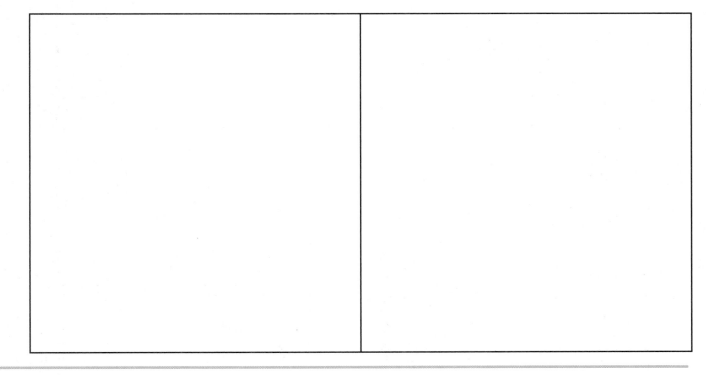

2 Circle one shape above that you made.
Write how many of each shape you used.

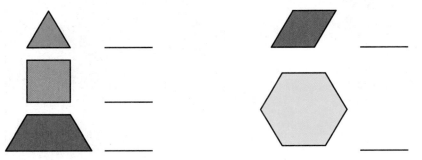

3 Color to show how to make this rectangle using other shapes.

Use 3 colors to show 3 shapes.

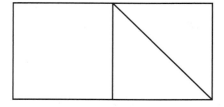

Use 4 colors to show 4 shapes.

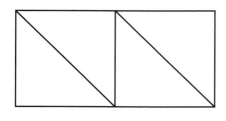

4 Circle the shape you can make if you put these two shapes together.

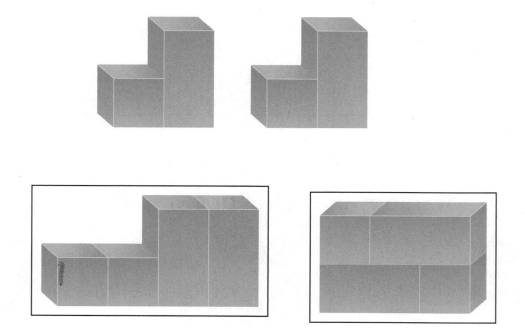

Understand Breaking Shapes into Equal Parts

Dear Family,

This week your child is exploring equal parts of shapes.

Your child will learn to divide circles, squares, and rectangles into halves and fourths. Your child will also learn how to put halves and fourths together to make circles, squares, and rectangles. This will help your child prepare to work with fractions in later grades.

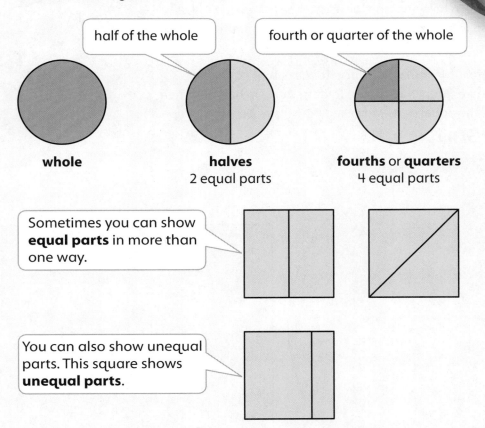

half of the whole

fourth or quarter of the whole

whole

halves
2 equal parts

fourths or **quarters**
4 equal parts

Sometimes you can show **equal parts** in more than one way.

You can also show unequal parts. This square shows **unequal parts**.

Invite your child to share what he or she knows about dividing shapes into equal parts by doing the following activity together.

Activity Breaking Shapes into Equal Parts

Do this activity with your child to practice working with equal parts of shapes.

Materials paper, pencil, scissors, and crayons or markers

Tell your child that you are going to pretend to divide food shapes into equal parts to share.

- Trace two copies of the circle and square below. Cut out each shape.

- Have your child color each shape to look like a food item. For example, a circle can be colored to look like a pizza or pancake. A square can be colored to look like a sandwich or cracker.

- Ask your child to fold one of the circles to make two equal parts so that each person sharing the "food" gets the same amount. Watch to see that your child folds the circle in half, and provide assistance as needed. Have your child trace the fold line with a crayon or marker. Ask what the equal parts are called (halves). Repeat with one of the squares.

- Then ask your child to fold the remaining circle to make four equal parts so that four people can share. Your child should fold the circle in half, and then in half again. Ask what the equal parts are called (fourths or quarters). Repeat with the remaining square.

Explore Breaking Shapes into Equal Parts

Learning Target

- Partition circles and rectangles into two and four equal shares, describe the shares using the words *halves*, *fourths*, and *quarters*, and use the phrases *half of*, *fourth of*, and *quarter of*. Describe the whole as two of, or four of the shares. Understand for these examples that decomposing into more equal shares creates smaller shares.

SMP 1, 2, 3, 4, 5, 6

Try It

Draw to show how you found 2 parts that are the same size and shape.

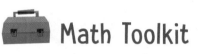 **Math Toolkit**

- paper rectangles and circles

Draw to show how you found 4 parts that are the same size and shape.

Connect It

Draw to show how you found 4 parts that are the same size and shape.

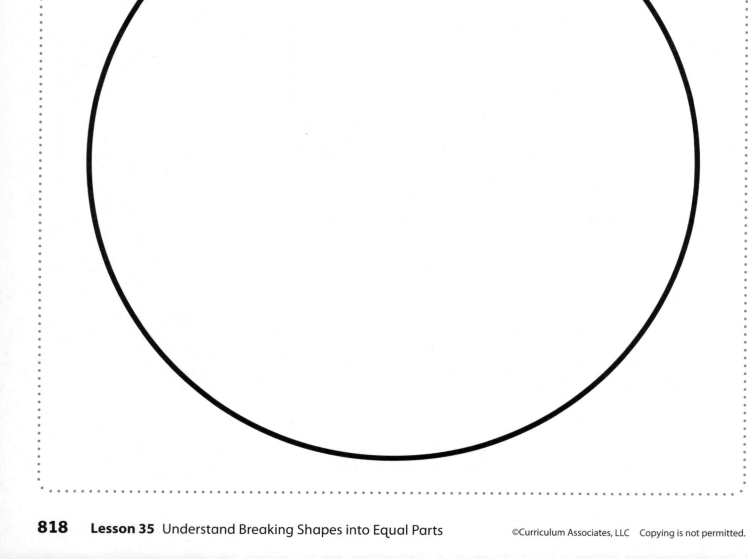

Prepare for Breaking Shapes into Equal Parts

1 Think about what you know about figures that are the same size and shape. Fill in each box. Use words, numbers, and pictures. Show as many ideas as you can.

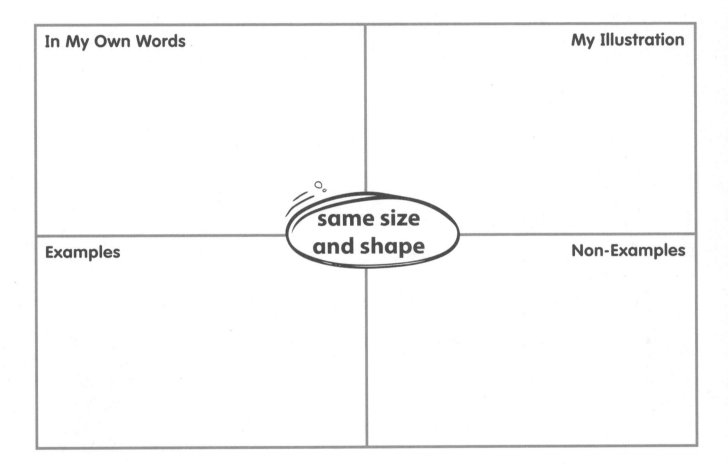

In My Own Words	My Illustration
Examples	**Non-Examples**

same size and shape

2 Ben says that his drawing shows 4 parts that are the same size and shape.
Do you agree? Explain.

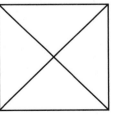

3 Solve the problem.

Draw to show how you found 2 parts that are the same size and shape.

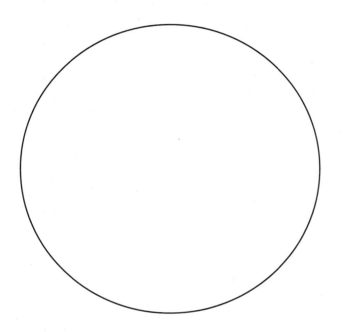

Draw to show how you found 4 parts that are the same size and shape.

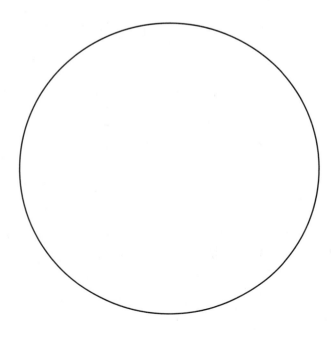

Develop Understanding of Breaking Shapes into Equal Parts

How can you break shapes into **equal parts**?

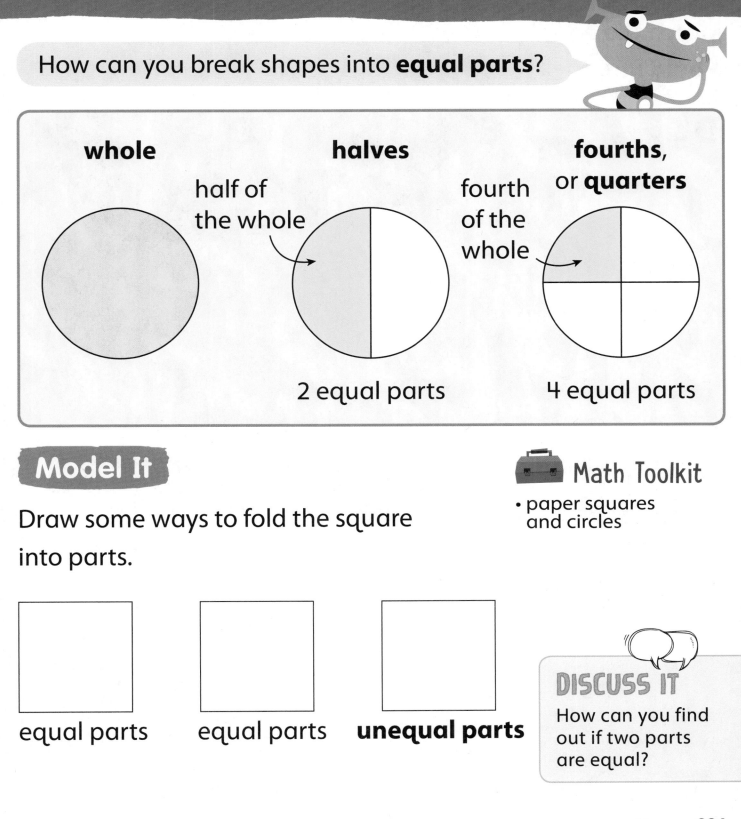

whole

halves

half of the whole

fourths, or quarters

fourth of the whole

2 equal parts

4 equal parts

Model It

Draw some ways to fold the square into parts.

🧰 **Math Toolkit**
• paper squares and circles

equal parts   equal parts   **unequal parts**

💬 **DISCUSS IT**
How can you find out if two parts are equal?

Connect It

Match the equal parts with the whole shape they would make.

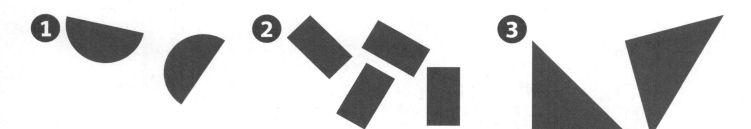

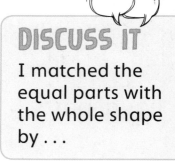
©Curriculum Associates, LLC   Copying is not permitted.

Practice Breaking Shapes into Equal Parts

Look at the Example. Then solve problems 1–8.

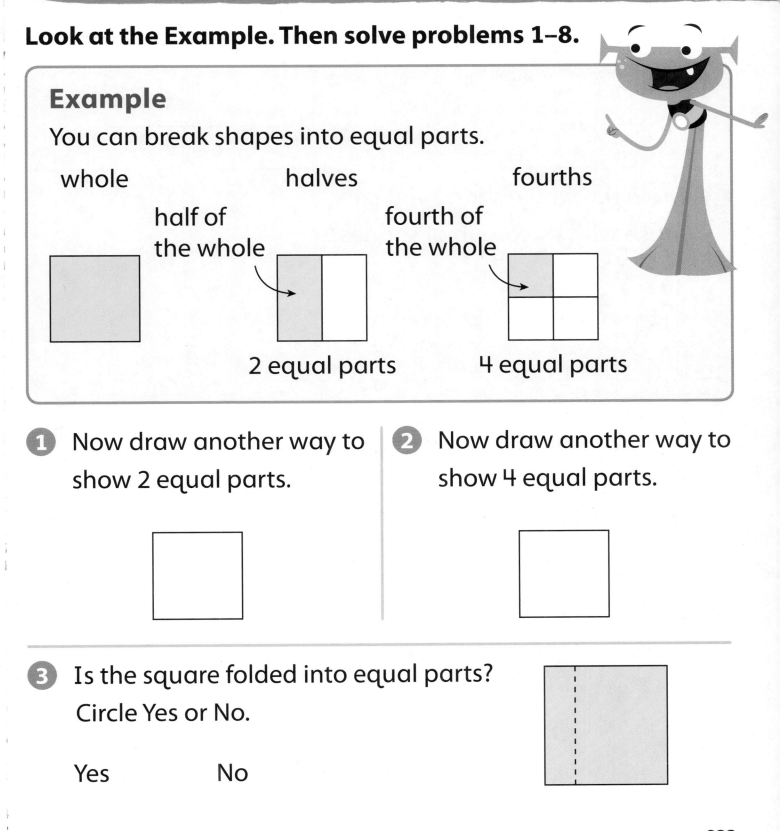

Example

You can break shapes into equal parts.

whole   halves   fourths

half of
the whole

fourth of
the whole

2 equal parts   4 equal parts

1 Now draw another way to show 2 equal parts.

2 Now draw another way to show 4 equal parts.

3 Is the square folded into equal parts?
Circle Yes or No.

Yes   No

4 Draw 2 equal parts.

5 Draw 4 equal parts.

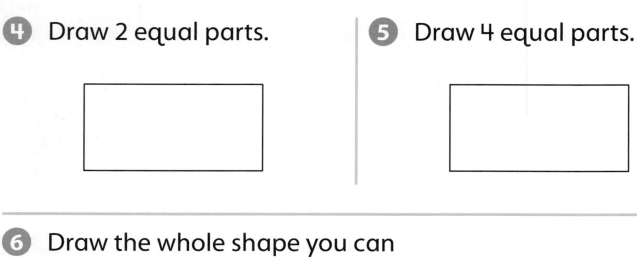

6 Draw the whole shape you can make with the group of shapes.

7 Draw the whole shape you can make with the group of shapes.

8 Draw the whole shape you can make with the group of shapes.

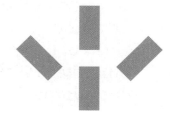

Develop Understanding of Breaking Shapes into Equal Parts

Model It

Use the circle and square. Fold them to make halves and fourths.

Math Toolkit
- paper squares and circles

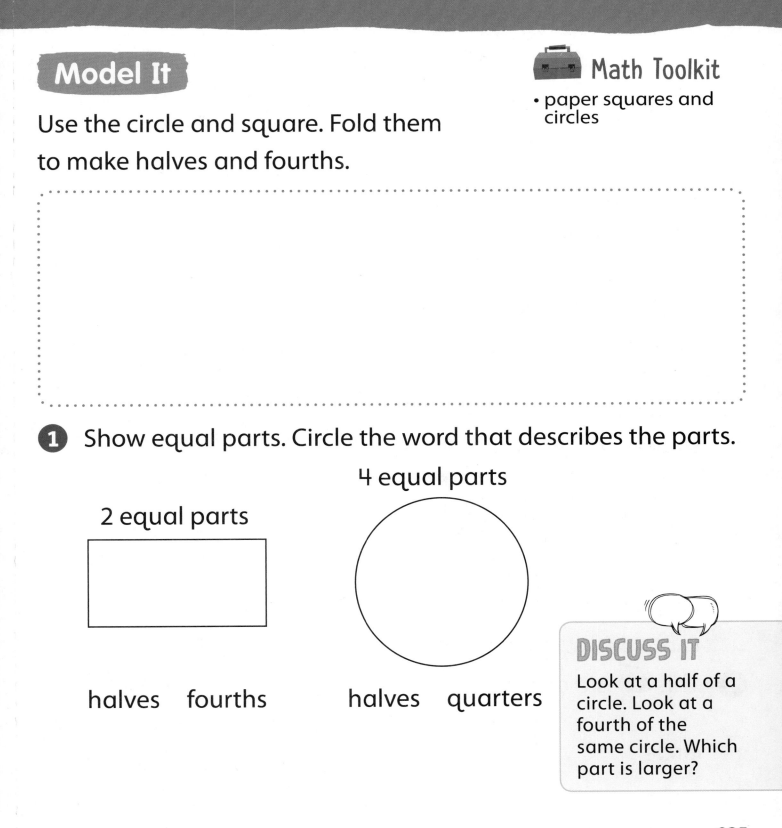

1 Show equal parts. Circle the word that describes the parts.

4 equal parts

2 equal parts

halves   fourths   halves   quarters

DISCUSS IT
Look at a half of a circle. Look at a fourth of the same circle. Which part is larger?

Connect It

2 You can think of a clock as 2 equal parts.

The clock shows 8:30 or _____ past 8.
Every half hour the minute hand travels _____
of the circle.

---

3 How many of these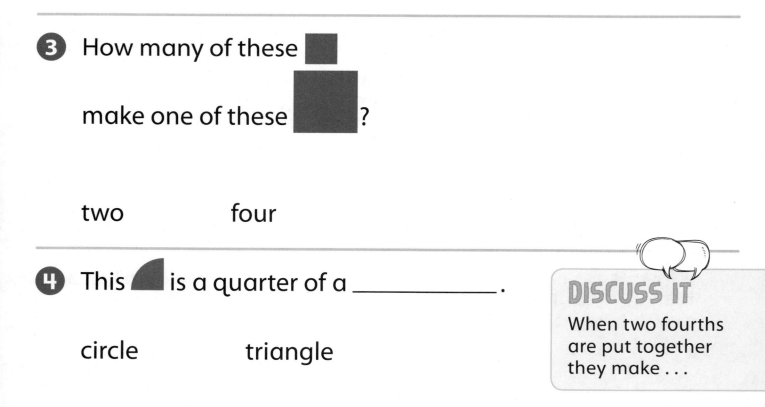

make one of these ?

two   four

---

4 This is a quarter of a _____ .

circle   triangle

Practice Breaking Shapes into Equal Parts

Look at the Example. Then solve problems 1–8.

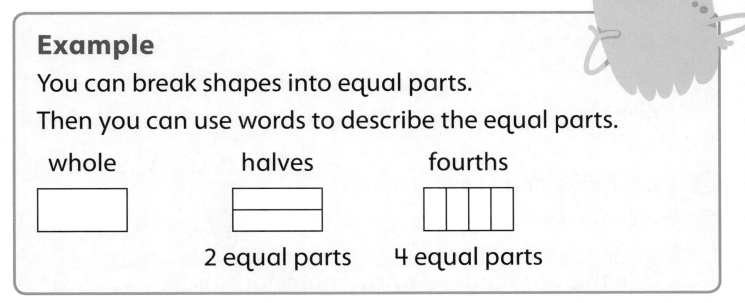

Example

You can break shapes into equal parts.

Then you can use words to describe the equal parts.

whole   halves   fourths

2 equal parts   4 equal parts

Circle the word that describes the parts.

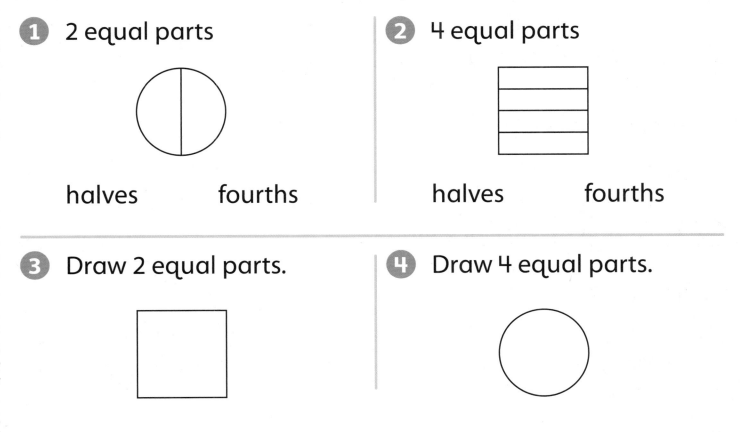

1 2 equal parts

halves   fourths

2 4 equal parts

halves   fourths

3 Draw 2 equal parts.

4 Draw 4 equal parts.

5 Draw 4 equal parts. Circle the word that describes the parts.

halves   quarters

6 How many of these fourths make a circle?

Circle the word that tells how many fourths.

four   two

7 This ◢ is half of a _____ .

Circle the word that names the whole shape.

circle   square

8 Each half of the clock represents a _____ hour.

It is 4:30.

To reach 5:00, the minute hand will move across _____ of the circle.

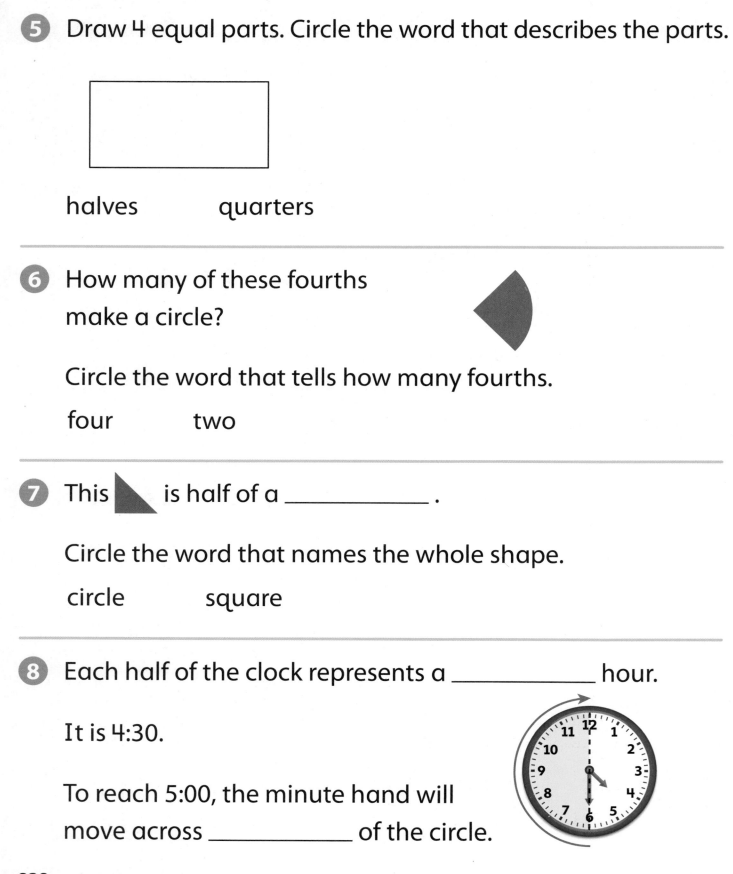

Refine Ideas About Breaking Shapes into Equal Parts

Apply It

1 **Explain** Jake's pizza is cut into 2 equal pieces.

Kim's pizza is cut into 4 equal pieces.

Whose pieces are smaller? How do you know?

Jake's pizza

Kim's pizza

2 **Identify** Write how many equal parts.

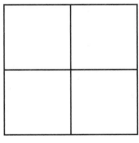

_____ equal parts

Two names for these parts:

_____

3 **Analyze** Buzz says that he shaded a quarter of this shape.

Do you agree? Why or why not?

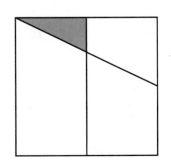

4 Think about breaking shapes into equal parts.

A: Ben and Manu each have a square paper.
They fold their papers in half in different ways.
Draw lines to show how they could each show halves.

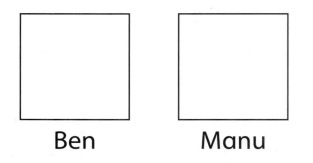

Ben   Manu

B: Maria and Latasha each have a square paper.
They fold their papers in fourths in different ways.
Draw lines to show how they could each
show fourths.

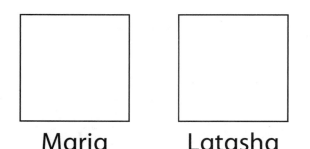

Maria   Latasha

In this unit you learned to . . .

Skill	Lesson
Use sides and corners to name shapes.	33
Put shapes together to make new shapes.	34
Break shapes into halves.	35
Break shapes into fourths.	35

Think about what you learned.

Use words, numbers, and drawings.

1 The math I could use in my everyday life is
_____ because…

2 One thing I could do better is…

Solve the problems.

1 Write how many equal parts.

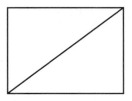

_____ equal parts

Write a name for these parts. _____

---

2 Jake's pizza is cut into 4 equal pieces.

Jill's pizza is cut into 2 equal pieces.

Which pieces are larger? Show how you know.

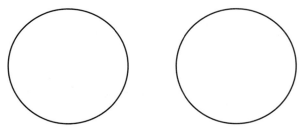

Jake's pizza   Jill's pizza

---

3 Draw 3 rectangles.

Make each one different in some way.

4 Zeke uses cubes to make this prism.
How many cubes does he use? Circle.

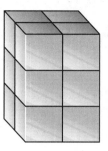

Ⓐ 6 cubes

Ⓑ 12 cubes

Ⓒ 16 cubes

5 Draw lines to show how many triangles are needed to make this hexagon.

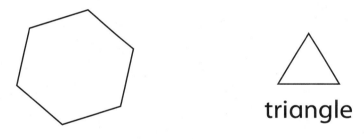

triangle

6 Circle all the reasons this shape is a rhombus.

Ⓐ It has 4 sides.

Ⓑ Its sides are the same length.

Ⓒ It has 1 square corner.

Ⓓ It is gray.

Put It Together

7 Put together 2 or 4 triangles like this ◣.
Make a shape with 4 sides. Describe the shape.

The shape is a _____.

It has _____ equal parts.

Circle the word that describes
the equal parts.

  halves   fourths

Use the shape you made.
Add some other shapes to make a new shape.

Draw the new shape.

Draw or write examples for each word. Then draw or write to show other math words in the unit.

circle a flat shape with no sides and no corners.

My Example

cone a solid shape that slopes from a circular face to a point.

My Example

corner a point where two sides of a shape meet.

My Example

cube a solid shape with 6 square faces and all sides of equal length.

My Example

cylinder a solid shape like a can.

My Example

edge a line where two faces meet in a solid shape.

My Example

equal parts parts of a shape that each cover the same amount of space.

My Example

face a flat surface of a solid shape.

My Example

fourths the parts formed when a whole is divided into four equal parts.

My Example

halves the parts formed when a whole is divided into two equal parts.

My Example

hexagon a flat shape with 6 straight sides and 6 corners.

My Example

quarters four equal parts of a whole.

My Example

rectangle a flat shape with 4 sides and 4 square corners. The opposite sides have the same length.

My Example

rectangular prism a solid shape with 6 rectangular faces.

My Example

rhombus a flat shape with 4 sides and 4 corners. All sides have the same length.

My Example

side a line that makes part of a flat shape.

My Example

sphere a solid shape like a ball.

My Example

square a flat shape with 4 straight sides of equal length and 4 square corners.

My Example

trapezoid a flat shape with 4 sides, where at least 1 pair of sides never meet.

My Example

triangle a flat shape with 3 straight sides and 3 corners.

My Example

unequal parts parts of a shape that do not cover an equal amount of space.

My Example

whole all of a shape, a number, or a group of objects.

My Example

My Word: _____

_____

_____

_____

My Example

My Word: _____

_____

_____

_____

My Example

Cumulative Practice

Name: _____

Set 1: Teen Numbers

Color and write the ones.

1 Show 14.

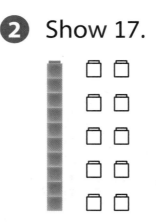

1 ten _____ ones

2 Show 17.

1 ten _____ ones

Set 2: Totals Greater than 10

Solve the problems.

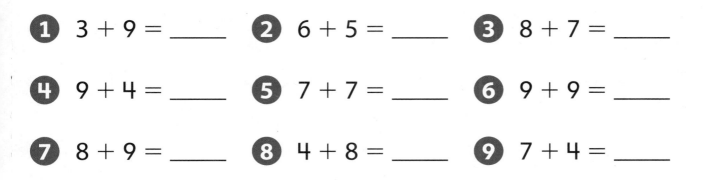

1 $3 + 9 =$ _____   **2** $6 + 5 =$ _____   **3** $8 + 7 =$ _____

4 $9 + 4 =$ _____   **5** $7 + 7 =$ _____   **6** $9 + 9 =$ _____

7 $8 + 9 =$ _____   **8** $4 + 8 =$ _____   **9** $7 + 4 =$ _____

Set 3: Make a Ten to Add

Complete the number bond and addition equations.

1 Find 6 + 8.

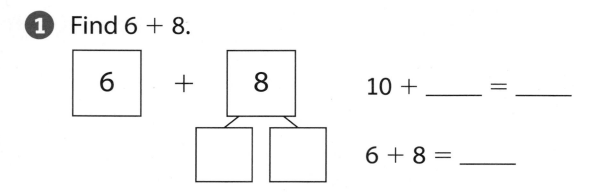

10 + _____ = _____

6 + 8 = _____

Set 4: Add Three Numbers

Solve the problems.

1 8 birds are on the shore. 5 birds join them.

Then 5 more birds join them.

How many birds are on the shore now?

_____ + _____ + _____ = _____

_____ birds

2 2 + 3 + 7 = _____

3 2 + 5 + 8 = _____

4 1 + 9 + 3 = _____

5 4 + 8 + 6 = _____

Set 5: Make a Ten to Subtract

Solve the problems.

1 Find 16 − 8.

16 − ____ = ____

10 − ____ = ____

16 − 8 = ____

2 Find 18 − 9.

18 − ____ = ____

10 − ____ = ____

18 − 9 = ____

3 Find 13 − 7.

13 − ____ = ____

10 − ____ = ____

13 − 7 = ____

4 Find 17 − 8.

17 − ____ = ____

10 − ____ = ____

17 − 8 = ____

Set 6: Unknown Numbers

Find the missing numbers.

1 ____ − 8 = 3

2 5 + ____ = 13

3 ____ + 9 = 17

4 ____ − 8 = 4

Set 7: Word Problems to 20

Solve the problems.

1 Ally has 6 fewer crayons than Fred.

Ally has 9 crayons.

How many does Fred have?

_____ crayons

2 16 crows are on the lawn.

Some fly away. Now there are 8.

How many fly away?

_____ crows

Set 8: True and False Equations

Circle the true equations.

1 $6 = 5 + 2$ **2** $5 = 5$ **3** $7 - 4 = 7 + 4$

$7 + 6 = 6 + 7$ $5 + 3 = 5 - 3$ $5 + 5 = 8 + 2$

$6 - 2 = 1 + 3$ $7 - 3 = 6 - 2$ $8 - 3 = 3 - 8$

Cumulative Practice

Name: _____

Set 1: Tens

Fill in the blanks.

1 5 tens is the same as _____ groups of 10.

2 7 tens is the same as _____ groups of 10.

First color. Then write how many tens.

3 Show 30.

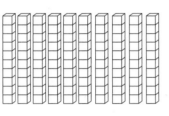

_____ tens

4 Show 80.

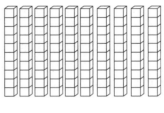

_____ tens

Set 2: Count to 120

Fill in the blanks to count on.

1 Count by ones: 92, 93, _____, _____, _____, 97

2 Count by ones: 98, _____, _____, 101, 102, _____

3 Count by ones: 89, _____, 91, _____, _____, 94

4 Count by ones: 108, _____, _____, _____, 112

Set 3: Tens and Ones

Fill in the blanks.

1 Show 38 in different ways.

38 is 3 tens _____ ones.   38 is 2 tens _____ ones.

38 is 30 + _____.   38 is 20 + _____.

2 Show 56 in different ways.

56 is 5 tens _____ ones.   56 is 4 tens _____ ones.

56 is _____ + _____.   56 is _____ + _____.

Set 4: Comparing Numbers

Write <, >, or = in the circles.

1 7 tens 5 ones   7 tens 8 ones

_____ ◯ _____

2 54 ◯ 54   **3** 59 ◯ 78   **4** 48 ◯ 47

5 92 ◯ 90   **6** 44 ◯ 72   **7** 77 ◯ 77

Set 5: Add Three Numbers

Fill in the blanks to answer each word problem.

1 Lucy made 7 pink paper hearts.
She made 4 red paper hearts and
3 blue paper hearts.
How many paper hearts did Lucy make?

_____ + _____ + _____ = _____

_____ paper hearts

---

2 Jack and Mia each have 6 toy trucks.
Lin has 3 toy trucks.
How many toy trucks do they have?

_____ + _____ + _____ = _____

_____ toy trucks

Set 6: Find Unknown Numbers

Find the missing numbers.

1 $9 + \_\_\_\_ = 18$

2 $14 - \_\_\_\_ = 8$

3 $12 = 5 + \_\_\_\_$

4 $\_\_\_\_ - 9 = 8$

Set 7: Add in Any Order

Complete the number bonds and write equations.

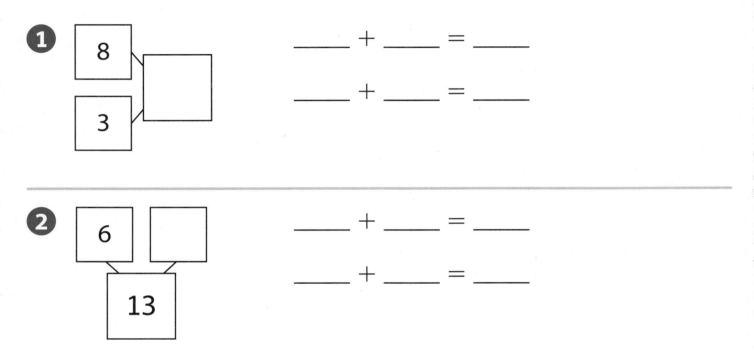

1

| 8 |
| 3 |

_____ + _____ = _____

_____ + _____ = _____

2

| 6 | |
| 13 | |

_____ + _____ = _____

_____ + _____ = _____

Set 8: Missing Addends

Find the missing addend to subtract.

1 Find 9 − 7.

$7 + \_\_\_\_ = 9$

$9 - 7 = \_\_\_\_$

2 Find 12 − 5.

$5 + \_\_\_\_ = 12$

$12 - 5 = \_\_\_\_$

3 Find 15 − 9.

$9 + \_\_\_\_ = 15$

$15 - 9 = \_\_\_\_$

Set 1: Add Tens

Solve the problems.

1 20 + 30 = _____

2 30 + 60 = _____

3 40 + 40 = _____

4 70 + 20 = _____

5 50 + 40 = _____

6 30 + 50 = _____

Set 2: Subtract Tens

Solve the problems.

1 50 − 40 = _____

2 40 − 20 = _____

3 60 − 30 = _____

4 90 − 50 = _____

5 80 − 30 = _____

6 50 − 50 = _____

Set 3: Find 10 More and 10 Less

Solve the problems.

1 37 + 10 = _____

37 − 10 = _____

2 82 + 10 = _____

82 − 10 = _____

3 46 + 10 = _____

46 − 10 = _____

Set 4: Add Tens to Any Number

Add. Show your work.

1 Find 23 + 20.   **2** Find 48 + 30.   **3** Find 50 + 33.

23 + 20 = _____   48 + 30 = _____   50 + 33 = _____

Set 5: Add Two-Digit and One-Digit Numbers

Add. Show your work.

1 Find 36 + 7.   **2** Find 48 + 6.

36 + 7 = _____   48 + 6 = _____

3 Find 62 + 7.   **4** Find 57 + 7.

62 + 7 = _____   57 + 7 = _____

Set 6: Add Two-Digit Numbers

Add. Show your work.

1 Find 52 + 27.

2 Find 34 + 18.

52 + 27 = _____

34 + 18 = _____

3 Find 36 + 47.

4 Find 68 + 25.

36 + 47 = _____

68 + 25 = _____

Set 7: Compare Numbers

Write <, >, or = in the circles.

1 42 ◯ 21

2 48 ◯ 84

3 33 ◯ 33

4 74 ◯ 78

5 53 ◯ 54

6 44 ◯ 36

Set 8: Solve Word Problems

Solve the problems. Show your work.

1 Laura has 6 more peaches than Molly.
Molly has 9 peaches.
How many peaches does Laura have?

_____ peaches

2 Paulie has 14 balls.
Gerry has 8 balls.
How many fewer balls does Gerry have
than Paulie?

_____ fewer balls

3 Ian has 15 stamps.
He gives some away. Now he has 8 stamps.
How many stamps does Ian give away?

_____ stamps

Set 1: Order Objects by Length

Circle the shortest object. Put an X on the longest object.

① ②

Circle the shortest object. Put an X on the tallest object.

③ ④

Set 2: Compare Lengths

Fill in the blanks with *longer* or *shorter*.

①

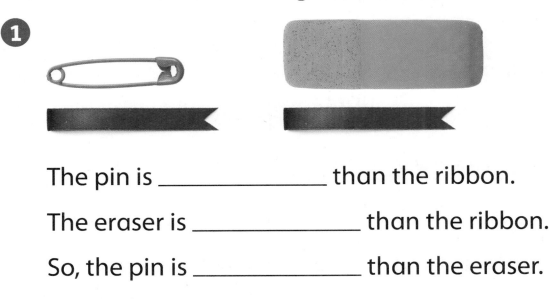

The pin is _____ than the ribbon.

The eraser is _____ than the ribbon.

So, the pin is _____ than the eraser.

Set 3: Measure Length

Measure the length using paper clips.

1

The comb is about _____ paper clips long.

2

The fork is about _____ paper clips long.

3

The crayon is about _____ paper clips long.

4

The paint brush is about _____ paper clips long.

Set 4: Add With Two-Digit Numbers

Solve the problems. Show your work.

1 Find 56 + 9.

56 + 9 = _____

2 Find 78 + 5.

78 + 5 = _____

3 Find 37 + 51.

37 + 51 = _____

4 Find 48 + 28.

48 + 28 = _____

Set 5: Count to 120

Count on to solve the problem.

1 70 counters are in the box.
There are more outside the box.
How many counters altogether?

_____ counters

Set 6: Make a Ten to Subtract

Complete the number paths. Make a ten to subtract.

 1 Find 14 − 7.

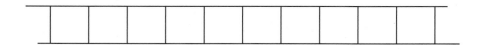

14 − 7 = _____

2 Find 13 − 8.

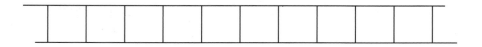

13 − 8 = _____

Set 7: Make a Ten to Add

Complete the number bond and equations.

1 Find 6 + 9.

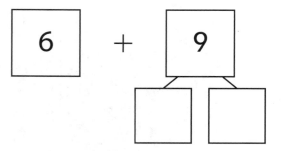

10 + _____ = _____

6 + 9 = _____

Glossary/Glosario

English	Español	Example/Ejemplo

Aa

add
to put together groups to find the total.

sumar
juntar grupos para hallar el total.

$6 + 2 = 8$

---

addend
a number being added.

sumando
número que se suma.

$4 + 5 = 9$
↑   ↑
addends

---

addition equation
an equation with numbers, a plus sign, and an equal sign. An equation tells that two things are equal.

ecuación de suma
ecuación que tiene números, un signo más y un signo de igual. Una ecuación dice que dos cosas son iguales.

$3 + 4 = 7$

English	Español	Example/Ejemplo

addition table
a table showing addition facts.

tabla de suma
tabla que muestra sumas y sus resultados.

1 + 1 2	1 + 2 3	1 + 3 4	1 + 4 5	1 + 5 6	1 + 6 7	1 + 7 8	1 + 8 9	1 + 9 10
2 + 1 3	2 + 2 4	2 + 3 5	2 + 4 6	2 + 5 7	2 + 6 8	2 + 7 9	2 + 8 10	
3 + 1 4	3 + 2 5	3 + 3 6	3 + 4 7	3 + 5 8	3 + 6 9	3 + 7 10		
4 + 1 5	4 + 2 6	4 + 3 7	4 + 4 8	4 + 5 9	4 + 6 10			
5 + 1 6	5 + 2 7	5 + 3 8	5 + 4 9	5 + 5 10				
6 + 1 7	6 + 2 8	6 + 3 9	6 + 4 10					
7 + 1 8	7 + 2 9	7 + 3 10						
8 + 1 9	8 + 2 10							
9 + 1 10								

analog clock
a clock that uses hour and minute hands to show time.

reloj analógico
reloj que muestra la hora con una manecilla de la hora y un minutero.

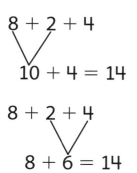

associative property of addition
when the grouping of three or more addends is changed, the total does not change.

propiedad asociativa de la suma
cambiar la agrupación de tres o más sumandos no cambia el total.

$$8 + 2 + 4$$
$$10 + 4 = 14$$
$$8 + 2 + 4$$
$$8 + 6 = 14$$

English	Español	Example/Ejemplo

Cc

cent (¢)
the smallest unit of money. 100 cents is equal to 1 dollar.

centavo (¢)
la unidad de dinero más pequeña. 100 centavos es igual a 1 dólar.

1 cent   1¢

circle
a flat shape with no sides and no corners.

círculo
figura plana que no tiene lados ni esquinas.

column
group of objects or numbers that go from top to bottom.

columna
grupo de objetos o números que van de arriba abajo.

column

31	32	33	34	35	36	37	38	39	40
41	42	43	44	45	46	47	48	49	50
51	52	53	54	55	56	57	58	59	60

English	Español	Example/Ejemplo
commutative property of addition numbers can be added in a different order and the total will be the same.	**propiedad conmutativa de la suma** sumar números en distinto orden no cambia el total.	$4 + 6 = 10$ $6 + 4 = 10$
compare to decide if numbers, amounts, or sizes are greater than, less than, or equal to each other.	**comparar** determinar si un número, una cantidad o un tamaño es mayor que, menor que o igual a otro número, otra cantidad u otro tamaño.	28 is greater than 21. 40 is equal to 40.  The length of the pink collar is less than the length of the orange collar.
compose to make by putting together parts. You can put together numbers to make a greater number or shapes to make a new shape.	**componer** combinar partes para formar algo. Se pueden combinar números para formar un número mayor o figuras para formar otra figura.	 The two triangles make a square.

English	Español	Example/Ejemplo
cone a solid shape that slopes from a circular face to a point.	**cono** figura sólida que se inclina desde una cara circular hacia un punto.	
corner a point where two or more lines meet.	**esquina** punto donde se encuentran dos o más rectas.	Corner
count on start with one addend and count to find the total.	**contar hacia delante** comenzar desde un sumando y contar para hallar el total.	4 5 6 $4 + 2 = 6$
cube a solid shape with 6 square faces and all edges of equal length.	**cubo** figura sólida que tiene 6 caras cuadradas y todos los lados de igual longitud.	
cylinder a solid shape like a can.	**cilindro** figura sólida con forma de lata.	

English	Español	Example/Ejemplo

Dd

data
a set of information that is collected.

datos
conjunto de información reunida.

Favorite Toys

---

decompose
to break into parts. You can break apart numbers and shapes.

descomponer
separar en partes. Se pueden separar en partes números y figuras.

The rectangle is broken apart into four smaller rectangles.

---

difference
the result of subtraction.

diferencia
el resultado de la resta.

$9 - 5 = 4$
4 is the difference.

---

digit
a symbol used to write numbers.

dígito
símbolo que se usa para escribir números.

0, 1, 2, 3, 4, 5, 6, 7, 8, and 9 are digits.

---

digital clock
a clock that uses digits to show the time.

reloj digital
reloj que usa dígitos para mostrar la hora.

9:30

---

dime
a coin with a value of 10 cents (10¢).

moneda de 10¢
moneda con un valor de 10 centavos (10¢).

10 cents   10¢

English	Español	Example/Ejemplo

dollar ($)
a unit of money. There are 100 cents in 1 dollar ($1).

dólar ($)
unidad de dinero. Hay 100 centavos en 1 dólar ($1).

←1 dollar

$1

doubles
an addition fact with two addends that are the same.

dobles
suma que tiene dos sumandos iguales.

$4 + 4 = 8$

doubles plus 1
an addition fact where one addend is 1 more than the other addend.

dobles más 1
suma en la que un sumando es 1 más que el otro.

$4 + 4 = 8$ ← doubles
$4 + 5 = 9$
↑
doubles plus 1

Ee

edge
a line where two faces meet in a solid shape.

arista
recta donde se encuentran dos esquinas de una figura sólida.

Edge

equal
having the same value, same size, or same amount.

igual
que tiene el mismo valor, el mismo tamaño o la misma cantidad.

$=$

3 = 3

English	Español	Example/Ejemplo
equal parts parts of a shape that each cover the same amount of space.	**partes iguales** partes de una figura que ocupan el mismo espacio.	2 equal parts 4 equal parts
equal sign (=) a symbol that means *is the same as*.	**signo de igual** (=) símbolo que significa *es lo mismo que*.	1 + 3 = 4 equal sign
equation a mathematical sentence that uses an equal sign (=) to show that two things are equal.	**ecuación** oración matemática en la que se usa un signo de igual (=) para mostrar que dos cosas son iguales.	$8 + 7 = 15$

Ff

face a flat surface of a solid shape.	**cara** superficie plana de una figura sólida.	Face

English	Español	Example/Ejemplo
fewer a lesser amount.	**menos** cantidad menor.	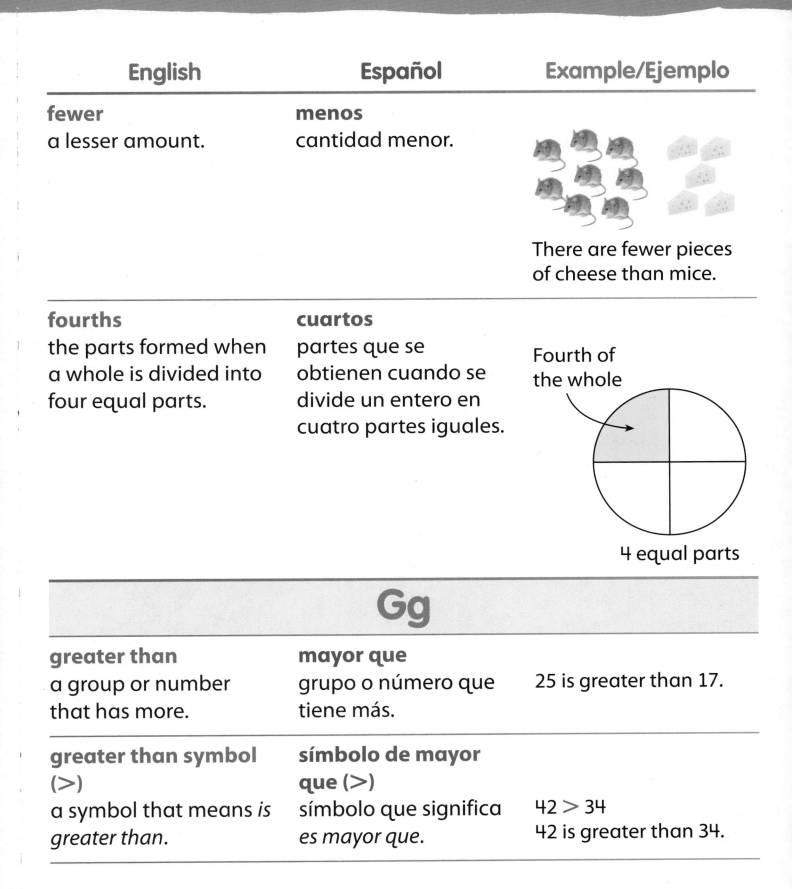 There are fewer pieces of cheese than mice.
fourths the parts formed when a whole is divided into four equal parts.	**cuartos** partes que se obtienen cuando se divide un entero en cuatro partes iguales.	Fourth of the whole 4 equal parts

Gg

greater than a group or number that has more.	**mayor que** grupo o número que tiene más.	25 is greater than 17.
greater than symbol (>) a symbol that means *is greater than*.	**símbolo de mayor que (>)** símbolo que significa *es mayor que*.	42 > 34 42 is greater than 34.

English	Español	Example/Ejemplo

Hh

half hour
a unit of time. There are 30 minutes in one half hour.

media hora
unidad de tiempo. Media hora equivale a 30 minutos.

(clock showing 4:30 / digital 4:30)

half past
a time that is 30 minutes after an hour.

y media
tiempo que es 30 minutos después de una hora.

(clock showing 4:30 / digital 4:30)

halves
the parts formed when a whole is divided into two equal parts.

medios
partes que se obtienen cuando se divide un entero en dos partes iguales.

Half of the whole

2 equal parts

hexagon
a flat shape with 6 straight sides and 6 corners.

hexágono
figura plana con 6 lados rectos y 6 esquinas.

English	Español	Example/Ejemplo
hour (h) a unit of time. There are 60 minutes in 1 hour.	**hora (h)** unidad de tiempo. 1 hora equivale a 60 minutos.	 1 hour = 60 minutes
hour hand the shorter hand on a clock. It shows hours.	**manecilla de la hora** la manecilla más corta de un reloj. Muestra las horas.	 Hour hand

Ll

length how long something is.	**longitud** cuán largo es algo.	length
less than the group or number with fewer, not as much, not as many.	**menor que** el grupo o el número que tiene menos o que no tiene tanto o tantos como otro.	17 is less than 25.

Glossary/Glosario A11

English	Español	Example/Ejemplo
less than symbol ($<$) symbol that means *is less than*.	**símbolo de menor que ($<$)** símbolo que significa *es menor que*.	$61 < 68$ 61 is less than 68.
longer greater in length.	**más largo** que tiene mayor longitud.	The blue line is longer than the red line.
longest greatest in length.	**el más largo** que tiene la mayor longitud.	The blue line is the longest line.

Mm

make a ten a strategy that uses numbers that add to ten.	**formar diez** estrategia en la que se usan números que suman diez.	Move 2 counters into the 10-frame. $8 + 5 = 13$

English	Español	Example/Ejemplo
measure to find length, height, or weight using a known unit.	**medir** hallar la longitud, la altura, o el peso usando una unidad conocida.	The line measures about 2 paper clips long.
minute (min) a unit of time. There are 60 minutes in an hour.	**minuto (min)** unidad de tiempo. 60 minutos equivalen a 1 hora.	60 minutes = 1 hour
minute hand the longer hand on a clock. It shows minutes.	**minutero** la manecilla más larga de un reloj. Muestra los minutos.	Minute hand 

English	Español	Example/Ejemplo
more, more than the greater number, quantity, or amount.	**más, más que** el número o la cantidad más grande.	 There are more skates than sticks.

Nn

English	Español	Example/Ejemplo
nickel a coin with a value of 5 cents (5¢).	**moneda de 5¢** moneda con un valor de 5 centavos (5¢).	 5 cents · · · · 5¢
number bond a drawing with a total and number partners.	**enlace numérico** dibujo que muestra un total y una pareja de números.	 3 · 5 · 8

English	Español	Example/Ejemplo

Oo

o'clock
to tell time for an hour.

en punto
cuando el reloj marca una hora en particular.

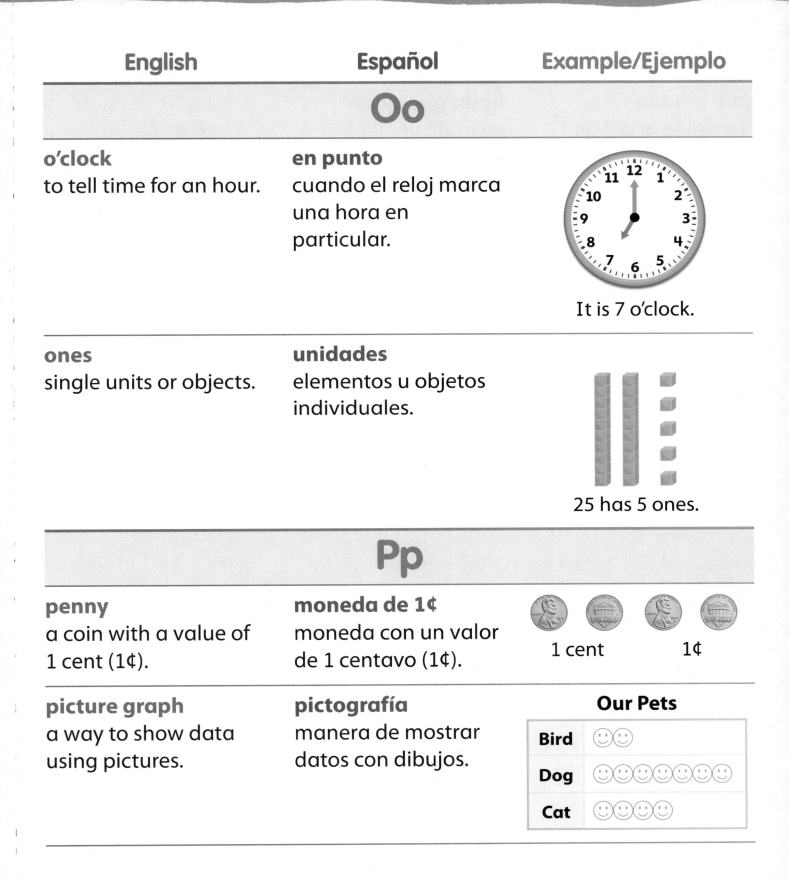

It is 7 o'clock.

ones
single units or objects.

unidades
elementos u objetos individuales.

25 has 5 ones.

Pp

penny
a coin with a value of 1 cent (1¢).

moneda de 1¢
moneda con un valor de 1 centavo (1¢).

1 cent   1¢

picture graph
a way to show data using pictures.

pictografía
manera de mostrar datos con dibujos.

Our Pets

Bird	☺☺
Dog	☺☺☺☺☺☺
Cat	☺☺☺☺

English	Español	Example/Ejemplo
place value the value of a digit based on its position in a number.	**valor posicional** valor de un dígito según su posición en un número.	32 is 3 tens 2 ones. 32 is 30 + 2.

Qq

quarter a coin with a value of 25 cents (25¢).	**moneda de 25¢** moneda con un valor de 25 centavos (25¢).	25 cents 25¢
quarters four equal parts of a whole.	**cuartos** cuatro partes iguales de un entero.	← Quarter

Rr

rectangle a flat shape with 4 sides and 4 square corners. The opposite sides have the same length.	**rectángulo** figura plana que tiene 4 lados y 4 esquinas cuadradas. Los lados opuestos tienen la misma longitud.	

English	Español	Example/Ejemplo
rectangular prism a solid shape with 6 rectangular faces.	**prisma rectángular** figura sólida con 6 caras rectangulares	
rhombus a flat shape with 4 sides and 4 corners. All sides have the same length.	**rombo** figura plana que tiene 4 lados y 4 esquinas. Todos los lados tienen la misma longitud.	
row a group of objects or numbers that go from left to right.	**fila** grupo de objetos o números que van de izquierda a derecha.	91 92 93 94 95 96 97 98 99 100 101 102 103 104 105 106 107 108 109 110 111 112 113 114 115 116 117 118 119 120 └Row

Ss

English	Español	Example/Ejemplo
shorter lesser in length or height.	**más bajo** que tiene una altura menor que la de otro objeto. **más corto** de menor longitud.	The yellow pencil is shorter than the blue pencil.

English	Español	Example/Ejemplo
shortest least in length or height.	**el más corto** el que tiene la menor longitud.	The red pencil is the shortest.
side a line that makes part of a flat shape.	**lado** recta que forma parte de una figura plana.	← Side
sort to group objects by how they are alike.	**clasificar** agrupar objetos según características similares.	The shapes are sorted by color.
sphere a solid shape like a ball.	**esfera** figura sólida con forma de pelota.	

English	Español	Example/Ejemplo
square a flat shape with 4 straight sides of equal length and 4 square corners.	**cuadrado** figura plana que tiene 4 lados rectos de igual longitud y 4 esquinas cuadradas.	
subtract to take from, take apart, or compare.	**restar** quitar, separar, o comparar.	$7 - 6 = 1$
subtraction equation an equation with numbers, a minus sign, and an equal sign. An equation tells that two things are equal.	**ecuación de resta** ecuación que tiene números, un signo menos, y un signo de igual. Una ecuación dice que dos cosas son iguales.	$5 - 2 = 3$
sum the result of addition.	**suma** el resultado de la suma.	$4 + 8 = \mathbf{12}$ **12** is the sum.

English	Español	Example/Ejemplo

Tt

taller
greater in height.

más alto
que tiene mayor altura.

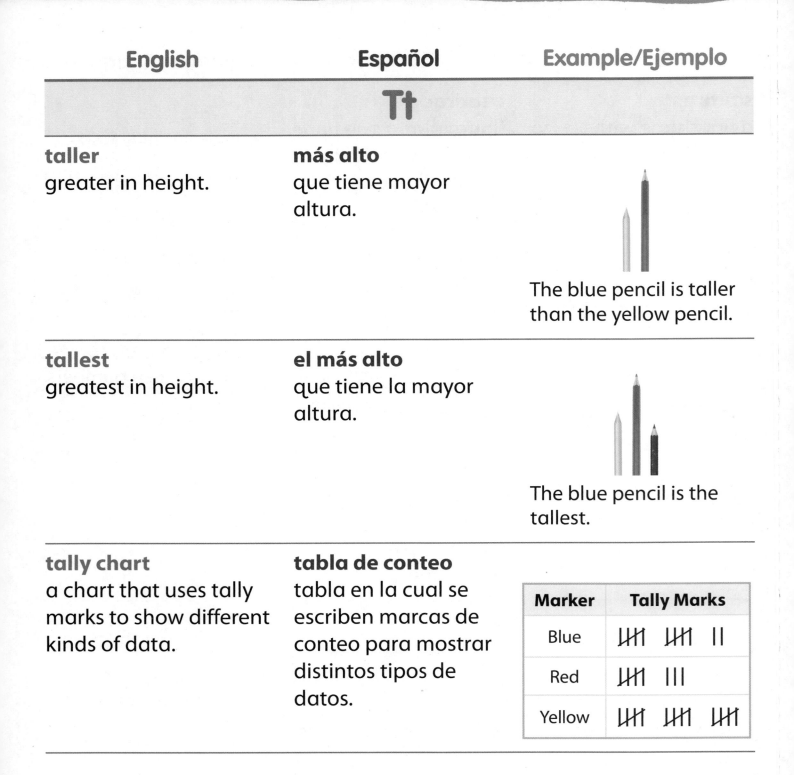

The blue pencil is taller than the yellow pencil.

tallest
greatest in height.

el más alto
que tiene la mayor altura.

The blue pencil is the tallest.

tally chart
a chart that uses tally marks to show different kinds of data.

tabla de conteo
tabla en la cual se escriben marcas de conteo para mostrar distintos tipos de datos.

Marker	Tally Marks		
Blue	ЖЖ	ЖЖ	II
Red	ЖЖ	III	
Yellow	ЖЖ	ЖЖ	ЖЖ

English	Español	Example/Ejemplo
tally marks marks that are used to record data.	**marcas de conteo** marcas que se usan para anotar datos.	<table><tr><th>Marker</th><th>Tally Marks</th></tr><tr><td>Blue</td><td>卌 卌 ||</td></tr><tr><td>Red</td><td>卌 |||</td></tr><tr><td>Yellow</td><td>卌 卌 卌</td></tr></table>
teen number a number that is 1 ten plus some ones.	**número del 11 al 19** número formado por 1 decena y algunas unidades.	11, 12, 13, 14, 15, 16, 17, 18, 19 are teen numbers.
tens groups of 10 ones.	**decenas** grupos de 10 unidades.	25 has **2 tens**.
total a number you get when you add two or more numbers.	**total** número que se obtiene al sumar dos o más números.	4 + 8 = 12 **12** is the total.

English	Español	Example/Ejemplo
trapezoid a flat shape with 4 sides, where at least one pair of sides never meet.	**trapecio** figura plana que tiene 4 lados, en la que al menos un par de lados nunca se encuentran.	
triangle a flat shape with 3 straight sides and 3 corners.	**triángulo** figura plana que tiene 3 lados rectos y 3 esquinas.	

Uu

English	Español	Example/Ejemplo
unequal parts parts of a shape that do not cover an equal amount of space.	**partes desiguales** partes de una figura que no ocupan la misma cantidad de espacio.	The square is divided into 4 unequal parts.
unit a part that is used to measure. Each part for one kind of unit has the same length.	**unidad** parte que se usa para medir. Todas las partes de un mismo tipo de unidad tienen la misma longitud.	You can use tiles as a unit of measure.

English	Español	Example/Ejemplo

Ww

whole
all of a shape, a number, or a group of objects.

entero
toda una figura, todo un número, o todo un grupo de objetos.

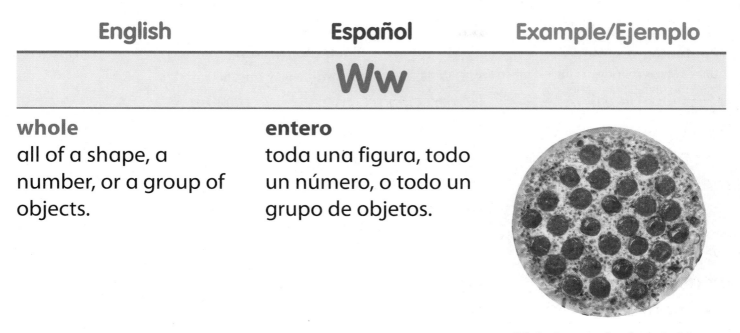

This is a whole pizza.

Acknowledgments

Common Core State Standards © 2010. National Governors Association Center for Best Practices and Council of Chief State School Officers. All rights reserved.

Photography Credits

United States coin images (unless otherwise indicated) from the United States Mint

Images used under license from **Shutterstock.com**.

iii ArtMari, Dirk Ercken; **iv** chuchiko17; **v** iris wright; **vi** Valentin Agapov, Africa Studio; **vii** Anest, Eric Boucher, udovichenko; **viii** Nenov Brothers Images, anaken2012; **1** Africa Studio; **3** Mary Rice, Blanscape, PITAKSUNTI, Xkunclova, Voraorn Ratanakorn, Nicola Bertolini, Seregraff, Nailia Schwarz; **4** Alena Stalmashonak, Mikkel Bigandt, Elisa Putti, Minerva Studio; **5** photka, Happy Together; **6** Mega Pixel; **8** Benjamin Simeneta, DenisNata; **9** Jenn Huls; **10** Jenn Huls, Liskus; **11** Ermolaev Alexander, Natasha Pankina; **12** JasminkaM; **15–16** FabrikaSimf; **17** KhanunHaHa; **21** HeinzTeh, Marques, PhawKStudio; **22** Marques; **23** Be Good, Triff, Etaphop photo; **24** Mega Pixel, Levent Konuk; **25** Irin-k; **26** Worraket, smilewithjul; **27** Dima Moroz, goir; **28** Hamurishi, VINCENT GIORDANO PHOTO, Gts, Prostock-studio; **30** BW Folsom, Natasha Pankina; **32** Peter Hermes Furian; **33** Naypong Studio; **34** Iasha; **35** Alexander Mak; **36** Yellow Cat, Kitzcorner; **38** Food Travel Stockforlife, seksan wangkeeree, bergamont, Duplass; **39** doomu; **40** jirateep sankote; **41** Dakalova Iuliia, Nadiia Korol; **42** Maks Narodenko, Kyselova Inna; **44** Mikkel Bigandt, Alena Stalmashonak, Elisa Putti; **45** timquo, HomeStudio; **46** Irina Rogova, studiovin, Lotus Images, Vilor; **48** goir, Dima Moroz; **49** Dima Moroz, Eric Isselee, Lyekaterina; **50** Wision; **51** chiaro; **52** Africa Studio, mamuangmay; **53** Mr Aesthetics; **54** photosync; **56** Mr Aesthetics; **57** nito; **58** Marie C Fields; **60** Hayati Kayhan; **63–64** Jakub Krechowicz; **65** Niferure; **68** Mindscape studio; **70, 72** chuchiko17; **75** Fablok; **76** Tanya Sid; **77–78** Erik Lam; **80** irin-k; **85** MriMan, Niphon Subsri, kostolom3000, kuroksta; **86–88** kuroksta; **89** Hedzun Vasyl; **91** Claudio Divizia, artnLera; **92** Prostock-studio, artnLera, NPeter, Dotted Yeti; **94** qingqing, mhatzapa; **96** mhatzapa, Lano4ka, Kristina Shevchenko; **97** KittyVector; **98** Ruslan Ivantsov; **103–104** PhawKStudio; **105** Kostenko Maxim, mhatzapa; **112** Vadim Sadovski, mhatzapa; **115** Lano4ka, inxti, Vetal; **116** Denphumi, Lano4ka, DeanHarty; **118** Ukki Studio; **120** Lano4ka, media point inc; **121** Lano4ka, niwat chaiyawoot; **122** Lano4ka, CrackerClips Stock Media; **123** Nataliia K; **124** wk1003mike, BoxerX, Lano4ka, Paul Orr; **125** wk1003mike, Andrey Lobachev, Dan Kosmayer; **126** Lano4ka, Mega Pixel; **127** BalancePhoto; **128** PaPicasso; **130** Lano4ka, Vereshchagin Dmitry, Vetal; **133** Tatiana Popova, umarazak; **134** makeitdouble, Lano4ka; **135** Tim UR; **136** Doug McLean, LYekaterina; **137** Triff; **139** Kyselova Inna, matkub2499; **140** P Maxwell Photography, I'm Mock-up, photka; **141** Kamenetskiy Konstantin; **142** Chris Renshaw; **144** Susan Schmitz; **145–146** Maryna Kulchytska; **147** Anteromite; **148** smilewithjul, Robert J. Beyers II; **149** goir, Khumthong; **150** Ermolaev Alexander, bergamont, Natasha Pankina; **152** Vorobyeva; **153** Viktar Malyshchyts; **157** Cherdchai charasri, Patchareephoto, Dirk Ercken, Ernst Photography; **158** Yurii Vydyborets; **159** Triff; **160** Cheers Group, punnaphob; **161** titelio; **162** Richard Peterson; **163** Sandratsky Dmitriy, photo one; **164** onair, Sandratsky Dmitriy, photo one; **165** Napat, Christian Musat, Eric Isselee, KITSANANAN, Praisaeng, Giedriius; **166** Coprid; **167** MirasWonderland, Gelpi; **168** Birgit Reitz-Hofmann;

Front Cover Credits

©Joel Simon/Digital Vision/Getty Images

Illustration Credits

All Illustrations by **Tim Chi Ly**

169 TerraceStudio; **170** Andrienko Anastasiya; **172** Lotus_studio, Mikael Damkier, Michiel de Wit, Lukas Gojda; **173** Eric Isselee; **174** photka; **175** Ragnarock; **176** Egoreichenkov Evgenii; **177** TRINACRIA PHOTO, Ksenia Palimski, leungchopan, Paleka; **178** napatsorn aungsirichinda, etraveler; **179** Audrey M Vasey; **180** Tsekhmister, azure1; **181** Anna Kucherova, Zhukov Oleg; **185** photka; **186** ppart; **187** chuchiko17; **188** Preto Perola, fieldwork; **189** doomu; **190** photosync; **192** Andrew Burgess; **196** Fotofermer, irin-k; **197** chuchiko17; **200** Hurst Photo; **203** kosmos111; **204** natalia pak, FabrikaSimf, runLenarun; **206** Mark William Penny, threeseven; **208** Robyn Mackenzie, Natasha Pankina; **214** jefftakespics2; **219** Nisakorn Neera; **224** Nata-Lia; **227** nikkytok; **237** Vitaly Korovin; **239** chuchiko17; **240** Nik Merkulov, EHStockphoto; **249** chuchiko17; **255** paitoon Meetee; **256** Riccardo Mayer, photka; **257** Annette Shaff; **258** marchello74; **261** Edwin Verin; **262** Dan Kosmayer; **267** FabrikaSimf; **268** Vladimir Prusakov; **274** Rob Wilson, Tiwat K; **278** paitoon Meetee; **279** irin-k; **281** jocic; **282** photosync, Natasha Pankina; **284** serg_dibrova; **285** Kwadrat; **286** Kwadrat, owatta; **287** Andrei Shumskiy; **288** Unconventional, Candus Camera, Slawomir Zelasko; **289** Rose Carson; **290** Photo Melon; **291** aboikis; **292** Pshenichka; **293** Lars Christensen; **294** photosync, Wonderful Future World; **296** Eric Isselee, mhatzapa, olnik_y; **302** Gelpi; **303** Narong Jongsirikul; **304** lord_photon; **305** Rose Carson; **306** Nenov Brothers Images; **308** bogdan ionescu; **309–310** Dora Zett; **311** Africa Studio; **312** Olga Rom; **315–316** Africa Studio; **317** Imageman, Johan Swanepoel; **319** Sergio Hayashi; **320** Jiri Hera; **324** Jiri Vaclavek; **326** Krasowit; **328** Prostock-studio, Africa Studio, enterphoto; **329** Mit Kapevski, ivansekretov; **330** nixki; **332** Kucher Serhii, MirasWonderland; **333** kustomer; **334** YolLusZam1802; **335** Andrew Olscher; **339–340** Low Sugar; **341** Joe Techapanupreeda; **350** spe; **351** RTimages; **352** N.Vector Design; **353** NATTANOP APICHITTRAKUL; **354** Eric Isselee; **356** Arnoud Quanjer; **357** unpict; **358** Svetlana Foote; **363** Diana Taliun; **364** Anna Kucherova; **375** creaPicTures, DMS Foto, Juneisy Q. Hawkins, puttsk; **376** Jaroslav74, Adrianhbr, NamoChonburi, Ukki Studio, jiangdi, Peter Vanco, Lapina, Africa Studio, Erik Lam; **377** Jiri Hera; **378** photomaster, Madlen; **380** Eric Isselee; **381** HomeStudio, Ilya Andriyanov, Noophoto, Fer Gregory; **382** Fer Gregory; **383** schankz; **384** mmstudiodesign; **386** Andy Piatt; **387** Africa Studio; **388** Valentyn Volkov; **389** schankz; **390** Kletr; **392** paperbees; **394** LittleMiss; **396** BEEE, Cristina Jurca, Pakhotin Andrey, Tatiana Mirlin, jsabirova; **398** design56; **399** Chones, Photo Melon; **400** Brooke Becker, Suradech Prapairat; **401** chuchiko17; **404** pukach, Alexey Broslavets, loskutnikov; **405–406** Rose Carson; **409** Super Prin, Butterfly Hunter; **410** Fesus Robert, N7atal7i, Eric Isselee, Jagodka; **411** Pavel Hlystov; **412** Oksana Kuzmina, Iriskana; **413** Feng Yu, shooarts; **414** RFvectors, Elena Pronenko, robinimages2013, ajt; **416** Kelvin Wong; **417** Mega Pixel, Chones; **418** Evgeniya Uvarova, Eric Gevaert; **419** Tsekhmister, Eric Isselee, photomaster; **420** Callipso, Super Prin, Tatyana Vyc, Evgeniya Pautova; **421** Eric Gevaert;

422 Family Business, Ianych, Tsveta Nesheva; 423 Viktor1; 431 MAHATHIR MOHD YASIN; 433 Antonia Giroux; 434 Irina Rogova, sss615, Tiwat K; 435 Kostsov; 436 gresi; 438 Svitlana-ua; 444 Lightspring; 447 Vladimir Wrangel, mhatzapa; 448 Jacqui Martin, Madlen; 461–462 mekcar; 464 Iasha, Elena Schweitzer, Andrii Horulko, Jr images; 465 Andrii Horulko, Quang Ho; 466 Ruth Black; 472 Andrii Horulko, Maris Kiselov, Candus Camera, drebha; 473 Pete Spiro, Claudio Divizia; 474 exoticartz; 491 David Franklin; 492 Ernst Photography; 493 Africa Studio; 494 Olga Guchek; 495 Quang Ho; 496 iris wright; 497 bogdan ionescu; 498 Richard Peterson; 501–502 Yeti studio; 507 Denise Torres; 512 George Filyagin; 514 creativestockexchange; 530 Svitlana-ua; 537 Anton-Burakov; 538 Ambient Ideas; 539 urfin; 540 Andrey Burmakin; 542 Fat Jackey; 552 nimon, NickKnight; 555 nimon, PinkBlue; 556 nimon; 560 nimon; 561 Low Sugar, Natasha Pankina; 571 Rudmer Zwerver; 573 exopixel; 574 ziviani, oleschwander; 575 Masterchief_ Productions; 576 Mega Pixel; 578 Valentin Agapov; 579 Alex Romantsov; 580 Ching Design; 581 Gunnar Pippel, balabolka; 585 Romariolen, Tim UR, Iiskus; 586 Lisovskaya Natalia; 587 Lotus_ studio; 590 bluehand, redchocolate; 591 Diana Taliun; 592 Andy Piatt; 595 Lersak supamatra; 596 FabrikaSimf, MichaelJayBerlin; 598 mayakova, Seregam; 599 Eric Isselee; 600 Olhastock; 611 STILLFX; 613 HeinzTeh; 614 aradaphotgraphy, Carolyn Franks; 615 Tatiana Popova; 616 Africa Studio, primiaou; 618 nanantachoke, Natasha Pankina; 619 Eric Isselee; 620 Tooykrub, Lalahouse; 621 valzan, smilewithjul; 625 wk1003mike; 626 Mike Flippo; 627 Yellow Cat, Tish1; 631 Andy Piatt; 632 BOONCHUAY PROMJIAM, Angeliki Vel; 634 Hong Vo, smilewithjul; 636 Madlen, smilewithjul; 637 chuchiko17; 638 chuchiko17, Astarina; 639 Petr Vaclavek; 640 Jiri Hera, Tiwat K; 643–644 Wasanajai; 645 BW Folsom; 646 Kotomiti Okuma, Iriskana; 648 Mike Truchon; 649 Roman Samokhin; 650 Sinelev; 652 IrinaK, ExpressVectors; 653 Meng Luen; 654 Bachkova Nataliia, Iriskana; 659 ULKASTUDIO; 663 elbud; 664 Natykach Nataliia, smilewithjul; 666 Cheng Wei; 667 Ivonne Wierink, timquo; 668 STILLFX, timquo; 673–674 Lizard, Petr Kratochvil; 674 Tatiana Popova; 676 topseller; 683 Claudia Paulussen; 685 Andy Piatt; 691 iskrinka74; 693 Olinchuk, SFIO CRACHO, Udovichenko; 694 GotziLA STOCK, MARGRIT HIRSCH, Alexander Rybalka, Yellow Cat, Iuchunyu; 695 Dakalova Iuliia; 696 photka; 697 Yellow Cat; 698 Studio DMM Photography, Designs & Art; 699–700 STILLFX; 701 Yellow Cat; 702 Ian 2010, Igor Kovalchuk, Damir Kabirov, Eric Boucher; 703 Eric Isselee, Palokha Tetiana, Dora Zett, Pavel Hlystov, STILLFX; 704 Bryan Solomon, normallens, Andrey Medvedev; 705 Artem Shadrin; 706 Astock Productions, Udovichenko; 707 Madlen, Tatjana Romanova, Africa Studio, Keizt Photography, COLOA Studio, Vilor; 708 Rich Carey, Jan Martin Will, Eric Isselee, Madlen, STILLFX, Eric Boucher; 709 TRINACRIA PHOTO, Nataliia Dvukhimenna, Mega Pixel, Vilor, ElenaR, haru, pzAxe; 710 Eric Boucher, Palokha Tetiana, STILLFX; 711 Eric Boucher, STILLFX; 712 Nebs, Timmary, Thammanoon Khamchalee, Anest, Protasov AN; 713 Yellow Cat, Bryan Solomon, normallens; 714 Plateresca, Astock Productions, udovichenko; 715 Ioskutnikov; 716 Picsfive, Iggy Yorke, Pavel Hlystov, Food Travel Stockforlife; 717 donatas1205, Picsfive; 718 Coprid, schankz, little birdie, Picsfive; 720 JasonCPhoto, Bluegrass Imagery; 722 Lucie Lang, Yellow Cat; 723 donatas1205; 724 donatas1205, timquo, Picsfive; 725 terekhov igor, Elena Anikina; 726 Iablonskyi Mykola, Bill45, trubitsyn, Alex Coan, Picsfive; 727 Picsfive, Svetlana Happyland, DJ Srki, dragon_art; 728 icolourful, Svetlana Happyland, Picsfive, Andrey_Kuzmin, Udovichenko; 729 elenovsky, photo one; 730 Bokeh Blur Background, elenovsky, photo one; 731 Madlen, Bokeh Blue Background, Eric Boucher; 732 Irina Barilo, Bokeh Blur Background, Dan Kosmayer, urfin, Katharina Scharle; 733 somdul, elenovsky, Dan Kosmayer, Katharina Scharle; 734 Bokeh Blur Background, MirasWonderland, Osadchyi_I; 735 urfin, Tarzhanova; 736 JDCarballo, Sergiy Kuzmin, Happy Stock Photo, gillmar; 737 SkaLd, InGreen, Eric Isselee, Yellow Cat, Eric Boucher, Picsfive; 739 Allocricetulus, StockPhotosArt, travis manley; 740 optimarc, Mega Pixel, Anest, nortongo, Katharina Scharle; 741 Lucie Lang, Dan Kosmayer; 742 margouillat photo, Dan Kosmayer, sergign, Anton Starikov; 744 Picsfive; 746 Picsfive, Africa Studio, valkoinen; 747 Yellow Cat; 748 matkub2499, StockPhotosArt, Picsfive; 749 revers, Eric Boucher, Tanakorn Moolsarn; 750 somdul, Africa Studio, nortongo, Dan Kosmayer; 752 terekhov igor, Hedez, Yellow Cat, Dan Kosmayer; 753 exopixel, Kirsanov Valeriy Vladimirovich, Eric Boucher; 754 Valentina Razumova, MichaelJayBerlin, Sondre Lysne; 755 Polryaz, Dan Kosmayer, Picsfive; 756 Oleksandr Lysenko; 757 troyka, shooarts; 758 Jiang Zhongyan, timquo, Dan Kosmayer, revers; 765 NizamD; 767 Nenov Brothers Images; 768 cherezoff, topform, Handies Peak, Richard Peterson, Birgit Reitz-Hofmann, Marcus Miranda; 769 Tang Yan Song; 772 bogdan ionescu; 775 OnlyZoia, GalapagosPhoto; 781 Nenov Brothers Images, topform; 784 Evgeny Karandaev; 791 Bankrx; 792 Vitaly Zorkin, Lu Wenjuan; 793 Vereshchagin Dmitry; 794 Mega Pixel, Odua Images, Natasha Pankina; 798–799 Anaken2012; 800 melnikof; 804 wk1003mike; 815 Boonchuay1970; 816 Lisovskaya Natalia; 820 COLOA Studio, Anna Kucherova, Rin Ohara; 829 Prostock-studio, Pixelbliss; 831 Sapunkele, siamionau pavel; A4 Yellow Cat; A6 titelio, Jiri Vaclavek, kitzcorner; A7 nimon, Valerii__Dex; A9 Tsekhmister, azure1; A11 Ruslan Ivantsov; A13 EHStockphoto; A14 Paleka, TRINACRIA PHOTO; A17, A18, A20 Peter Hermes Furian; A22 Ruslan Ivantsov; A23 bestv

Student Handbook, appearing in Student Bookshelf and Teacher Guide only: HBi ArtMari, Pixfiction, Rawpixel.com, Disavorabuth; **HB1** Africa Studio; **HB2** iadams; **HB3** Palabra; **HB4** Tero Vesalainen; **HB5** Harvepino; **HB8** Chiyacat; **HB9** Kyselova Inna, Markus Mainka; **HB11** Disavorabuth; **HB19** Rawpixel.com

i-Ready Classroom
Mathematics

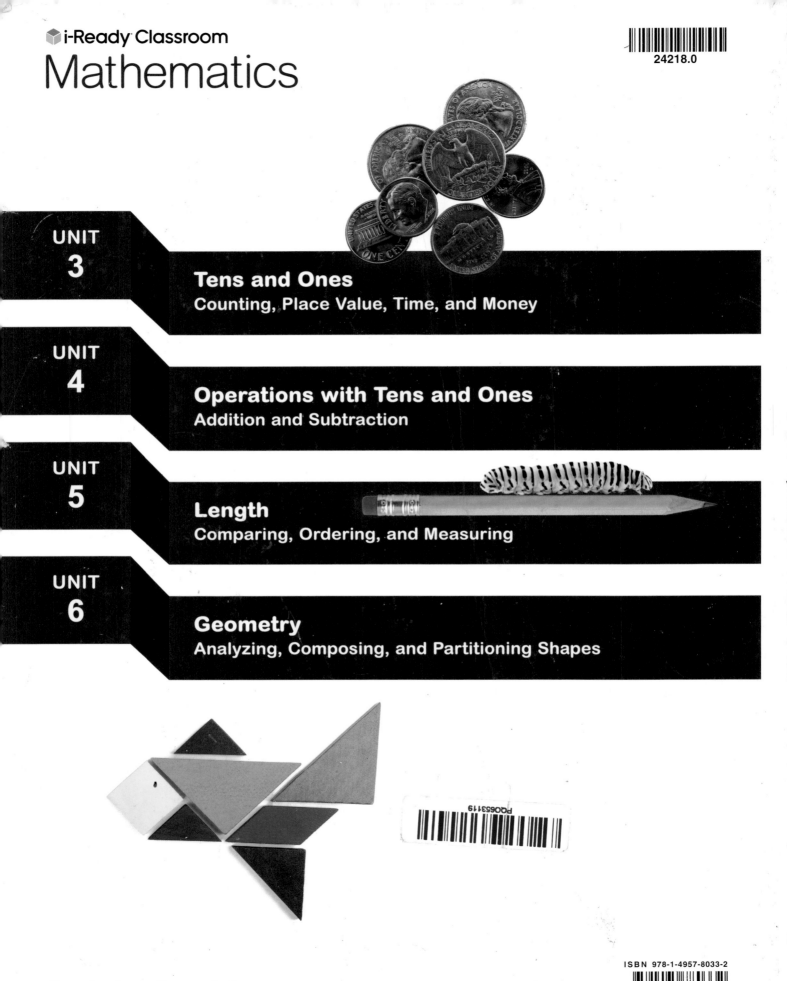

Curriculum Associates 800 225-0248 CurriculumAssociates.com

ISBN 978-1-4957-8033-2

24218.0